✳ ✳ ✳

"The Oak Ridge Boys are *the* quintessential American Music Group!"

President George H.W. Bush

"If these boys singing doesn't get you fired up...Then your wood must be wet."

General Chuck Yeager

"When I see those tour buses and gear trailers parked at their office in Hendersonville, Tennessee, I always think to myself, *YES...the BOYS are home!* When I drive by and see those buses are gone I always think, *The world is just fine! The BOYS are out there somewhere singing!*"

Marty Stuart
singer, musician, and country-music historian

✳ ✳ ✳

★ ON THE ROAD WITH ★

Joseph S. Bonsall

HARVEST HOUSE PUBLISHERS
EUGENE, OREGON

Scripture quotations are taken from the New American Standard Bible®, © 1960, 1962, 1963, 1968, 1971, 1972, 1973, 1975, 1977, 1995 by The Lockman Foundation. Used by permission. (www.Lock man.org)

Lyrics to "This is America" by Norah Lee Allen used by permission of First Time Around Publishing.

Cover by Left Coast Design, Portland, Oregon

Front cover photo © Jarrett Gaza Photography

ON THE ROAD WITH THE OAK RIDGE BOYS
Copyright © 2015
Published by Harvest House Publishers
Eugene, Oregon 97402
www.harvesthousepublishers.com

Library of Congress Cataloging-in-Publication Data
  Bonsall, Joseph S.
  On the road with the Oak Ridge Boys / Joe Bonsall.
      pages cm
  ISBN 978-0-7369-6419-7 (pbk.)
  ISBN 978-0-7369-6420-3 (eBook)
  1. Oak Ridge Boys. 2. Country musicians—United States—Biography. I. Title.
  ML421.O2B68 2015
  782.421642092'2—dc23
  [B]
                                                                    2014035335

Printed in the United States of America

        15 16 17 18 19 20 21 22 23 / LB-CD / 10 9 8 7 6 5 4 3 2 1

TO OUR PRECIOUS MOTHERS…

Lillie Bonsall
Lorette Allen
Ruth Golden
Victoria Sterban

"All that I am, or hope to be, I owe to my angel mother."
—Abraham Lincoln

CONTENTS

Prologue:

A PHENOMENON

"Living Our Dreams"

When I was first approached about writing another book about the Oak Ridge Boys, I wasn't really sure whether I could take it on. Writing is an all-consuming art, and although I've managed to write quite a few books over the years, this task seemed daunting.

Several years ago I wrote my heart out about the Oak Ridge Boys in a coffee-table book called *An American Journey*. I thought that book was the whole story. But my wife, Mary, inspired me to keep writing about the group, and I'm not sure she even realizes it.

It was a summer afternoon, and I had to leave early that evening for a concert at a big Midwestern state fair. Normally we'd leave at around midnight, but Darrick Kinslow, our tour director, set the departure time for six p.m. to give us plenty of time to arrive in Somewhereville, USA, to get set up and prepare for the huge grandstand show the next day.

Mary and I decided to eat dinner out early. We picked one of our favorite places, which just happened to be right across the road from our offices and the gathering point for our departure. We drove there separately so she could head for home after dinner and I could drive over to our parking lot, grab my stuff, and board the bus. As I remember, it was to be a four-day trip.

After dinner, Mary and I sat together in her truck in the restaurant parking lot and watched the constant activity across the street. The two big black Prevost tour buses had started and were now on high idle. Band guys and crew guys were arriving. Some arrived by themselves while others were dropped off by family members or friends. The life of the road musician leaving home was being played out right there in that parking lot, and it was exciting to watch it unfold.

I was just about to tell Mary goodbye when she turned to me and said something I've never forgotten. With teary eyes and a halt in her voice, she said, "You know, hon…that's a phenomenon going on over there. *You* guys are a phenomenon! It's so hard to believe you all are still out there performing at such a high level…it's just a phenomenon." After her voice trailed off, she regained her composure, kissed me, and added, "Now get going. You're *never* the last one on the bus!"

We both laughed, and I watched as she drove away in her big, white Silverado pickup, back home to a houseful of cats and, as usual, no husband for the next several days.

You have to realize that Mary Ann Bonsall never says much about the Oak Ridge Boys. Singing is what I do and what I've always done, so for me to get on the bus and leave home is a natural part of our lives. But this particular evening seemed a little different somehow. Mary doesn't give props every day, so I must admit my heart was warmed as I parked my own truck and boarded the bus with a few shoulder bags, my laptop, and four days' worth of clean laundry and stage wear (clean jeans and some cool shirts).

As is usually the case, I greeted and was greeted back warmly by two of my fellow Oaks, Duane Allen and Richard Sterban. Then our fourth member, William Lee Golden, pulled into the lot, so I was indeed not the last one to board the big bus—our rolling home away from home.

I threw my stuff into my designated area on the back couch, hung my clothes in my closet, and decided that even though it was early I would crawl in my bunk and get some sleep. I had worked hard on my farm the past few days, and I was tired. My stomach was full as well, so I settled in, pulled the covers up to my chin, and just lay there for a while.

I could hear the guys laughing and cutting up in the front lounge. Richard already found a baseball game on the TV in the back lounge, and Darrick, or DK as we call him, was already on the phone, talking to tomorrow's promoter. Our driver pulled away from the office, the other bus full of band and crew followed, and suddenly we were off. Buses on the move…time to ride…time to sing again. It has never gotten old—no, not once!

Leaving home is always hard though, and as we rolled through the early Tennessee evening I felt myself drifting off into a wonderful and much-needed sleep. I could still hear Mary's voice echoing, "You guys are a phenomenon…a phenomenon…"

Her words made me realize there really *is* still a lot more to write about the Oak Ridge Boys.

1

OCTOBER '73

"Jesus Is the Man for the Hour"

SAMMY HALL

*I*t was mid-October, 1973, but I remember it as if it were yesterday. It was about ten in the morning as my flight was landing in Cincinnati, and I was about to open what would become an exciting and very long chapter in my life.

I had spent the better part of the past seven years in Buffalo, New York, singing and promoting gospel music with my cutting-edge little gospel band, the Keystones. I was having fun, but I was also starving to death. I might have stayed in Buffalo forever singing with the Keystones, but thank God, I didn't. What influenced my decision to board the plane and fly away from the Niagara Frontier on that autumn day?

One reason was that my first wife, Barbara, was pregnant, and my bills, which were way overdue, were weighing heavily on me. Especially the one that was earmarked "Rent"!

But it wasn't all about money. I had always managed to somehow keep singing and still pay my bills, and even as a young man of 25 years, my faith in God to provide was strong. I believed (and still do) in the saving power and guiding grace of Jesus Christ, and I was stepping out in faith with the assurance that God was guiding my path.

As my plane touched down, I was excited to no end to see the big, brown Silver Eagle bus parked in the airport lot. Just seeing the bus nicknamed Chocolate and knowing it was there to pick me up was mind-boggling for this Philadelphia kid who had dreamed of someday singing in a great harmony group. And on *this* day I would be joining my absolute favorite group in the world—and a gospel group at that—the mighty Oak Ridge Boys!

Yes, I already loved this group even before I was a member. They not only sang great but also were cool. There was just nobody like the Oak Ridge Boys. I still feel that way more than 40 years later.

The Boys were all there to meet me too. There was my longtime friend Richard Sterban, whom I knew from my Philly days. He had been an aspiring singer from New Jersey, selling men's clothes in a department store. We had sung together for several years in the Keystones, but then he joined J.D. Sumner and the Stamps Quartet and toured with Elvis. Richard had joined the Oak Ridge Boys only a year earlier, and I was stoked about singing with him again.

There was Duane Allen, a man I had long loved and respected. Duane had produced a dozen albums for our little Keystone group in his own studio and on his own label. He had always believed in what I was doing and in me. Besides that, he was a great singer, and now I was going to sing alongside him—*wow*!

William Lee Golden had always been "Bill" to me in those days. He and I had worked out many reciprocal promotions over the years. I would book the Oaks up north, and he would bring the Keystones south to take part in some of the great music festivals of that day. But our relationship was much more than that. Bill was a dreamer and a visionary, and late-night phone conversations with him from my little apartment in Buffalo always left me encouraged. He made me feel that just maybe I had what it took to take my talent to another level.

Bill Golden had called me and told me that their longtime tenor, Willie Wynn, was leaving the Oak Ridge Boys and that they had unanimously chosen me to take his place.

We all shook hands, hugged, laughed, and boarded Chocolate. We headed straight to a clothing store called Dino's, where they bought me a bunch of new clothes to wear onstage. We then drove to Columbus, where we were to perform that very night. For the rest of the afternoon we rehearsed and worked out harmony parts for the concert.

That night, suddenly, there I was—singing onstage with the Oak Ridge Boys, shaking like a leaf in my new green platform shoes. I was so nervous that I was sweating through my brand-new Dino's sport coat. But overall the evening went well. I didn't hit any major clams, and the guys seemed happy with their choice to hire me and move me to their base in Nashville.

I'll never forget that night. It's as fresh in my mind as if it happened yesterday. I can easily conjure up every vision, every emotion...even every song. The show was promoted by my longtime friend Sonny Simmons and took place in an outbuilding on the Ohio State Fairgrounds. We opened with "Jesus Is the Man for the Hour." I remember feeling that God's hand was on my life, leading me down a new path. I had always dreamed this would happen but never imagined it could really come true.

We were young and strong and fearless, and the road ahead, though rocky at times, would be paved with incredible success and music-making history. But all I could think about that night, and most nights thereafter, was that I was now an Oak!

The next night we played for Sonny again back in Cincinnati, but the excitement had me so zoned out, the concert remains somewhat of a blur. I do remember a fan who had loved Little Willie asking Duane Allen when the regular tenor was coming back.

In those early days, I didn't know where all of my dreams would lead me. Becoming an Oak was the only dream I had, and now I *was* an Oak. Today, I'm well into my sixties, and I'm *still* an Oak! For more than four decades I've been an Oak, still singing right alongside Duane, William, and Richard. And honestly, after all these years, I love those guys today more than ever. I'm so thankful to God for great health and these many blessings down through the years.

Writer and author Bill Gaither could have easily been thinking of the Oak Ridge Boys when he wrote the great song "Loving God, Loving Each Other."

2

THE BOYS

"Loving God, Loving Each Other"

*I*t's amazing that after all of these years people still call us "the Boys." On every level this is quite magical—and fun as well! "The Boys are in town!" "The Boys are back!" "Let's take this idea to the Boys!" "The Boys rock!" Our recent live album is even called *Boys Night Out*. And on it goes. It sure makes sense somehow, though between the four Oak Ridge Boys, we have thirteen children, seventeen grandchildren, and two great-grandchildren. Oak Ridge *Boys*? Right!

So who are the Boys? Let's start with William Lee Golden, from Brewton, Alabama—the most distinct character who has ever walked on the planet. His look, his swagger, and his tender demeanor make him one of the most beloved members of any group anywhere. The man is well into his seventies now and still has the energy and vocal power of someone much younger. When he yells out (as he often does), "I feel like singing all night!" he's not kidding.

"The only thing more important than singing in harmony is living in harmony."

WILLIAM LEE GOLDEN

William Lee joined the Oaks in 1965 after a stint with the Future Farmers of America Quartet and the local Pilots Trio. He had honed his talents at a young age by playing and singing with family members. Also while young he grew to love and appreciate the Oak Ridge

17

Boys of that day. They became a huge influence and guiding force in his young life. Back then, the Oak Ridge Boys recorded with Warner Brothers, and William was heavily influenced by the energy and style he heard on those early records.

Only Golden could have approached the group and convinced them that he alone could bring a certain amount of class and distinction to what they were doing—and he was right. All these years later, he's still doing just that every night onstage.

The man most assuredly walks to the beat of his own drummer, and that's what makes him unique. He's probably the most unpredictable of all of us onstage. He may stand still for a while and then literally explode across the stage. On a whim he just might go out into the audience and shake hands with people for a few songs…or he may not. He's truly an individual, and I sincerely believe the Oak Ridge Boys would have been hard pressed to make it to the big time without him.

William Lee is also a successful artist and a first-tier photographer. When we're on tour, he spends a lot of time on his laptop, reviewing and honing the thousands of photos he's taken. One never knows when he'll take one of those photos and turn it into a beautifully painted landscape that will grace his next art show.

Creative, energetic, unique, and more eclectic than anyone you know…that's our William Lee Golden!

★ ★ ★

Duane Allen is the man we call the Ace, and that moniker seems to fit him just right. He actually got this nickname from a *Mayberry* episode in which Barney Fife uttered the words "Call me Ace, I like that!" For years Duane actually wore a shirt that said "Call me Ace!" (Now his T-shirt usually reads, "Don't be a pinhead!")

Like Golden, Duane grew up in a hardworking farm family that loved to sing. Also like Golden, his father was a man of the earth who counted it an honor and a blessing to farm the land and provide for his family.

I've heard Duane say many times that when his brothers and sisters all came home, they had enough members (counting Mom and Dad) to have a double quartet, and they sang all day and night. Being the youngest, he would take whatever harmony part was left, feeling around to find the right part to sing. That experience would ingrain his love for great harmony singing down to his very soul.

Duane's love for pure singing, coupled with the high moral ground gleaned from his upbringing in Taylortown, Texas, would have a huge effect on his life and his future. He studied classical music in college. His *Songs of Inspiration* radio show aired in Paris, Texas, where a bridge was named in his honor in 2014. He also sang in a popular local gospel quartet called The Southernaires.

The Ace would eventually head to Knoxville, Tennessee, and join the popular Prophets Quartet before moving to Nashville in 1966 to take the lead singer job for the Oak Ridge Boys. The rest is history. Nobody has had more effect on the growth of our group than Duane Allen. He is the ultimate song man. More than anyone, the Ace knows a good song when he hears one, and the Oaks have benefited from this over and over as the years and the hits have flown by.

Duane is a real leader, and his sharp business acumen has guided the Oaks down many a successful pathway. I dare not think where we might be today if not for his constant input and dedication to doing all things right. While William is off taking pictures or painting and Richard is in the broadcast booth calling balls and strikes for the Triple-A Nashville Sounds or the Vanderbilt Commodores, and while I'm pecking on this computer keyboard or playing banjo (earning my Ban-Joey nickname) or bush hogging a field or petting one of our cats, Duane is working the business of the Oak Ridge Boys. He is a 24/7

"We've had a wonderful career, and we're *still* having a wonderful career, so the business as a whole has impacted all of our lives. I would hope that somewhere along the line we've done something to contribute to it, to make it better for those who follow us."

DUANE ALLEN

guy—so much so that I think when he sleeps he's still thinking about the next project. This is just how the guy rolls, and we all benefit from his tireless efforts. He's better than any of us at thinking things through and coming up with the right answer when only the right answer will do.

Duane loves dogs, tools, old cars…and listening to songs. He has a great farm in Sumner County, Tennessee, where many abused and forgotten animals have found a home. He also happens to be one of the greatest voices in the history of music and should probably be in the Smithsonian.

Duane Allen is also a great communicator. He's terrific at letting folks into our world. His Facebook presence is proof of that. Everyone loves the Ace. I know I do! After all, Duane and his wife, Norah Lee, put me up at their place until I could find my own apartment when I moved to Nashville to become one of the Boys.

Duane's also a fine writer. In 1971, Duane, along with coauthor Jesse Burt, wrote an in-depth book called *The History of Gospel Music*. It's hard to find now, but if you really search the Internet, you may find a copy. It's well worth looking for and well worth reading.

Our bass man, Richard Sterban, was born in Camden, New Jersey, and raised in a Christian home in nearby Collingswood. He lost his hardworking dad early on, but his mom, Victoria, kept the family ship on a steady course, and her influence on Richard shows up in his life to this very day.

Richard attended Trenton University and was a founding member of the original Keystone Quartet, of which I became a part. In fact, he hired me to sing with the Keystones when I was just 19.

Then, in the early '70s, Richard left the Keystones to join J.D. Sumner and the Stamps Quartet, who would go on to back up Elvis Presley on the biggest rock-and-roll tour of its day.

In 1972, Richard left the Stamps and the King to join the Oak Ridge Boys. His is an amazing story that he and his friend Steve

Robinson chronicled quite well in a book called *From Elvis to Elvira*—a great read!

Richard's good looks and amazing voice have paid many dividends for the Oak Ridge Boys over the years. He has become the most well-known bass singer in the history of music—not only from his added touches on monster hit songs, like "Elvira" and "Bobbie Sue," but also for his soulful solo work on songs like "Dream On," "Down Deep Inside," and Christmas classics, including "I'll Be Home for Christmas" and "'The Christmas Song."

Richard is not only a great and unique talent but also a good friend and a good man. He is as steady as it goes…honest and true and always fun to be around.

> "Singing bass is not like singing any other part. It takes a certain mindset. You must be totally relaxed and very confident to be able to sing low notes on a consistent basis."
>
> RICHARD STERBAN

I might add that the man is consumed by baseball. College, minor league, major league…it doesn't matter. I would guess that he'd even stop at a Little League game just to watch and to spread some positive cheer among the players.

He does that on every level, and if Richard wasn't singing bass with the Boys, he could probably be found in a broadcast booth somewhere calling balls and strikes or adding colorful commentary to the game he so loves.

Richard also does a ton of interviews for the Oaks. He talks to local press and radio, and he fronts most of the dates we play. In this day and age of instant social networking, it's still important to actually talk to people, and Richard is the best at this. He's always willing to use his personal time to do whatever it takes to keep pushing the Oak Ridge Boys forward.

And did I mention…the man can *evermore* sing bass!

✳ ✳ ✳

Joe Bonsall? Well, that's me. I find it much easier to write about the other guys, but I'll take a small shot over the bow to introduce myself.

I was born and raised in Philadelphia and have loved to sing since I was little. My mom and dad were both World War II veterans, as chronicled in my book *G.I. Joe and Lillie*, and though my dad had a crippling stroke at age 39, my mom always encouraged me to press forward. Along with Jesus Christ, she deserves much of the credit for anything I am today, and Jesus might not have been in the picture at all if not for my mom. Mom was a down-on-her-knees praying woman. It's hard to be afraid, even if your father just had a debilitating stroke, when you hear your mom praying for you in the next room.

Truth is, all four of us Oaks had great moms. I hope you noticed I dedicated this book to our four precious moms. Richard's mother, Victoria Sterban, was the last living Oak Ridge Boy mother. She died recently at age 94 and joined Lillie, Lorette, and Ruth on that far bank of Jordan, awaiting their sons' arrival. Until that day, we each thank our moms. We are what we are because of them! Yes, I can honestly say that we are mommas' boys as well as Oak Ridge Boys.

One reason my mother prayed so hard for me was that I grew up in a rough neighborhood in Philly. A few years ago we found ourselves in Philadelphia, so my sister loaded up her car with me, William Lee Golden, Darrick Kinslow, and Sherman Halsey, the son of our manager, and drove us to my old Kensington neighborhood at two o'clock in the morning—a rather dangerous undertaking. Sherman grew up in a small Kansas town and lived in Los Angeles and Nashville for years, but he had never seen the likes of Kensington at two a.m. He kept saying two things over and over. "You grew up *here*?" and "I wish I had my camera!"

I mentioned in chapter 1 that I joined the Oak Ridge Boys in 1973 after singing in the Keystones. (I had also had my own Faith Four Quartet.) When legendary gospel music tenor Willie Wynn left the Oaks, they thought of me. And for four decades, the Boys have always been there for me—and for each other.

In March of 1974, I had been an Oak for only a few months. The night before my daughter Jennifer was born, we were in Wichita,

Kansas, and about to head out toward western Canada. The guys pooled together all the money they had and gave it to me so I could fly to Nashville the next morning. It was very selfless of them, and it meant the world to me. Duane's wife, Norah Lee, picked me up at the airport and took me to the hospital to see my baby girl, Jennifer, for the first time. I got there an hour after she was born, and except for a dent in her head that the doctor assured us would round out, she was just beautiful. I then flew back to Montana and checked into a hotel to wait for the bus to come through. I remember falling into a deep sleep long before the knock on the door. There stood all the guys and the whole band, smoking cigars with little pink ribbons on them. As I lit one up and headed for the idling bus, I thought I would never forget that moment—and I never have! I do love my fellow Oaks!

"The Oak Ridge Boys have been called a gospel quartet singing country music with a rock and roll band! So be it!"

JOE BONSALL

Apart from the Oaks, I love cats, I love to write, I love my farm, I love my banjo, and I love my family. I always try to bring a positive approach to the table, and if you follow the group on Twitter, most often you're hearing from me.

About 17 years ago, Mary and I bought a 350-acre farm on the Kentucky–Tennessee border, and this has become my fortress of solitude. There's a lot of work to do out there, but I thank God every single day for this piece of heaven on earth. Someday, very far on down the road, I will probably shut that gate and never leave! What's easier—sitting in a hotel room all afternoon or dragging a huge rotary cutter behind a John Deere across a weedy field? The hotel room, of course—but I would always rather be on my tractor!

So there you have us—the Oak Ridge Boys. Through all these many miles we've traveled and everything we've been through together for more than 40 years, we haven't really changed much as we've gotten older. Singing, doing things right, honoring God and families in our lives…these things are still what really matter the most to each of us.

The Oak Ridge Boys constantly rise up above the four individuals who share that name. We're all just spokes in one big wheel, and we each realize that. We know our part and revel and celebrate in this unique brotherhood. Everything we do as individuals is aimed at one common cause—to keep the Oaks going strong. We were all fans of the Oaks before we became members, and we have taken the Oak Ridge Boys' name and brand into the history books. No small thing from a bunch of young kids who all just dreamed of singing in a group one day!

3

THE SONGS

"Three Minutes of Magic"

DUANE ALLEN

*E*very song is a story, and there's a story for every song. And it seems for every song, there's a question—where did that song come from? Who wrote it? What made you decide to record it? How do you figure out who sings lead? Did you know it would be a hit when you recorded it?

So many good questions, and people love to hear the answers because songs are important to folks. Nothing marks time and space in a person's life like a great song that holds a special meaning. You know what I'm talking about. You've heard a favorite song from the past and instantly reveled in sweet memories from an earlier time in your life.

People also often ask us if we ever get tired of singing these same songs. The answer is no! Absolutely not, and I'll tell you why. To a man or a woman of music, a song can be magic. In fact, Duane calls a good song "three minutes of magic," and a well-crafted song is just that.

When a performer is fortunate enough to write or find a song with that three minutes of magic, the song moves in and takes up residence deep within his or her very being. If others find that song meaningful as well, the power of that magic grows into something that becomes simply unforgettable for years—or in our case, decades.

The truth is, we never get tired of a great song. The Oak Ridge Boys have tried our very best over these many years to record and to sing truly memorable and meaningful songs. Doing so has paid great dividends. One of those dividends is the ability to stay popular for a very long time.

When the intro kicks in to "Y'all Come Back Saloon," I still get excited because *boom*—it's 1977 again, and in my mind's eye I can see a bunch of young guys enjoying their first big hit record after having made the move from gospel to country. With the success of "Saloon," we were on our way, and whenever we sing it today, tons of memories rush in like a flood.

> "The most important thing you can do for your career is to record three minutes of magic! The next best thing you can do is to follow that up with *another* three minutes of magic! Recording great songs is the key to longevity."
>
> **DUANE ALLEN**

We walked into a truck stop back in those early days and were blown slam away when we heard "Y'all Come Back Saloon" playing on the jukebox. So blown away, in fact, that we stayed right there for more than an hour, feeding quarters into the machine and listening to ourselves. It's a wonder we didn't get beat with a tire iron!

This little song—written by Sharon Vaughn, produced by Ron Chancey, and chosen as our first big single on what was then ABC Dot Records (soon to become MCA)—was not only blaring out of a truck-stop jukebox but also setting a peg for all that was to come.

All these years later, many people still tell us they remember where they were the first time they heard "Saloon." Many of these folks are top executives in the music industry who say that their first thought was always, *Wow…well, here come the Oak Ridge Boys!*

Three minutes of magic!

★ ★ ★

We've been pretty good at finding those three minutes. We've had more than 50 charted songs, most of them landing at number one or at least in the top five or ten. In fact, the Oak Ridge Boys have charted albums and singles in five different decades now. As of 2015, we've sold 41 million albums. That's a lot of magic!

In addition, our shelves are full of awards for which we are very thankful: Grammys, Country Music Association Awards, Academy of Country Music Awards (including the coveted Cliffie Stone Pioneer Award), Gospel Music Association Dove Awards…just to name a few. We're members of the Gospel Music Hall of Fame, the Vocal Group Hall of Fame, and the Grand Ole Opry. We're also honorary members of the Barbershop Harmony Society.

As if that weren't enough, to our own amazement, we each have collected some individual awards over the past four decades.

- William Lee Golden is a member of the Alabama Music Hall of Fame.

- Duane Allen is a member of the Texas Gospel Music Hall of Fame and the Texas Country Music Hall of Fame. (The Texas Country Music Hall of Fame was kind enough to induct the other three of us as honorary members.)

- Richard Sterban and I are members of the Philadelphia Music Alliance Hall of Fame.

Are awards important? Lord knows there are more award shows than ever, and I'm not certain they're all necessary. However, when your peers or the music public decides that what you're doing is relevant and well done, that's a very special honor. It's like a huge pat on the back from people who matter to you. So yes, winning an award is rewarding on many levels, and I'm thankful for each one on my shelf. I remember sleeping with my first Country Music Association (CMA) award. Yes, I did.

One award, though, has eluded us—the prestigious Country Music Hall of Fame. I'm not sure if this will ever happen, but if it ever did, it would be the greatest of all honors! Perhaps one day it will happen. I can only hope we are still breathing oxygen if it does!

✳ ✳ ✳

Everyone has their favorite Oak Ridge Boys song, and memories of some kind always accompany the music. Whether it's "Thank God for Kids," "Elvira," "American Made," "Make My Life with You," "I Guess It Never Hurts to Hurt Sometimes," or perhaps "I Wish You Could Have Turned My Head (and Left My Heart Alone)," there's sure to be a song in our catalog that will move the listener—and us onstage as well.

We wouldn't be singing today without the help of some of the finest songwriters in the world, many of whom reside right here in Nashville. They've always been good to us by sending us their best efforts or in some cases getting together and writing one "just for the Boys."

Maybe you've never heard of some of these guys—Paul Overstreet, Roger Murrah, Dave Loggins, James Dean Hicks, Sonny Throckmorton, Randy VanWarmer, Michael Foster, Jimbeau Hinson, Gary Burr, Dallas Frazier, and so many more great writers—but they have sat down many times with just a guitar and a pencil and pad in their hands and have, quite frankly, written our entire career. *We've* certainly heard of them and are very thankful.

As the great songstress Tricia Yearwood assured us, "The song remembers when." Well, yes it does, and we *never* get tired of singing…and remembering!

> ✦ ★ ✦
>
> "Music is an instrument from God, and it has a way of touching people and moving people. If done in the proper way it can move people and touch people for the good."
>
> RICHARD STERBAN

Here's a good example. A young girl came up to me in a Walgreens recently and told me how much the song "I Guess It Never Hurts to Hurt Sometimes" meant to her when her daddy died. She was in tears because she never thought she would ever get to see me to thank me personally. This song seems to have brought comfort to many people during times of loss. Randy VanWarmer wrote it when his own father passed away, and I'm honored to sing it. Sadly, Randy himself lost a battle with leukemia a few years ago as well. He was just 49 years old.

That song was also my own mother's favorite, and I sang it to her on her deathbed. To this day, I think of her and of Randy whenever I sing it. That's just one small example of how meaningful one little song can be—to the writer, the singer, and the listener.

We could tell stories about how all our songs were written, why we recorded them, or the effect they've had on people.

Sometimes we record a song because of the effect it's had on us. For instance, back in the mid-1970s, we often listened to the Staple Singers on our bus. All four of us are fans of black gospel music, and Duane has a huge collection of recordings from some of the best artists in that genre. We loved hearing Mavis Staples sing "I'll Take You There" and "Respect Yourself." We always vowed that one day we would record one of the Staples' songs, and when we finally did in the mid-'80s, it hit big-time. It's still a joy to see a huge crowd of people shaking each other's hands while we sing "Touch a Hand, Make a Friend."

That's why it was also a great thrill for us to record "Take the High Road" with the Blind Boys of Alabama a few years back. Jamey Johnson produced that project, and we jumped at the chance to do it.

Sometimes the song simply carries a great message. Grand Ole Opry star Bill Anderson once wrote a song for us that asks, "Did I Make a Difference?" It's a great song, and the answer lies somewhere inside your own heart. One *can* make a difference every day by just doing things right and being kind to people. It might not seem earth-shattering at that moment, but by shining your light every day, you can be a blessing when you don't even realize it. Every person carries some kind of burden—sickness, marriage problems, financial worries, spiritual uneasiness…or they just may be walking beneath a dark cloud without even knowing why. When these people see your countenance radiating a more positive and Christlike demeanor, the results can be amazing. So try putting your own problems on a lower shelf if you can and strive to be a blessing to others. You *can* make a difference.

Another memorable song for us is "Thank God for Kids." I believe that William Lee Golden's recording of that song was one of the great moments in American music history. He's still creating historic moments when he sings it onstage. Our Cajun brother Eddie Raven wrote this little song and recorded it in 1972, and it has been magic for us ever since we recorded it in 1981 for our first MCA Christmas album.

Many folks tell us they grew up listening to this holiday album, and for them we still sing many of those songs during our Christmas shows. But this one song was the flagship tune of the project. MCA wanted to release it as merely a Christmas song, and a funny thing happened they hadn't counted on. "Kids" went cruising right on past the Christmas season and became a number one hit record for us. Now, William Lee can evermore pound out some great songs—"Ozark Mountain Jubilee," "Roll Tennessee River," "Louisiana Red Dirt Highway," and many others—but what he does with his voice on "Thank God for Kids" is just wonderful, and it's always a highlight of the show.

✦ ✦ ✦

Of course, there's another key person involved besides the songwriter when producing three minutes of magic, and that's, well, the producer. We've been blessed with some great producers through the years, notably our very capable Ron Chancey. If you haven't heard of some of the songwriters I mentioned above, you're even less likely to have heard of some of our great producers.

Ron Chancey produced every gold and platinum album that hangs on our walls. Everyone has a lot of solid creative input during the recording process, but the producer is the one who separates the wheat from the chaff and adds the special touches that can mean the difference between a good record and a *great* record. Ron has always had the special ear, touch, and magic that resulted in hit after hit for us. We call Ron the Fifth Oak for his friendship and constant input.

Another key man in our success is our manager, Jim Halsey. We call him our godfather because he has guided our career and inspired us on every level since 1975. I'll never forget these words Jim spoke 40 years ago: "The Oak Ridge Boys are just three minutes away from being country music superstars." Turned out he was right. And every year since then, his mantra has been, "This will be the biggest year we've ever had!" Ron, Jim, and our record company executive, Jim Foglesong, are among the biggest reasons the Oaks grew from a gospel quartet into hit makers.

> We were all in the historic Woodland Sound Studios in early 1982, working on that first big Christmas album. We were trying to get the vocals right on "O Holy Night," and it just wasn't happening. We were worn out, so we told Ron we would take a short break to go to the bathroom. Instead, we walked out the side door, jumped in our cars, and drove home. Ron sat behind the audio console in the control room for a long time before he realized we weren't coming back!

Of course, we've had plenty of success with other producers as well. Richard Landis produced some wonderful tracks for us, and we all loved working with him. Landis is the one who worked out our being part of the movie soundtrack for *My Heroes Have Always Been Cowboys* with our rendition of the Righteous Brothers' "Soul and Inspiration."

Once when Richard visited us in Lake Tahoe to talk about an upcoming project, he was given a hotel room that adjoined mine. Well, before he arrived, my wife, Mary, and I filled his bed with peanuts. When he checked in around two a.m. and finally crawled into bed, he almost had to be rushed to the hospital because he was highly allergic to peanuts. That's the night we almost killed producer Richard Landis!

The legendary Jimmy Bowen produced several big hit songs and many very popular albums for the Oaks in the late '80s, and songs like "It Takes a Little Rain," "This Crazy Love," "Beyond Those Years," "No Matter How High (I Get)," "Gonna Take a Lot of River," and "True Heart" are still a big part of our lives today. It was a thrill to work with Jimmy Bowen. I mean, after all, this guy had produced Frank Sinatra!

Young David Cobb took us down some roads we might not have traveled on our own. Just think of our hits "Seven Nation Army" and "Boom Boom," the latter written by the great John Lee Hooker. We became good friends with David after he invited us to sing with Shooter Jennings on a project, and working with David has been a great experience for all of us. He's a young man with a ton of vision and talent, and he's also a heck of a guitar player! Shooter Jennings wrote the title song for the Cobb project and called it "The Boys Are Back."

Michael Sykes has had a tremendous impact on many of our projects with Spring Hill Music over the past 15 years. His production ideas are always fresh and crisp, and he puts his heart and soul into every project. Michael's creative hand has guided some of our best work over the past decade.

Then there's our friend Ben Isaacs of the legendary gospel and bluegrass group the Isaacs. Ben is a master of harmony and acoustic arrangements and a joy to work with on every level. He has won many Producer of the Year honors from several organizations, and he is most deserving of every accolade he has received. We love Big Ben!

Our own Duane Allen has a great producer's heart and an expert ear for hearing exactly what we should sound like on a given project. His hand is heavy on *every* project, and he probably doesn't ever get the credit he deserves for his mastery. Many of our projects might not have come together in the first place if not for Duane's constant behind-the-scenes work on our behalf.

Duane was a crucial part of our studio album *It's Only Natural*, which is sold exclusively at Cracker Barrel Old Country Store. The album was totally off the table until Duane went to Lebanon, Tennessee, to talk with the powers that be at this great American company. If not for Duane and the relationship he built with marketing guru Julie Craig, Cracker Barrel would not be in our lives at all.

Although we never tire of our songs, we are open to times of change and are always trying to stay fresh. In 1983, Ron Chancey felt we needed a fresh approach as we were preparing to record our *Deliver* album. So instead of booking us at Woodland Sound Studios, where we had recorded the previous eight albums, he booked us in Rick Hall's legendary Fame Studios in Muscle Shoals, Alabama. (Ron did this kind of thing once before—on the 1978 *Room Service* project—when he took us to Los Angeles to record a few tracks just to get a different feel.) Famous guitarist James Burton's licks on the big hit "Cryin' Again" was proof positive that Ron made the right decision. The Muscle Shoals experience would also prove to be the right move because the legendary players there added a special touch to *Deliver*, and it paid off big-time.

The documentary film *Muscle Shoals* is a must-see for anyone who loves music and music history. It traces the famous Muscle Shoals sound and chronicles artists from the Rolling Stones to Aretha Franklin making the trip to this little place to work with the soulful players who created that special magic. They're known as the Muscle Shoals Rhythm Section, or the Swampers, as Leon Russell called them. There was Barry Beckett (keyboards), Roger Hawkins (drums), David Hood (bass), Jimmy Johnson (guitar), Pete Carr (guitar), and Spooner Oldham (organ). We had such a blast down there making music! We stayed at the Holiday Inn for almost a week and hung out at Fame Studios all day, every day.

I remember Jimmy Johnson's mother coming by with fresh biscuits and homemade barbecue. We would sit around and eat and laugh with the players and then go in to the studio and cut a rockin' track. Many times we would go back in the early evening and do vocal work alone with Ron. The magic can be felt big-time on the hits "I Guess It Never Hurts to Hurt Sometimes" and "Ozark Mountain Jubilee" and on the other tracks on *Deliver*.

Ron wanted to capture more of that magic, so he took us back to Muscle Shoals for the following MCA project, *Step On Out*. It was like coming home, and I think this time it felt even better than the previous time, if that were possible. The magic and love and fun were there again as we recorded more big hits, like the Billy Barber song "Little Things," the aforementioned "Touch a Hand, Make a Friend," and the incredible Rick Giles–George Green song "Come On In (You Did the Best You Could Do)," which rocked then and rocks now.

Other notable Oaks' classics recorded in the Fame Studios sessions included our version of Robbie Robertson's "Ophelia" as well as "Roll

Tennessee River," written by Russell Smith and David Loggins. This song still appears on our set list from time to time, and it's fun to hear William Lee Golden throw his Alabama-born soul into every line.

"Roll Tennessee River" made a lot of sense to us because the locals down there believe that the music actually comes from the Tennessee River as it rolls by Muscle Shoals. Old Indian legends say that if you listen carefully, you can hear the river sing. I know this much—recording at Fame Studios with the Muscle Shoals Rhythm Section is the most fun I have ever had creating music in my entire career! So I say yes, the river is *singing*!

Of course, it doesn't always work out so well. Sometimes we miss a few gems along the way. Three minutes of magic we wish had been ours turn out to be for someone else. These are the ones that got away from us. Mark Chesnutt had a big hit in 1992 with "Bubba Shot the Jukebox," but we had a chance at that first. We turned it down because we just didn't want to sing about a guy shooting a jukebox. It was a great song for Mark though!

Sometimes when we miss out on a song, it's not our fault. The Oaks were on RCA records for about two years and two albums, and except for the megahit "Lucky Moon," those projects were not really very successful. Almost immediately after we were signed to RCA, the label went through a ton of executive changes at the top, and we just never clicked with the new guys. For example, their head of A&R (artists and repertoire) turned down a bunch of good songs we really wanted to record. The head of A&R at a record label helps an artist and producer decide what song is right for them and the label, and our A&R guy turned out to be…well, let's just say he no longer works in the music business.

One day Duane Allen careened into my driveway with a cassette tape (remember those?) of a demo by songwriting genius David Loggins. Together we listened to "She Is His Only Need," and we were both so excited. We had an RCA project coming up, and we wanted to record this masterpiece of songwriting. We just *knew* it was a hit song, but the A&R guy said, "No, it's not right for a group," and he tossed it aside. We were just dumbfounded. The next year, when Wynonna Judd began her solo career, that song was her first big hit. Case closed.

In the same A&R meeting, Duane brought to the table a song especially written for us by Roger Murrah and Randy VanWarmer called "I'm in a Hurry." We absolutely *loved* this song, but it seemed to give the A&R guy a headache, so he gave it to the group Alabama instead. You know how that story ends.

Duane also had in his bag of tricks a new Gary Burr song called "That's My Job." Yep, the big-deal record exec said, "You guys have 'Thank God for Kids' and have played that family thing to the hilt. It's not for you!" He tossed it aside, and Conway Twitty picked it up. He recorded a masterful version of "That's My Job," and we've cried about it ever since.

Gary Burr is a masterful songwriter. We've recorded many of his songs over the years, but "Make My Life with You" is just a bit more special than most, especially with Duane Allen singing lead. I can't tell you how many wedding proposals have taken place on our stage over the years, and thankfully, whenever we've allowed this to happen, she has always said yes. (*Whew!* That could be an awkward moment if she said no.) I'll bet this song has been played at more weddings than any of our other songs. When the Ace sings it live, it's just as tender and moving as it always has been. The a cappella chorus at the end always brings the house down.

One more story from that magical meeting with the A&R guy. A group called the Marcy Brothers, whom we knew quite well, had recorded a song called "Achy Breaky Heart." We heard it and thought it was pretty cool. We wanted to put our own special touch on it, but of course, the A&R guy said, "No, it's too gimmicky," and threw it in the trash. Billy Ray Cyrus took this gimmicky song and…well, you know how *that* story ends as well!

The lesson here for young artists is this. Do *not* trust record label executives to drive and influence your music and your career. Be true to yourself and to what you believe to be right, and you'll go a long way. Except for that fateful meeting at RCA that day, we've always done just that. We learned a lot of hard lessons that day, and we've applied the experience to our own decision-making process ever since. *You must make music you believe in.* If a record label doesn't believe in what you're doing, you need a new record label. We left RCA soon after that meeting and never looked back. Now, don't get me wrong—RCA is an institution of music with an enormous amount of history. But we just never experienced the magic there that we did in all our years at MCA.

Had things gone differently, and had we recorded those five songs we wanted to, I'll bet we would still be on RCA Records today and selling more units than Elvis during his tenure there.

A few other songs *almost* made it. Over the past few decades we've had several songs that received a ton of play on radio outlets in medium-sized and small towns as well as classic country stations (we're considered classic now, you know). One such song was "Hard to Be Cool in a Minivan" from the *Front Row Seats* album on Spring Hill Music. This song was written by Rory Feek of the husband–wife singing team of Joey and Rory. It was a ton of fun to sing, and everyone else seemed to love it too. We figured if it had been released in the early '80s, it would have been a monster. Our timing was just off on that one. As a funny side note, our manager, Jim Halsey, pitched the song to all of the major automotive companies producing minivans. We thought it might be a cool jingle, but as it turned out *not* being cool in a minivan wasn't the message they wanted to convey. Oh well…it was worth the shot.

One night we were up late at Compass Point Studios in Nashville, working on our *Boys Are Back* album with producer David Cobb, when Jamey Johnson came by. Jamey hadn't hit it big yet as a performer, but as a writer, this former Marine from Alabama was scoring some big hits with songs like "Give It Away" for George Strait and "Honky Tonk Badonkadonk" for Trace Adkins. His soon-to-be-released, self-written song "In Color" would very quickly propel him to critical heights, but on this night he just sat in a circle with the Oaks and David Cobb and played us some songs he had written.

When he played a song called "Mama's Table," school was out. We just loved it! We made him sing it over and over to us, and we actually recorded it the next day. "Mama's Table" has become a classic Oaks' song that was never a hit record but is a beloved song to many people to this very day. Everyone has a great memory of their mama, and most mamas sat their families around the table to eat and talk and laugh. The song should have been a monster hit!

"Whatcha Gonna Do" certainly fits into the could-have-been-a-big-hit category as well. We recorded it on our special Cracker Barrel project, *It's Only Natural.* But again, even though we hired a bunch of extra promotion companies to help us push this song, it again failed to gain any traction on major radio stations that reported to Billboard. In fact, a dear friend who was a DJ in a major market gave it a spin—and almost lost his job. The suits told him, "We play only *young* country at this station, and playing any records by the Oak Ridge Boys is absolutely forbidden!"

Ah. So now we're forbidden even though recording new and relevant music is still very important to us. It keeps us fresh, and it keeps our stage show fresh as well. We know where we stand in the big picture now, and we have no complaints. We've had a ton of success in radio over the years, for which we are very grateful. There is no guarantee that an act will have hit records for its entire career, and we're good with that. With big radio being run by just a handful of corporate owners these days, personable DJs and real program directors have become things of the past, and an older act finds this a very difficult nut to crack. When one guy sitting in Kansas City decides what is played on 120 major stations, the writing is on the wall. It's a different paradigm from what we knew in the business, but none of us is crying about it. We just keep on singing.

A fan recently tweeted, "Radio station W___ never plays the Oaks anymore." We answered, "We are very thankful for all the years they did."

Besides, most all of our music can be found online at iTunes or somewhere else. There are so many great songs sleeping on most of these projects. It's fun for the casual fan, the Oaks scholar, and yes, us too, to dig into the catalog and find buried gems. I could give directions, but I'll let you hunt and find your own three minutes of magic. Years and years of recording have amassed quite a collection of very cool and meaningful songs that you may not have heard yet. Enjoy digging.

Of course, of all our many songs, there's one song that we *must* sing…even at our Christmas concert. You know what that is!

4

ELVIRAL

"Let's Sing 'Elvira'!"

*L*et's face it, in a book about the Oak Ridge Boys, "Elvira" obviously deserves its own chapter.

I call this chapter "Elviral" with good reason. I can't take credit for the term though. On a recent swing through Florida, we decided to take in an afternoon spring training game between the Phillies and the BoSox. My longtime friend Steve Robinson was visiting us, and we started to talk about what a phenomenon "Elvira" was for us back in 1981.

I mentioned something about the way songs and videos and such go viral in this age of social networking and YouTube, and Steve said, "Well, *that* song went *Elviral!*"

Going viral is easier now than it was in 1981. Cable TV was just getting underway back then, and even MTV was brand new. There was no Facebook or Twitter or YouTube or Instagram. But now, if you can get your cat to play an acoustic bass for 15 seconds, you can become an Internet sensation.

The Oaks were already riding high as we entered 1981. We had piled up a dozen number one singles, and five gold albums hung on our wall. We were touring with Kenny Rogers and Dottie West on the Full House tour—the first big arena tour in country music history—and we were winning our share of awards. We were pretty much recognized as the hot young act of the day.

As the story goes, late one night a song plugger for Acuff-Rose Music by the name of Ronnie Gant heard a bar band in Texas singing "Elvira," and he immediately thought of the Oaks.

Now keep in mind, Dallas Frazier's song, which had once been a regional hit for him, had been recorded over and over since he first wrote it in 1964. Rodney Crowell had a version out, and so did Kenny Rogers & the First Edition.

When Dallas wrote the song, he took the name Elvira from a street in Madison, Tennessee. Yes, there *is* an Elvira Street—check it out on Google Maps!

"Elvira" wasn't Dallas's only big hit as a songwriter. In 1960, years before we made "Elvira" a hit, a group called The Hollywood Argyles took Dallas's novelty song "Alley Oop" high on the charts. Remember that one? I do!

Ronnie acted on his hunch and presented "Elvira" to Ron Chancey. Ron's reaction was, "The Oaks have never done anything like this before. If Joe sings the verses and Richard bombs the 'oom-pa-pa,' this thing just might turn out really cool." Well, Richard did great on the "oom-pa-pa," even adding a silent "H" to the phrase "hhhhh-ooom." Without Richard's distinctive bass vocals, "Elvira" wouldn't be what it is.

We recorded the song as part of our *Fancy Free* album project, which we were already hard at work on, and a funny thing happened along the trail. As usual, we wanted to try out a few new songs on our live show, so one night we stuck "Elvira" in the middle of a set in Spokane, Washington. The result was an audience reaction that was… um…*viral*!

After a few more nights like that with "Elvira" blowing all of our big hits off the stage, we came home and asked MCA to release the song as a single. They did so in February 1981, and it became a huge hit on country radio right on through June. The single sold more than a million copies, and the album went platinum on just country radio airplay, which was unheard of back then.

Next we released "Fancy Free," our second single from the album, to country radio, and as "Fancy" was racing up the country charts, "Elvira" was spilling over to the pop charts. The song was played in heavy rotation throughout the summer and well into the fall of that year on every pop radio station all over this country and abroad.

We found out just how big a song could be, and this had a profound effect on our group. Because of lots of TV exposure from the *Tonight Show*, the CMA Awards, the ACM Awards, and just about every other major television music program, people came to know it was the Oak Ridge Boys who were singing the song, making the entire phenomenon even that much bigger for us.

"Elvira" won every music award given in 1981 except the Gospel Music Association Dove Award—and had even that happened I wouldn't have been surprised. It won Country Music Association Single of the Year, Academy of Country Music Single of the Year, a Grammy, a Jukebox Award for the most plays, and on and on. "Elvira" filled our walls and shelves with honors.

An odd one is our inclusion in the *Guinness Book of World Records*. At one Vanderbilt University football game, everyone in the stadium was given a kazoo. At halftime, the Oak Ridge Boys led the crowd in a booming kazoo rendition of "Elvira." It was the largest crowd ever to play a song on kazoos all at once—a record that may never be broken.

We have accumulated a lot of "Elvira" stories down through the years. In 1982, we made our first trip to Alaska, with a big Monday night Labor Day show scheduled in Anchorage. Well, the presenting radio station decided to celebrate "Labor Day Weekend with 'Elvira'," and they played "Elvira" nonstop for three days before we arrived! My friends, this measures out to be 72 hours of continual booming bass singer licks over the airwaves. I thought they might throw ice balls at us when we landed in Anchorage, but the promotion seemed to work because the arena was filled to capacity that night. *Whew!*

I sure felt sorry for women named Elvira in 1981. They probably either loved us or wanted to plant claymore mines beneath the stage. I have to believe they got it good from everyone. During our shows, we often find that an Elvira is in the audience. We have been known to check their driver's license first and then bring them onstage as we sing it. What a hoot that is!

One interesting "Elvira" experience involves the Mormon Tabernacle Choir. We were in Salt Lake City to film a patriotic television special for our friends at Feed the Children. The choir was part of this very moving and wonderful event. We performed several of our great songs from the *Colors* album, backed by a full orchestra and the Mormon Tabernacle Choir. Wow—it was one of the greatest nights ever!

Earlier that afternoon during rehearsals, someone brought up the idea that "Elvira" might make for a nice moment in the show that night. But word immediately came down from the hierarchy or whoever that "Elvira" must *not* be performed in this sacred place in front of this sacred choir. Well, that night after we performed our patriotic songs with flags waving and the choir singing, we took our bows and started to exit stage right. And then the Mormon Tabernacle Choir members themselves began to chant "Elvira!" It was unbelievable. So of course, we went ahead and sang it and brought the house down. This was the only time that "Elvira" was performed by the Mormon Tabernacle Choir! The hierarchy? Never heard a word from them, and the TV show came off great. However, we did have to help our godfather, Jim Halsey, up off the ground. I think he fainted.

In our concerts, "Elvira" usually ends the show, usually with "Bobbie Sue" as a follow-up encore of sorts. We've tried placing it in different sections of the set list, including as an opener on just a few occasions, but it really works best at the end.

We still hear "Elvira" played on occasion at some major- and minor-league ballparks and a few NFL stadiums. And everyone always sings along. There is nothing like being at a game and hearing "Elvira" blaring over the speakers. It never gets old!

No doubt about it, "Elvira" changed everything for the Oak Ridge Boys. We had been a very successful country music act, but now we were a household name. It went viral with every age group too. It was *the* monster hit that every music act would love to have, and we're still feeling the results of it more than three decades later. We can't walk through an airport or down the street without somebody singing "Elvira" at us. The single of "Elvira" sold well over two million copies, and the *Fancy Free* album zoomed to double platinum status in no time at all. It still sells today! Yep, it's still Elviral.

✳ ✳ ✳

Which begs the question, what other songs have gone viral, and why? There are plenty, of course. "Achy Breaky Heart" comes to mind. Perfect timing for a good-looking young guy with a mullet to hit it big with a catchy tune.

"Macarena"? This is unexplainable on every level.

All of the early Elvis songs and Beatles' recordings went nuts because of radio play, TV, and the charisma of the icons themselves.

From the 1940s to the present, you can pick out songs that became part of the soundtrack of our lives. Steve Robinson reminded me that "Convoy" by C.W. McCall went big because of CB radios. Remember those? Kenny Rogers has had more than a few long-lasting songs. I'll just say "Lucille" and "The Gambler" and stop right there, but there are quite a few more on Kenny's hit list.

In the year of "Elvira," other hit records were making big noise as well, including "Celebration" and "Bette Davis Eyes." Nobody is making much of a deal about those two songs now, but Rick Springfield is still out there rocking the heck out of "Jessie's Girl." It's amazing how some songs endure over time.

Just a word about Lee Greenwood's viral hit "God Bless the USA." It was early in 1984, and brother Lee was on the bill with us at Bally's in Las Vegas. Right before Lee took the stage, he says to us, "Hey guys, I wrote what I think is a pretty cool little song about America. I just recorded it a few weeks back, and I'm going to give it a try onstage tonight. I'm anxious to see what you think."

Well, the results were similar to our Spokane performance of "Elvira." When Lee got through the first verse and chorus, the usually reserved Vegas crowd were up on their feet cheering. It was so cool to be there with Lee that first night. And that's another song that has held up over the years. It's become almost another national anthem.

Every performer wishes they had a song like "God Bless the USA," "The Gambler," or "Elvira." Just today I ran into a young mother who claims that her little three-year-old girl loves "Elvira." A while back, a rocking drummer named Dan Nelligan, who played for the popular group STEMM out of Buffalo, New York, told us that the Oaks were his heroes and that "Elvira" had started it all when he was just seven years old.

Recently the super country vocal group Little Big Town added a bluesy rendition of "Elvira" to their stage show. They have even performed it on the stage of the Grand Ole Opry, and people just go bananas when they realize these kids are singing our song. We all think it's pretty cool and count it a huge honor.

So it would seem that our little song has been passed down through generations. Perhaps it's a big reason the Oak Ridge Boys are still around. Our music, our shows, and our own American spirit have been passed down from grandparents to parents to young couples and even on to their children. We see them all at our shows—still singing "Elvira" with the Boys!

5

THE SHOW

"Touch a Hand, Make a Friend"
HOMER BANKS, RAYMOND JACKSON, AND CARL HAMPTON

I was once asked in an interview what I did to prepare for a show. What was my personal routine? How did I prepare mentally? What kind of frame of mind was necessary for me to walk out on the stage and perform for thousands of people? The young woman conducting the interview was serious. I closed my eyes, found my center, and answered to the best of my ability.

"I keep a magic amulet in my pocket. It is said to have been found at the foot of Mount Olympus. Fifteen minutes before each show, I face the mystic east and rub the amulet while thinking about King Zeus. At the same time, I reflect on dolphins and the deep blue sea. I eventually imagine myself as a dolphin—or perhaps a whale—floating freely in a deep blue vortex. As my mind clears, I swim to the surface feeling fulfilled, if not somewhat wet. Then I'm ready to sing."

"That is so beautiful," the interviewer said, wiping away a tear. "You *are* serious, right?"

"Nah," I said. "Actually, I just roll on out there and sing. Although I *do* have several stuffed owls in my tour bus bunk, and they watch over me while I sleep at night."

I felt sorry for the girl until she bopped me in the face with her microphone!

The truth is, the Oak Ridge Boys have been doing this for a long time, and our approach to a show rarely changes. When it's time to sing, we just roll on out there and sing because that's what we're really all about. It's what we do. We sing. We are song men, harmony men, men of music!

In most cases, we've traveled a good distance to sing, and we're there for one reason—to hit that stage and put on a great show. I didn't come to Syracuse, New York, to visit the state fair, as nice as that is. I came to *sing*!

When the lights dim, the theme music begins to play, and our band members take up their positions, it's just as exciting today as it has always been throughout our long history. We know that people have gathered (and paid their hard-earned money) to hear us sing our songs, and we never take one person in the audience for granted. When I write that every song is a story, well, even more so, every person in that audience—from the front row to the nosebleed section—is a story as well, and I think about that many times as we're singing to them.

Concertgoers usually find that certain songs are meaningful to them on some level. Some will need to hear a message of love and hope, and a lot of our songs are designed to provide just that. I believe most people come to a show because it's a good getaway for them—a couple of hours of music and fun that take them away from their daily grind and whatever problems they're facing. Bills, kids, taxes, politics, bad news on TV…whatever it is, I've always believed that the power of a good, live music show can free a soul for just a little while, and we all need that freedom on occasion. I know I certainly do!

Several times in our history, our music has played a meaningful role in helping people through tough times. The greatest example dates back to World War II and the very founding of the Oak Ridge Boys.

It happened like this. V-E Day was celebrated on May 8, 1945, ending the war with Nazi Germany in Europe while the bloody war in the Pacific against Imperial Japan rolled on and on. From the time the atom was split in 1932, many notables had been exploring theories of nuclear fission and what it might mean. Albert Einstein once wrote in a letter to President Franklin Roosevelt that a nuclear reaction would begin its own chain of events and inspire a whole new way to look at weaponry and war for all time.

Einstein explained in his letter that uranium was indeed a new source of energy. When plutonium was then discovered in 1941, FDR set in motion a plan to develop an atomic bomb. From 1941 through 1944, most of this work was done in secret in the town of Oak Ridge, Tennessee. The project was code-named Manhattan, and while thousands of military personnel, scientists, and their families labored at the Oak Ridge Labs in total secret, only one music group was allowed inside to perform—a Knoxville-based gospel–bluegrass band called the Georgia Clodhoppers. They would enter the secret facility on a Saturday night, and on a makeshift stage, they would sing and pick and bring some much-needed hope and fun to those who were sequestered there. Eventually this group would become known as the Oak Ridge Quartet. These men were literally the forefathers of the Oak Ridge Boys of today.

History tells us that the brutal war with Japan would end because of the work of those dedicated men and women of Oak Ridge, and after the war, the quartet that had kept them going would move on to Nashville and continue singing and making music history.

We four have visited the secret installation in Oak Ridge and stood on the very spot where the original group performed. There was also a street named after us, which we all thought was pretty cool—Oak Ridge Boys Way. How about that!

In our earlier days, some people in the business thought the Oak Ridge Boys needed a name change. They thought it sounded hokey or backwoods or hillbilly or something. In fact, some of our earlier Columbia singles actually just say the Oaks. Now that's a nice nickname, but we never succumbed to the pressure. We were and are the Oak Ridge Boys!

I believe a name is what you make it. I remember the first time Lady Antebellum opened a show for us. I thought, *Lady what? What kind of a name is that?* Well, Little Big Town and Lady Antebellum are a couple of the finest singing groups out there today, and their songs are amazing. So you see, a name *is* what you make it! Think the Beatles! Point made!

People in the entertainment business, especially the Hollywood movie-making crowd, often believe that everything they do is so important. I find that music people aren't quite as bathed in self-importance, but we all tend to get a bit narcissistic sometimes when talking about the importance of singing or writing songs. Contrary to what I may have implied in the paragraphs above, we are not exactly splitting the atom here, and after all, it *is* just music.

However, our show and what we do carries a bit more weight at times, as we learned during the most horrifying piece of our nation's recent history—9/11.

We all remember where we were and what we were doing when right there on our TVs we witnessed the mass murder of thousands of American citizens. Within hours the headlines in the morning paper that day vanished and became meaningless. What seemed oh so important to us the day before became irrelevant after the terrorist events in New York City, Washington DC, and Shanksville, Pennsylvania.

All of the Oak Ridge Boys were moved to tears, overwhelmed with feelings of grief, patriotism, and rage—probably just as you were. But we were faced with a unique situation. We had to leave town that night for a show the next afternoon in Branson, Missouri, at the famous Grand Palace Theater.

How in the world could we ever get through that? We were drained. We were spent. At one point I thought we might even cancel the trip—a first, as far as I could remember—and in my heart, I was okay with that. A few concerts over the years might have been called off because of weather and such, but for us to call and say we're not coming? This never happens. If guys are sick or injured, we've proven over the years that we are still able to persevere and get the job done. It's part of our

DNA to press forward regardless of the circumstances. But this was a challenge like none other we'd ever faced.

We got on the phone with Jim, our manager. All five of us were on the conference call, and like the rest of America, our emotions were pretty raw. First, as always, Jim led us in a word of prayer. He prayed for our nation, for the grieving families, and for the Oak Ridge Boys.

I remember feeling a bit better after that prayer, and then, like the great life coach he is, Jim explained that some moments in our lives were special, and this was one of those. He said he had no idea how many people would show up at the Grand Palace tomorrow, but those who did just might need us more than ever.

"Your music is positive and lifts the soul," he said. "The Oak Ridge Boys represent America more than any other act out there today, and today America needs to hear you sing!"

Well, after that, we couldn't get to the bus fast enough! I was wide awake in the middle of the night on the way to Branson, so I crawled out of my bunk, opened a fresh page, and wrote a statement that would be read before the show the next day. I said in part that we were counting on Jesus Christ on this day to lift all of us and that it was our prayer that everyone in attendance would be glad they gathered on this occasion—and that included those of us onstage.

After the concert began and I read the statement, we made it clear that we all needed each other on this dark day, and when we sang "Amazing Grace," the 1400 or so in attendance stood as one and applauded. It was a great and memorable evening on that September 12, 2001, and yes, for those of us gathered inside that theater, that show was important.

✵ ✵ ✵

We love to be the ones performing a concert, but we all love music by other great performers as well. Let me get personal here for a minute. I was once asked by a major magazine to name the five best live concerts I'd ever seen and explain why I thought they were the best. Here's what I wrote.

1. Bruce Springsteen and the E Street Band, Cleveland, Ohio, 1984

Now, I've seen the Boss nine times over the years, but this concert was the first time. I had been turned on to his music with the *River* album in 1980—later than many of his fans, but then I bought everything he had recorded. For several years he was about all I listened to, so when I got the chance to see him live that first time, it was the greatest concert I'd ever seen. The Boss rules!

2. Johnny Cash, the Canadian Expo in Toronto, Canada, 1971

I had no idea then that in a few years I'd be touring with John as a member of the Oak Ridge Boys and that we would become good friends. Driving from my home in Buffalo to Toronto to see the Man in Black live, I was as excited as a little boy on Christmas Eve. Halfway through the show it poured rain. I mean *sheets* of rain...but Johnny never stopped! He even walked out onto a long ramp and sang in the pouring rain for about another hour. To this day I have never seen anything like it. I caught my death of cold after that night, but it was worth it!

Forty years after that concert, I'd be standing on a stage sharing a few words at Johnny's induction into the Country Music Hall of Fame in 2011. Amazing, isn't it?

In my tribute to Johnny I told the story of the day our publicist sent us some questions to answer from a fan magazine. Most were the usual questions, asking about our favorite foods, favorite colors, and the like. But one of the questions was different: "Name the one artist in the music business who has affected or inspired you more than any other."

It didn't take long for me to come up with the name Johnny Cash. The Oak Ridge Boys might not even be here today if not for him. In the mid-1970s, when nothing was going right for the Oaks, John and June kept us going. Yes, John booked us on many shows and recording sessions, but our personal time with him was even more meaningful. We often sat in a circle and sang gospel songs, read Scripture, and talked about faith and perseverance, believing in yourself, and trusting Jesus Christ in all things.

Even though we knew him well, Johnny just seemed larger than life to the Oak Ridge Boys.

During John's funeral, a family member looked into the casket and said, "I only hope that all of those things you believed in so strongly are indeed happening for you right now." Of course, as Christians, we know that heaven is real. We therefore know that all those things *are* indeed happening for Johnny. While here on earth, he stood taller than any one of us, and today in glory, he stands even taller.

That was Johnny Cash.

3. Elvis, Buffalo, New York, 1972

Richard Sterban would join the Oaks in October of that year, but on this night he was onstage singing with J.D. Sumner and the Stamps Quartet, backing Elvis. I remember thinking that was so very cool. In fact, Richard provided my tickets for the show. I had been an Elvis fan all my life, and that night at the Buffalo Memorial Auditorium, he looked and sang great. I would see Elvis a few more times before he passed in 1977, but that first time seeing him live was just incredible. I can still hear every song! He *was* the king!

4. Neil Diamond, Nashville, Tennessee, 1976

Just extraordinary! *Hot August Night* has always been one of my all-time favorite albums, and to see Diamond at last was really something. Great music, full orchestra, kicking band—and big, *huge* sound. Neil's 12-string guitar sounded just incredible, and his voice and energy and songs were unforgettable. I wanted it to never end!

5. The Oak Ridge Boys, Wilmington, Delaware, 1969

Willie Wynn, Duane Allen, William Lee Golden, and Noel Fox. It was the most cutting-edge gospel act one could ever imagine. They had just recorded their award-winning *Light* album, and they energized the whole room.

When the Boys hit the stage with a full band and began to sing the Bill Anderson song "Great Great Day," I felt like shouting. I had enjoyed all their albums and knew every song they sang. And their power and energy and total coolness were such as I had never seen before. Oh, I had seen other gospel groups and was a big fan of many of them, but this was a whole new paradigm. This group was so good that I figured if they really wanted to, they could be a major music act. History proved I was right. But that night, I didn't need proof. They already were major. What a show! I was in awe of the Oak Ridge Boys that night, and even though I've been singing with them for more than four decades, I'm *still* in awe of this group.

Of course, there might be another reason that concert is a favorite of mine. The opening act that night was none other than the Keystones of Buffalo, New York, with yours truly singing tenor and Richard Sterban singing bass. We were honored and stoked to be a part of this show with our heroes, the mighty Oaks. Over the preceding several years the Oaks had become the most popular group in southern gospel music, and they accomplished this by putting on an incredible show and singing great songs. Until that night I had never seen anything like them, and in five years I would become part of their continuing legacy and history. It's still mind-boggling.

A funny side story: The Oaks, as usual, had a beautiful Silver Eagle bus parked by the stage entrance. After years of hoofing the road in cars and vans and such, the Keystones also now traveled by tour bus. It was an early model General Motors 4104—silver and blue with a black back. The back was black because the old bus threw oil everywhere. We had to keep an entire bin full of cases of oil because we had to stop so often to add oil to the engine.

We also had an air-bag leak. When we shut the engine down, all the air leaked out, and the bus tilted to one side. So we did two things before we arrived that night for the Oaks' show. First, we washed the back of the bus—and discovered it was blue as well! Second, when we pulled up behind the Oaks' bus, we parked with one side up on the curb. That way, when the air leaked out, the bus would look almost level. Hey, we were young and poor and having a ball, and we were about to open for the Oak Ridge Boys. Life was good, and the bus seemed level!

That night's show changed my life, and I also got to spend some quality time with William Lee Golden and Duane Allen. They thought the Keystones sounded really good, and they both took the time to talk to me. They gave me some advice so we could improve what we were doing, and they encouraged me to press on and not give up.

I often think of how different my life would be if not for the show in Wilmington, Delaware, that night at the Scottish Rite Cathedral Auditorium. But God always has a plan, and some events are beyond our understanding. Our daily lives are filled with what-ifs. What if I had taken this turn or made that decision instead of the one I made? What if I had gone right instead of left? So many things are simply unexplainable.

I believe the answer lies in following Jesus and living your life accordingly. There's no sense in us trying to figure out the chain of events that transpire over the course of our lives, but what *is* important is leaning on Him for constant guidance. I believe good things happen as we strive to seek God's will in our lives. So you don't need to figure out the what-ifs. Just be thankful for what is!

I just know that an Oak Ridge Boys' show gave me a fresh, new way to look at my life and my music. It inspired me to reach a little higher and gave me an opportunity to make new friends. It drew me closer to God and changed my life forever.

I believe that during each of our performances, someone is sitting in that audience for a reason, and sometime during that night's show, they will hear just what they need to hear. We try to affect people in a positive way, and God has blessed our efforts again and again for decades.

So we continue to get off the bus and roll out onto stages and sing our songs. We may be at a big festival, a fair, a theater, or a performing arts center; we may be singing hits or classics, gospel songs, Christmas melodies, or a few patriotic songs; but rest assured that when you see the four of us onstage, we're doing what we love to do more than anything else.

How important is the show? To some folks it's very important, and to others probably not so much. But to the Oak Ridge Boys, it's *everything.*

✴ ✴ ✴

So what does an Oak Ridge Boys' show look and sound like? Well, it's a fast-paced entertainment package that lasts about an hour and a half. We sing a lot of the big hits as well as classic Oaks' songs with very little stage chatter. Many times we include some gospel and patriotic songs. There are 23 to 26 songs on the set list on any given night, and the set list changes quite a bit with every show. We've kept a record of every set list over the past 15 years so that when we go back to a place we don't repeat too many of the same songs. Of course, "Elvira" is on every set list. It's the law!

The show is a clean show. A family show. Mom and Dad and the kids are there, and so are Grandma and Grandpa. The young country crowd is usually in attendance as well.

It's amazing how many times we hear someone say, "I was a big fan of the Oak Ridge Boys in my twenties. Went to shows, bought all their albums, and even had their pictures on my wall. In my thirties I drifted away from them, but into my forties I heard they were nearby and thought it would be fun to go see them again. I knew they'd bring back some fond memories, and guess what—I got hooked again! Now I buy their newer music and never miss a show. I even follow them on Twitter!"

God bless these people! They keep us as pumped up as we do them.

* * *

Because of our big tours with Kenny Rogers and the incredible success of our own concerts in the early 1980s, we never saw an empty seat for about six straight years! We don't see many empty seats today either, albeit we often play smaller venues than we did in the heyday of the '80s. Back then, we played mostly big arenas, and we certainly learned from Kenny Rogers how to put together a great package. Our most frequent supporting acts included Exile, the Forester Sisters, Lee Greenwood, T.G. Shepherd, the late Eddie Rabbitt, the Bellamy Brothers, Nitty Gritty Dirt Band, and Patty Loveless. In later years, the Judds, Randy Travis, and other acts got their start by opening for the Oaks.

Big arena acts today, such as Keith Urban and Brad Paisley, have also learned the value of a great package show. I think George Strait and Brooks and Dunn probably did it the best.

Nowadays we mostly go it alone, and there is value in that as well. An evening with the Oaks in a beautiful theater pays dividends to the real Oaks fan who only wants to hear the Boys sing. Once in a while though, a larger venue will package the Oaks with Kenny or Lee or the Bellamy Brothers, and those are always like family reunions.

The Oak Ridge Boys haven't toured overseas very often, but when we have taken our music to other countries, it's been quite memorable. We've been to Belgium, England, Finland, France, Monaco, Norway, the former Soviet Union, Sweden, Switzerland, West Germany, and of course, Canada. We've played every province in Canada except Newfoundland, where we were once booked for a festival but never made it because we got fogged in at the Halifax, Nova Scotia, airport.

We nearly crash-landed that day because of poor visibility, and after spending 14 hours in that airport, we began to wonder if we had indeed been killed and were now stuck in some kind of maritime purgatory, condemned to be forever playing games on our iPhones and eating peanuts.

So we never made it to Newfoundland, and we never flew out of Halifax either. Our tour director, Darrick Kinslow, sent a bus to pick us up and drive us up to Moncton, New Brunswick. From there we flew to the United States, where we had other commitments. Boy, was that a strange trip.

With the successful worldwide release of our live *Boys Night Out* album in 2014 on the Cleopatra Records label, we are most certain to start traveling internationally again. We have had quite a few overseas tour ideas on the table as of late, and I would guess that even as you are reading this tidbit, the Boys just might be singing in Portugal, where our live cut of "American Made" actually topped the charts! Number one in Portugal, baby! I've actually been doing interviews in Portuguese…sort of.

One memorable overseas tour was in the Soviet Union in 1976. Manager Jim Halsey worked out a deal with the Russians and our State Department to send Roy Clark and the Oaks behind the Iron Curtain for a bit more than three weeks as part of a cultural exchange program.

With the Iron Curtain firmly in place and Communism in full force, we performed in Riga, Latvia; Saint Petersburg (then known as Leningrad); and Moscow. We learned a lot about freedom as we moved among those who had very little. It was an educational and life-changing experience, and when we landed back in America, we each kissed the ground. We never did find out what America received in the cultural exchange, but Duane Allen is convinced it was Yakov Smirnoff.

6

THE BUS

"And We Ride!"

I've never written much about our tour bus over all these years, so consider this a short seminar on music acts and road travel. I mentioned earlier that the Oak Ridge Boys had a big, fancy Silver Eagle, and my Keystones group had an old money-pit of a bus that threw oil out the back. It was trying at times to keep that blue goose up and running! But we loved that old thing because it was a bus and not a car.

In this day, a few younger acts have undoubtedly achieved some quick success and transitioned immediately from singing in a bar somewhere to being on a major tour and riding in a big, customized, Prevost coach. However, most of the acts on the road today paid a lot of road dues before they were able to lay back in a comfy bunk berth complete with satellite television, DVD players, WiFi, and a nice cozy comforter.

First some history. The Blackwood Brothers and their illustrious bass singer, J.D. Sumner, are credited for first coming up with the idea of converting a passenger bus into a custom tour bus. A replica of that first Blackwood bus, which is believed to be a 1947 Aerocoach, is now on display at the Southern Gospel Music Hall of Fame and Museum in Pigeon Forge, Tennessee. Since the early 1950s, gospel acts have traveled in tour buses, and eventually country music acts and rock acts also realized that customized busing was the way to go.

To be clear, early country acts, such as Bob Wills and the Texas

Playboys, traveled by bus for years, but they just had regular bus seats in them and not sleeping quarters and other amenities.

The custom bus business is now huge. There are now many bus-leasing companies in Nashville alone, and they all do great business. They even lease buses to politicians. We lease our buses from Hemphill Brothers Coach Company, and working with Joey and the boys there is a sheer joy.

Growing up in Philadelphia, I once saw an old General Motors Silversides parked downtown with "Sam and Dave" scrolled out in big, blue letters on the side. They were Philly rhythm-and-blues masters. In fact, Sam Moore is a good friend today, and when I saw him recently I shared the story about seeing the bus as a kid and wondering if they were actually onboard.

Sam laughed and said, "Onboard? Heck, son, we were *living* on that thing!"

It's a good thing I didn't know that as a boy. I'd have started hyperventilating if I knew Sam and Dave were inside.

Another time, while living in Harrisburg, Pennsylvania, as a member of the Keystones, I saw Tammy Wynette's old brown-and-yellow Flexible Coach go by. This time I *did* hyperventilate! "Tammy is on there!" I gasped. At that time the Keystones were traveling in a Buick pulling a U-Haul, so Tammy's little Flex looked like the Taj Majal on wheels!

In my early days of singing gospel, I was a big fan of groups like the Gospel Couriers, the Blackwood Brothers, and the Statesmen Quartet. To see their bus parked outside an auditorium was downright exhilarating for a young wannabe big-time singer. I think people feel the same way when they see the Oaks' rigs pull into town. They're here! They're on that bus! There's a show tonight!

When I was in high school, I flunked geometry because instead of drawing trapezoids and such, I was drawing pictures of buses and stage plots. I was such a weird kid—and here I am, still writing about tour buses.

Most touring musicians have spent many a mile traveling in cars, cars pulling trailers, vans, vans pulling trailers, airport limos, converted bread trucks…Yes, I knew a gospel group called the ViCounts that once converted a bread truck. You could still faintly read Bunny Bread on the side.

✳ ✳ ✳

As I write this, I'm sitting in the back of the Oaks' big black Prevost bus, and I assure you we have all learned over these years how to travel in style. At our age and with the many miles we've endured, comfort is an absolute must!

So what do the Boys do on the bus? Duane is sitting in the front lounge, talking business on his iPhone while posting on his Facebook page. William Lee Golden is in his usual spot with his big Nikon camera plugged in to his laptop, downloading pictures he took recently at some Midwestern state park. Tour director Darrick Kinslow is sprawled out on the front couch multitasking like a chambermaid. His iPad, laptop, and iPhone are all going full speed. I might add that all three guys up front are also watching Fox News on DirecTV.

The front lounge consists of two televisions, DVD and satellite DVR players, and lots of sound gear. A double refrigerator and several drawers and cabinets are filled with road food and everyday necessities. The kitchenette includes a sink, a microwave, and a built-in cooler full of ice and drinks. A nice bathroom is up there as well. To the front of the lounge, cordoned off by a dark curtain, is the jump seat (complete with its own TV) and the driver's cockpit, with a customized seat.

Walking from the front lounge toward the back of the bus, behind a push-button automatic sliding door (think *Star Trek*) is the sleeping area. Our bus has six bunks, five closets, and lots of drawer space for each guy. The bunks are stacked two high, so they're very roomy. Each bunk has its own entertainment system and individual satellite TV feed, complete with headphone jacks. As you walk through the open door, William Lee's bunk is on the bottom left, and Darrick sleeps in the upper berth. To the right are closets and drawers for stage clothes. A bit farther back is Richard's lower bunk to the left and my top bunk above that. To the right, Duane sleeps on the bottom, and above him is the guest bunk, which sometimes houses a guest or occasionally our operations manager, Jon Mir. But for the most part it catches more junk than Sanford and Son's old garage, including my well-worn and often-played banjo.

Next comes another Captain Kirk sliding door, and voilà, you have the back lounge. It's much like the front except there's a bit more couch space as well as extra closet space. We also have a smaller fridge back there, another built-in cooler, and another complete entertainment unit. Right now, Richard is sitting to the left, watching a major-league ball game on the big TV while watching a Vanderbilt University game on his iPhone.

I might add that each section of the bus has its own climate control. Front and back, left and right. Duane can sleep in relative warmth while Ban-Joey here has snow falling inside his bunk. Since we have a hotel room all to ourselves each day we're on tour, we've never needed a shower on the bus, but I might add that most solo acts have showers, and the back room is usually configured into a fancy, private bedroom big enough for just one. We always call that the Hillbilly Superstar room!

We're running two buses now, and the only difference between the band–crew bus and ours is that their middle area has more sleeping accommodations and not quite as much closet space. The bunks are stacked three high instead of two high. Not for the faint of heart or the claustrophobic! That bus also pulls a huge trailer full of gear, and on some occasions our bus also pulls a trailer.

With audio gear so much more compact now than in earlier years, we can usually fit everything we need in the trailers. But on our Christmas tours, which are much bigger productions, a big truck becomes a necessity.

In the heyday of the early 1980s, we ran four buses and two semi-trucks full of gear. It took two buses to carry our entire crew back then, except for the time we tried a strange bus we called the Wooly Worm. It looked like two buses hooked together by an accordion. The guys sitting in the back could see the guys sitting up front turn a corner before they did. That was one strange bus, and the novelty of it wore off pretty quickly. It looked like a train going down the street, and parking it was nearly impossible!

Through the years, we've had our share of near misses and breakdowns. We've traveled in every kind of bus imaginable. Sometimes we owned our own buses, but in the past decade or so, leasing has worked better for us. We end up with state-of-the-art buses at a decent price, and let's face it, if the engine blows up, it's someone else's problem. For years we owned Silver Eagles, but they're not in production anymore. Ask any gospel or bluegrass band that's still running an Eagle today, and they'll tell you that getting parts is impossible. And let's face it, now that we've been in the big Canadian-made Prevosts, the old Silver Eagles seem like World War II submarines. The Prevost is wider and longer and roomier. We don't bump into each other when passing down the aisle. That's a good thing!

✳ ✳ ✳

By law, anyone who drives our bus must have a Commercial Driver's License, or CDL. Safety on the road is an absolute must for anyone who makes his or her living constantly traversing America's highways. Anything can happen anytime, and one often wonders about the law of averages, but we tend to just put these things in God's hands and try not to worry about them. We've been involved in quite a few close calls over the years, and believe me when I say that we're thankful for the traveling mercies God has provided over the decades. Sleeping in a bunk on a rolling bus can be a bit harrowing at times, especially if an unexpected swerve is involved.

We lost one of the greatest gospel music songwriters of all time in 2008 when our friend Dottie Rambo was killed in a bus crash. The driver swerved to avoid a wreck, lost control, and went off the road and down an embankment. Dottie was 82 years old and was killed on impact. There are many such stories, but losing Dottie was especially tragic as she was such a dear friend and such a good soul. So I say all of this to ask for an occasional prayer or two for those of us who make the highway our home. Thank you!

We have drivers now, but there was a day—for most gospel groups anyway—when everyone in the group took turns driving the bus, usually in shifts of two to three hours. One would pull over when his shift was over, go back and wake the next guy, and then crawl into his bunk. This routine repeated itself again and again. Everyone chipped in and did their part.

✴ ✴ ✴

The story goes that back in the '60s, our predecessors in the earlier Oak Ridge Boys were quite the pranksters. One time after a driving shift, Herman Harper (the bass singer) pulled off the main road and drove about six miles. He then pulled into an old farm and drove the bus up a hill and into a barn, where he shut it down and turned off the headlights. He proceeded to wake my predecessor, Willie Wynn, and then went to bed. A very weary and not quite awake Willie settled into the seat and started up the bus, and when he turned on the headlights he found himself looking directly into eyes of several dairy cows. Lucky it wasn't a farmer with a shotgun!

This is the same group that put Limburger cheese on another act's manifold, and the same group that let a bunch of crickets loose on the Speer Family bus while they were onstage. Or was it grasshoppers? Anyhow, it was brutal!

Pranks seem to be part of the fun of touring. Recently Darrick and I went to see our gospel singing friends the Perrys in concert. It was a great show, and blessings were many.

We left a bit early, and we noticed that their bus was parked right by the stage door. We looked at each other and smiled. DK knows buses, so he found the keys, and we proceeded to move the Perrys' bus all the way around to the other side of the building.

We jumped in the car and drove off laughing. We laughed even harder later when we learned that Libby and Tracy and all came out of that stage door and thought someone had stolen their bus! It took them a while to find it, but it didn't take them long to figure out who the culprits were.

Nowadays, Duane is the one we must watch out for. He loves to scare people. When you get up in the middle of the night to honor nature, he can make himself small and hide in the bottom of your bunk and then yell when you get back in. One never knows when he will strike, but I swear he has stopped my heart on occasion!

One time we were parked outside a hotel where several senior-citizens' tours were staying. We had been in town playing a festival for several days, and I was just waking up on the bus and about ready to head for my hotel room.

(As a side note, I never sleep in a hotel room unless I have to. If the bus is there, I prefer my bunk to any strange bed. Stephen King once wrote that a hotel room is quite possibly the creepiest place on earth. Who knows what sort of stuff has gone on in there? Sick people? Dead people? Other things? Okay, I'm not really that paranoid. I just like the comfort, coolness, and quiet of my bunk on the bus.)

Well, on this morning I woke up on the bus, poured a cup of coffee, put my travel bag over my shoulder, and opened the door. There to my surprise were about 30 seniors, all lined up. As I got off, they began to pass by me and board the bus. I never said a word. I just kept going and let them board. I don't even know what happened when they realized that this wasn't their tour bus! I just thought it was funny and let them get a good laugh too when they discovered their mistake.

Back to our drivers. These poor guys drive all night and sleep most of the day. They rarely ever get to see a show.

Our long-time driver through the heyday of the early '80s and on into the '90s was Harley Pinkerman. Harley was a superstar driver. Everyone knew and loved Harley. He had once driven for Waylon Jennings, and he was a character for certain. He was as well known for his poker playing as he was for being a bus driver. Harley died way too soon of cancer in 1998, and his passing was very tough on all of us because we loved him so much.

Harley left a great legacy. There's a huge Christmas for Kids benefit every year in Nashville, and one of the highlights of the event is when all of the tour buses gather in Tennessee and run for the kids. It's amazing to see hundreds of tour buses all driving together for a great cause through our hometown of Hendersonville. Harley was one of the founders of this great event, and because of him, thousands of unfortunate children in middle Tennessee have a better Christmas. Even today, most all of the drivers, young and old alike, remember and respect Harley Pinkerman. RIP, Bub! We all miss you!

Driving a tour bus is easier nowadays than it was in the past. Modern Prevost tour buses have automatic transmissions. In Harley's day of standard transmissions, drivers had to double-clutch when shifting. I'll tell you, braking with your heel while tapping the accelerator with your toe and releasing the clutch on a steep hill...well, it's not for the squeamish.

When I was a young Keystone and drove our old bus, I wasn't very good at double-clutching. I cost us many a clutch throw-out bearing, and if people in a car behind me on a hill had known that a 21-year-old Philadelphia hoodlum was driving that big bus in front of them, they would have been worried. Thankfully I never backed over a station wagon full of hardworking Americans who were just going about their business!

I don't want to disparage bus drivers in any way by saying today's busses are easier to shift. That's not really the whole picture. Every day is different on a music tour. Musicians might have to go 200 miles one night and 600 miles the next night. They could drop anchor at a performing arts center one day and arrive at a county fair the next day. Some days the driver is enjoying sunny weather, and the next day he's fighting rain, hail, ice, or snow.

And the driver is responsible for more than just getting the act there safe and sound. He's in charge of keeping the bus clean and the shelves stocked with everyone's daily needs—favorite snacks, coffee, toilet paper, soft drinks...The driver's work is never done.

Our driver for 11 of the past 12 years was Billy Smith. Billy was not only a smooth driver who took good care of the Boys but also an entertainment business encyclopedia. We loved to try to stump him, especially on music trivia. Country, rock, jazz, bluegrass…he just always knew the answer. Billy was also a full-fledged Elvis impersonator known as Bill-*ee*! I'm serious! Unfortunately, we lost Billy in September of 2014. He was a fan favorite and loved by everyone. I'm certain that he's found Elvis by now and is getting some pointers. Until the day, Billy! Until the day…

In the mid-1970s, we were always looking for ways to make a few extra dollars. One day, Darrell "Curly" Jones, our bus driver at the time, had an idea. This was when we traveled on the bus called Chocolate— the four Oaks, our four-piece band, and one sound man by the name of Brad Harrison. The bus was so full that we actually built a special bunk in the back right over the engine for Brad. We called it the hell hole because it was so hot in there.

(Brad is now the president of Harrison Audio Consoles, who developed *the* sound board to have in most recording studios and concert venues for decades to come. A long way from sleeping in the hell hole on a bus called Chocolate.)

Curly found out that Olivia Newton-John was about to go on tour and might need a bus. We didn't have many dates at the time, so Curly leased our bus to Olivia. But there was a catch. We didn't have a bathroom onboard. We did, however, have a funnel in the back, near the hell hole, where the boys could honor nature. Using the funnel on a moving bus required talent, but that story is best left untold.

So Curly had a bathroom built for Olivia, and she leased our bus for several months. When we had dates to play, we borrowed either Roy Clark's bus or promoter Sonny Simmons' RV, or we rented something ourselves.

When Chocolate returned to us after Olivia's tour, we had a full-fledged bathroom. We, of course, named it the Olivia Newton *John*. Curly eventually left the Oaks to go into the bus business. His company was among the first of the premiere bus-leasing operations in Nashville.

As a footnote to this story, at a big MCA records soiree in New York City in 1982, I actually met Olivia. In fact, a picture of Olivia and me hangs on the wall of the Italian restaurant where the festivities occurred.

All I could think of, however, was the Olivia Newton *John*. She remembered the bus well and asked about the funnel. What a conversation to have with a superstar!

Here's another great story involving Chocolate during those gray days of the mid-1970s, when we had no gospel dates, no hit records, and no *dinero*. Most buses have destination signs on the front that say Detroit or New Orleans or some such city. Well, ours usually said Oak Ridge Boys. But we also had a whole scroll full of cool stuff we could use, and on two occasions in particular, our sign paid dividends.

Remember the 1973 oil embargo? At the time, we were in California, where truck stops would allow only ten gallons per vehicle. We would get our allotment at one truck stop, drive to the next one, and wait in line until we could get another ten gallons. The process was tedious to say the least. At that rate, getting from Fresno to Orange County took three days, so we did what any self-respecting gospel group would do. We turned the old sign crank to read, Johnny Cash Show.

You got it! Truck stops filled up our tank, believing that Johnny was on the bus.

"Is Johnny onboard?" gas-pump jockeys would ask.

"Yes, but he's asleep," we'd reply.

One other memory is even better. We flew to Sweden out of New York City for two weeks. Thank God we had some dates somewhere, although as I recall we pretty much broke even on that trip. But the girls were pretty and the meatballs were great.

We had nowhere to put the bus while we were gone, so Curly brazenly took the bus to Yankee Stadium and scrolled up our Governor's Staff sign. We took off to Sverige, hoping for the best. We were certain we would come home and find the bus towed and impounded, but security at Yankee Stadium actually guarded the "governor's" bus. In fact, they almost arrested Curly for breaking in when he came to pick up the bus. Somehow Curly convinced them he was the governor's staff driver. Pretty creative, right?

I wish I could share a few of the other signs we had on that scroll, but some things are better left unwritten.

We had several strange bus drivers in the days between Curly Jones and Harley Pinkerman. One guy named Jim Thompson was a kenpo karate instructor, and that worked out well for me because in my mid-twenties I studied martial arts—until I got tired of getting the stuffing beat out of me. It seemed silly to be learning self-defense techniques while getting my block knocked off every week. I could have done that by just staying in Philly.

One night we brought our bus-driving sensei onstage to present me with a new belt. To get a new belt, I had to show that I could take a kick in the stomach, so right there onstage (at a gospel show, no less) Jim did a flying backward crosskick that caught me right in the solar plexus. I flew backward about ten feet. I could hardly sing after that, but I did earn my blue belt. The crowd that night was astounded. And so was I!

Another interim driver was a big, tough, former long-haul trucker named Harvey. Harvey looked like a pirate, talked like a pirate, and drove like a maniac. One day we found black spots painted on the windshield of the bus. When we asked Harvey about them, he explained that he lined one dot up with the white stripes in the middle of the road and another dot on the side. He figured if he just watched the dots he would always stay in the middle of the road. We fired old Harvey. *Argh!*

Later, we had a driver for a few years named Jim "Pappy" Glass. His job was a tough one because we were running one of those tall MCI buses that had a lot of sway to them. Pappy handled it well, considering that the bus always felt as if it were being slammed by a tornado.

Pappy was also the patriarch of the gospel group the Telestials, and he was often on his cell phone, trying to book his little family group while driving our bus. We would sit behind him and listen in. When a preacher or promoter would turn him down, he'd get so mad that he'd hang up and grumble for the next 50 miles.

Pappy was also a taxidermist. One night he ran over a big owl that had flown in front of the bus. He stopped, picked up the dead bird, wrapped it in a towel, put it inside a cooler, and placed that in one of the bins of the bus. We were still out on the road for another several days, and it was the middle of summer. You guessed it. Pappy hadn't put any ice in that cooler, and *whoa*…the bus was soon reeking of dead owl.

Pappy was asleep at the hotel, oblivious to what was going on. I heard something I had never heard before in all my days on the road— Duane Allen was telling our road manager, "You call Pappy and tell him to get over here right now and get that dead owl off this bus!"

Boy, am I paraphrasing!

Another driver was named Dean Hartley, but we called him Elvis. He wore his hair in a distinctive Elvis pomp and even sneered most the time so as to resemble the King. He was driving our semi to a little place called Nashville North in Taylorville, Illinois.

(It was a small venue, but we played there every year like clockwork until it closed sometime around 2004. We stayed with other smaller venues that booked us when we were starving, including the Little Nashville Opry in Indiana. It was a payback of sorts to go in there in 1982 and see them make big money on us. These two venues stayed with us as well because we played them both for many years thereafter. The Little Nashville Opry burned down a few years ago, but we hear they're rebuilding it—maybe we'll be back there again one day!)

Dean pulled the semi alongside of Nashville North so the guys could unload the gear. Suddenly the cab of the semi started to sink down into a huge septic tank. It happened so quickly. They had to bring tractors in to haul the truck out of that hole, but the lasting memory of "Elvis" trying to get out of that cab as it was sinking into the kaka is the stuff of legend!

Reasons for a change in drivers is usually centered around our demanding road schedule, which is much more rigorous than most touring bands' itineraries. Many good men cannot keep pace with us. The day and age of drivers like Curly Jones, Harley Pinkerman, and Billy Smith are long gone. Those were men whose blood ran Oak Ridge Boys all the way and would stay behind that wheel through thick and thin because they loved and cared for this group more than they did for themselves. Yes, we had drivers like that. Men we will never forget.

As I've been writing this piece, a front tire blew out on our band–crew bus in Oklahoma. Fortunately they were slowing down. The tire literally exploded. A horrible fear for any road warrior is to have a front tire blow. Driver Tracy Denton had to actually stand up and wrestle the wheel as he pulled the bus over. If he had been going much faster, it might have jackknifed with the heavy trailer full of gear it was towing, and many injuries or worse might have taken place. We will always be thankful to the Oklahoma State Patrol and the Oklahoma Department of Transportation for their immediate response and help, but we are most thankful to our Lord God for His mercy and protection.

We made the show just fine. And when we asked the band and crew if they were okay, most of them admitted they slept through the whole thing. I was involved in a bus wreck in my early touring days, and I assure you that I would have woken up screeching! Thanks again, Lord!

Our trips are almost always safe and enjoyable. For me, this is the best-case bus scenario: We've been rolling all night, and I'm sleeping pretty well in my bunk when we arrive at our destination. After finding a good spot to drop anchor (usually a hotel parking lot), the driver shuts down the main engine. The big diesel grumbles to a halt, and the only sound that remains is the gentle purring of the generator, at which point I usually fall into yet a deeper and dreamier sleep. The bunk is dark and cold and quiet and...zzz.

A very long bus ride is called a "space trip." And on a space trip, our tour director, Darrick, usually has something very good cooking in the Crock-Pot. Say we sang in South Dakota the night before, and after the show we haul for home. That, my friend, is a space trip because we will probably not arrive home until early evening. It is also a day when the Crock-Pot will be rocking big-time!

It's also a day when the drivers really earn their keep. We do have relief drivers on a space trip—Darrick Kinslow and our lighting director, Dave Boots, have CDLs, and they both take driving shifts. And if need be, we will hire an extra driver to come out for these long hauls. Our logs are always in order, and we are always in concurrence with the law.

Well, that's our bus history. So when you see those big private tour buses roll into your town, the Oak Ridge Boys are indeed onboard and getting ready to sing…if we can just quit texting and tweeting and watching sporting events!

Things you will *never* hear said on the Oak Ridge Boys' bus:

"Duane Allen slept until noon."

"Richard Sterban is up with the chickens."

"Hey, Joe, bring that banjo on up here and play
   something for us."

"That's way too far between dates—we'll never make it."

"No, we don't want any food after the show."

"Bonsall just doesn't tweet very much anymore."

"There are never any good sporting events on."

"The Ace isn't on Facebook today."

"Nobody's hungry, so there is no need to stop."

"Richard is in the back of the bus playing a fiddle and
   eating a cheeseburger."

"The driver isn't lost."

"I'm out of ammo."

"We have a bunch of cheerleaders at the bus door."

"Golden is shaving!"

"That Carrie Underwood is one ugly chick."

"Darrick says the bus is clean enough…let's go."

"Let's leave the bus at home and take cars this week."

"I think we left Golden at a truck stop last night." No, wait…
   that *did* happen!

7

THE ROAD

"Highways, Hotels, and Late-Night Pizza"

That old highway does indeed roll on forever. Rodney Crowell knows what he's talking about—those white lines have been hitting us hard in the face for decades!

I was recently listening to my bluegrass friends Dailey and Vincent sing "Brothers of the Highway." The song is mostly about truckers—somewhat like "Roll On," written by Dave Loggins and recorded by Alabama—but traveling minstrels who have spent most of their life on the road can identify with any song about life on the road.

The Oak Ridge Boys are indeed "Brothers of the Highway," we still "Roll On," and we have even left Louisiana—yes, in the broad daylight (to quote a favorite song) on more than one occasion.

We have actually left every state in the early morning light at one time or another—except Hawaii. We've been to Hawaii, but as strange as it may seem, we've never put on a show there. We did a big private show on a beach once in Puerto Rico, but we've never sung on Waikiki.

I'm certain that the Oak Ridge Boys have burned up every Interstate highway and secondary road in the United States over all these decades—and lots of back roads as well. Most acts tour for only six to eight months and then might not go out again for a year or more. Most pop acts tour that way for certain. But the Oaks, the Charlie Daniels Band, the Bellamy Brothers, Willie Nelson, and Kenny Rogers really never stop touring. We may take a couple weeks off in January after the Christmas tour, and sometimes we may even take a little time off here and there in the spring. But we're usually out there playing from 140 to 160 dates a year.

Mile after mile of white lines, town after town, county after county, state after state. We have watched America go by from the windows of our bus for decades, just like in our own classic Oaks' song "Roll Tennessee River." And for those of us in travel mode, it's been a sheer joy all these years to look out on the amber waves of the greatest country in the world.

One of our friends and fans, Jeff Myers, brought up an interesting comparison between life on the road in the early days versus touring these days with many more perks.

Life on the road back then wasn't bad, but it *was* different. There weren't as many food or hotel chains back then, so the options weren't as varied. No Applebee's, Olive Gardens, Subways, Hampton Inns, and such. But we did have plenty of truck stops, pizza places, Holiday Inns, and Ramada Inns, and there were still plenty of Arby's and Dairy Queens. We even stopped at plenty of Colonel Sanders and lots of good mom-and-pop restaurants.

I do miss those "magic fingers" machines on motel beds a little. For just a quarter you could vibrate the whole room. I don't miss the Naugahyde though.

The biggest changes to road life all have to do with technology. In the old tour days we had a Mattel Intellivision video-game machine in the back of a crew bus, and we played archaic baseball on it all the time. We even had our own teams and leagues, and Richard acted as our commissioner, keeping track of standings and settling any disputes between the T Rat Cardinals, the Jim Krueger Pirates, the Joe Bonsall Phillies, and the Mark Bass Braves.

Now we watch the major-league baseball package on DirecTV as the *real* Cardinals and Phillies and Pirates and Braves play.

We have a hundred stations on our hotel-room televisions and hundreds more on the bus. And, of course, WiFi and handheld devices. As for video games, they make our old Intellivision console look like the first wheel.

We spent a lot of time back then reading books, magazines, and newspapers, throwing baseballs and footballs around Holiday Inn parking lots, going to movies, playing our video games, or whatever it took to pass the time and miles, just as we do today.

So much has changed, yet so much remains the same. Managing life on the road is an important part of what we do, and we have always found a way to make it work even when our iPhones are out of range. We've been to every major city and many, many small towns in America. We are, in fact, hard pressed to find a town where we haven't played, and on the occasion when we do find a new place to play, we always celebrate it (most recently, Fish Creek, Wisconsin, and Shaunavon, Saskatchewan).

✦ ✦ ✦

We have outlived well over a hundred of our concert venues. We're still here, but the likes of Ponderosa Park in Salem, Ohio; Lanierland Music Park in Cumming, Georgia; the Little Nashville Opry in Indiana; Mill Run Theater and Poplar Creek in Chicago; the Spectrum in Philadelphia; the Circle Star in San Carlos, California; and even the Starwood Amphitheater in Nashville are no more.

Our long history of performing in Las Vegas is littered with venues that are dead and gone, such as the Landmark and the Frontier Hotel. Bally's and Caesars' Palace are still there, but the Celebrity Room and the Circus Maximus showrooms where we once ruled are all gone.

I could go on and name them all, but you get the picture. Huge concert venues are long gone, but thousands of memories and songs are wrapped up in these venues for all of us.

Who can forget Mama Lois's homemade country cooking at Lanierland Music Park in Georgia? Or the water-gun fights with the audience every year at Ponderosa Park in Ohio? Or watching my own parents beam with pride and joy from the front row of the old Valley Forge Music Fair outside of Philadelphia?

We played for an audience of fine Minnesota folks at the old Carlton Theater before it was torn down and replaced by the Mall of America. The old ballpark where the Twins once played was right across the street from the Carlton, and we would always head on over there after a show to catch the last few innings of a ball game.

On March 5, 1978, Kenny Rogers and Dottie West hosted what was billed as the World's Largest Indoor Country Music Show with more than 60,000 fans in the Silverdome in Detroit, Michigan. The show was broadcast to millions by NBC, and we were thrilled to be a part of it. Well, I just read that the Silverdome is coming down and everything there from seats to concession stands is being liquidated. You can find a pretty cool video on YouTube of us singing "Just a Little Talk with Jesus" recorded that night in the Silverdome.

Another big, long-gone venue was the Astrodome. Once hailed as the Ninth Wonder of the World and home to the Houston Astros and the former Houston Oilers, it was also the home of the huge Houston Livestock Show and Rodeo. We played this great American event many times in the late 1970s and '80s. In fact, we held the one-day attendance record there for years by performing two shows in one day. (That record was broken years later by some guy named Garth.)

We have many great memories from that Houston rodeo. A huge round stage was lowered from the Astrodome ceiling, and the hot country artists of the day performed on that stage for about an hour right before the bull-riding events. This was long before ear monitors, and the echo was just incredible. As you started singing the second line of a song, the first line came back at you. It took some real concentration to be certain, and many an act went way off course in the center of that dome. I once slid off the grid while singing "I Guess It Never Hurts to Hurt Sometimes." It was pretty weird and somewhat embarrassing.

When an act was announced at showtime, they usually rode out to the stage in the back of a pickup or on a stagecoach. One year we heard that Garth Brooks actually ran through the dirt and mud to get to the stage, which is a very Garthian thing to do, so we decided to try it too.

"Ladies and gentlemen, here they are again—Houston Rodeo favorites and MCA recording artists, the Oak Ridge Boys!"

The band was already in place on the big, round stage and was starting to play the intro to "American Made" as the four us began to run through the dirt. It was slow going as we were getting bogged down in not only the mud but also lots of horse and bull poop. It took us forever to get there. We must have looked pretty funny from high up in the stands trudging toward that stage. When at last we arrived, we were somewhat exhausted. The band had been playing the intro over and over for what seemed like hours, and when Duane made it to the microphone at last and began to sing, we were laughing so hard we could hardly breathe, let alone sing. Our shoes and jeans were covered in mud and poop, and the whole big-time entrance thing was just a bad idea. I think that was the last year we played there.

Yes, the Astrodome is gone now, but the memories remain. I'll bet when they tore that thing down they could still hear some music rattling around in that huge ceiling. Maybe the first verse of "Never Hurts to Hurt" was still up there.

We've made so many memories, and the great thing about life on the road is that we constantly get to make new ones. You have to be around a long time to outlast that many concert venues, and I wonder sometimes how many of the great places we play today might one day vanish. We opened the Grand Palace in Branson, Missouri. What a stunning theater! It was once hailed as *the* showplace of the Midwest. Now it's vacant and full of spiders. It's very sad.

My daughter Jennifer once called to tell me she found a bunch of our old CDs in a bargain bin. It seemed to really upset her. I asked her if our new stuff was in the regular bin, and she happily replied, "Yes!" Well, there you go—one has to be around for a long time to be in the new section and the bargain bin at the same time!

Once I was walking with Ron Reed, a dear friend who pitched for the Philadelphia Phillies in the early '80s, in the parking lot after one of his games at the old Veterans Stadium (old ballparks go away as well). The Astros had lit him up pretty good that night, and as we walked by a bunch of baseball fans, they all began to boo and curse at Ron. These guys were brutal, but he didn't seem to mind even though his two young daughters were right there with us. I remember being thankful that I never get booed. Even when I'm fighting a cold and not singing my best, people are still out there smiling at me and applauding the Oak Ridge Boys. Nobody is yelling, "Hey, Bonsall, you stink! Get off the stage, ya bum!"

Well, there was that one time at a jazz festival in Switzerland where they booed us pretty bad. I'm not sure what these peaceful Swiss people were expecting, but it sure wasn't us! It was the only time in 41 years I can recall actually getting booed. That's a pretty good batting average in any league. To keep that streak alive I guess we need only to keep away from Switzerland—and we have.

As I mentioned earlier, we used to do more overseas tours than we've done recently. I referred to our Soviet Union tour with Roy Clark in 1976. The audiences had no idea what we were singing, but they smiled and responded positively to our harmony and sounds and energy. Roy Clark wowed them with his talents. The Ruskies had never seen anyone do *that* with a balalaika! The Iron Curtain was firmly in place at the time, and we learned a lot of things about *not* having freedom.

Recently we took part in a seminar on music and freedom at the Heritage Foundation in Washington DC, and our William Lee Golden, who never says much in this type of forum, really opened up. He gave the most moving dissertation on our experience in the USSR and how relevant it was to our appreciation of America and the freedoms so many take for granted. It was very moving and oh so true! We returned from the USSR as patriots, and that has never wavered.

So yes, the old highway has extended around the world a bit, but there are still many places we have not been, such as the Orient and Australia. Once a tour offer came in for Bulgaria, but we told our manager, Jim Halsey, "Man, we haven't been to San Diego in six years—why go to Bulgaria?"

This is typical Oak Ridge Boys. Going overseas is fun and rewarding and educational, but we would rather book shows in California before considering Bulgaria—or Switzerland!

These days the highway runs from the Colorado State Fair in Pueblo to the Norsk Hostfest in Minot, North Dakota. From the Jamboree in the Hills in Ohio to the Big Valley Jamboree in Camrose, Alberta, Canada. From a county fair in Iowa to the stage of the Grand Ole Opry, and from the Seafood Festival in Maryland to the Corn Palace in Mitchell, South Dakota. From the Pacific Northwest to the deep South, across the plains through the Midwest and on to New England, the Oak Ridge Boys are still out there singing. We're probably coming to your town soon, so plan on coming out to see us. Bring the whole family!

✴ ✴ ✴

As to the logistics of the actual concert, we usually arrive at our hotel in the morning. Each Oak has his own hotel room (I use mine sparingly) and his own routine for the day. Duane loves to spend time on the bus working the laptop and watching the news. He and tour director Darrick Kinslow are usually up early, and often most of the world's problems are discussed and solved right there in the front lounge long before the other three of us are even awake.

William Lee and myself are usually up next. We grab some coffee and our bags and head to our respective rooms. Richard always sleeps the latest because most times he stays up the latest.

Eventually everyone ends up with a decent meal and shower before boarding the bus for the venue at around five p.m. The band–crew bus has already been at the venue for most of the day. The crew has been setting up. The band may have been shuttled back to the hotel, or they may have decided to stay right there, especially if the venue is really nice with decent clean-up facilities.

A catered lunch and catered dinner is always provided, and the Boys usually arrive in time for dinner. There may be a sound check or a rehearsal—or not.

We all relax on the bus before the show, and if there's a meet-and-greet of sorts, we make sure we're dressed and ready for whatever time Darrick sets. After the show, we retreat back to the bus to chill and relax. If the next show is a good distance away, we might leave for the next town right after the load out. But most times, we'll go back to the hotel for showers and such and be back onboard before leaving time, which is often between two and five a.m., depending on how far we have to travel.

Drivers sleep most of the day and are always ready to get it on by the appointed time. The four Oaks are usually fast asleep in our bunks long before we roll on to the next town, where pretty much the same routine is played out again.

When we're on the road, a night off is never preferred. From a business standpoint, a night off costs us money. It's all outgo and no income, but once in a while it just happens. It's a part of road life.

A long distance to go between dates with a night off has its positive sides as well. Everyone gets off the bus for a few hours, cleans up, and has a nice dinner somewhere before resuming the bus ride to the show date.

Sometimes we try to plan that night off around a movie or a major-league ball game. Ah, that's the best. We check the team schedules to see if it works out right, and many times it does, so we swing by a major-league ballpark and watch some baseball. We really enjoy this and usually talk about each game we attend as well as that ballpark for years to come. If you have to have a night off, a night off at a ballpark is the best!

Of course, with all this travel, we've developed some traditions and have some favorite stops along the way. One tradition has to do with time. To the Oak Ridge Boys, the Central Time Zone in America is known as Tulsa time. Even when we're rolling home to Nashville, thanks to Don Williams's recording of Danny Flowers's great song, we always set our watches back to Tulsa time. "Gonna set my watch back to it 'cause you know I've been through it."

✳ ✳ ✳

One of my funniest memories wasn't really a road trip at all. It was 1978 and we were scheduled to be on the large Tom Turkey float in the Thanksgiving Day parade in New York City.

All four of us had watched this parade on television since childhood, and now we would be marching right down Broadway with all the huge floats, characters, bands, and Santa Claus himself. I think most kids in New York believe the Macy's Santa is the real Santa and all others are his helpers. Growing up in Philadelphia, I always believed that the real Santa resided at Gimbels department store. After all, would my mother lie to me?

On this day, we were having our own good time on Thirty-Fourth Street. We gathered in a celebrity holding area at around six that morning. Then we were herded onto a bus, where we sat for a long time making jokes with Patrick Swayze and John Ritter and enjoying the coffee and pastries on board.

Well, William Lee really started pounding the coffee. We all did, but Golden loves his coffee in the morning and really hit it hard.

Suddenly we heard the five-minute call. We each took a turn in the bathroom in the back of the bus—except for Golden, who was still slugging down a last cup of Maxwell House.

We proceeded to board the huge Tom Turkey float. You see it every year, right near the front. The huge bird bows up and down, and his tail feathers gyrate from side to side. This year, the four Oak Ridge Boys gathered in the front of the float, where we would wave and lip-sync "Callin' Baton Rouge" and "Come on In" for the next two and a half hours. This would prove to be known as one of the coldest Thanksgivings in New York City history. It was about 19 degrees with a very cold breeze, which brought the windchill factor to somewhere around unbearable.

As soon as the Tom Turkey float got going, Golden turned to us and asked, "Is there a bathroom on this thing?"

There is no need to go into details here. I will tell you that by some miracle, he *did* make it to the end of the parade. We would go on to appear in the Macy's Day Parade a few more times over the passing years, but riding the Turkey Float on this frigid morning in the Big Apple and pretending to sing in front of thousands of cheering fans and a live network TV audience while WLG was suffering in pain was one of the funniest times that I can ever remember. I ached from laughter. William Lee failed to see the humor.

★ ★ ★

One of the true joys of the road life is in finding great places to eat. Our favorite stops usually involve great food we've discovered down through the years—sushi in Los Angeles, salmon in Washington, cheesesteaks in Philly, chowder in Boston, grouper in Florida, chili in Cincy, pizza in New York City, barbecue in Memphis, or crab cakes on the Chesapeake. You always owe it to yourself to take the time to stop and smell the calories. Just make sure you're taking your statins!

When we're anywhere near Chicago, we always visit Garrett Popcorn Shops. Even if it's 50 miles out of the way, we will still roll into Chi-Town for Garrett's. We have also been known to swing over by the old Medinah Temple and pick up something at Pizzeria Due. The best deep-dish pizza in Chicago.

Another great tradition is dinner after a show in Atlantic City at Angeloni's II Restaurant and Lounge on Arctic Avenue. Our friendship with Allen Angeloni dates back decades to the days when Richard used to have a condo in Atlantic City. He and his wife, Donna, became friends with Allen and dined there often. Regardless of where we're playing in Atlantic City, Angeloni's stays open late for the Boys! It is simply the best Italian restaurant in the country.

Then there's Vic and Anthony's Steakhouse at the Golden Nugget in downtown Las Vegas. There's one in Houston as well. Simply put, this is the best dining experience in America. Honorable mention goes to Manny's Steakhouse in Minneapolis and Spencer's for Steaks and Chops in Spokane!

Whenever we play a casino date—and that's quite often—the first thing Darrick will do after we arrive is check to see if they have a great steakhouse, and the really nice places always do. The Oaks have a

tradition of dining together about an hour after the show to celebrate…
well, to celebrate whatever needs celebrating!

Hey, this is the road! This is living the life of a traveling showman.
This is what we dreamed about from childhood. We are all about keeping those dreams alive!

✦ ✦ ✦

Cruising the Caribbean with the Boys? Yep, we have taken part in
three huge cruise events, and there are certain to be more in the future.
We have hosted a couple Rally-at-Sea cruises on our own, and we
have also participated in the Country Music Cruise, where we shared
the stage and the ship with several other major acts, such as Martina
McBride, Charlie Pride, the Roys, the Gatlin Brothers, and many more.
Here's an excerpt from one of my Cruise Muse diaries:

> I'm very happy to be breathing in the tropical air after such
> a hard winter. I'm happy to be a part of this great Oak Ridge
> Boys cruise event as well, and right now I'm happy to be sitting here on my little private deck, staring out into the abyss
> as I write.
>
> A ship passes in the night. The only experience that is even
> close to a ship passing in the night on the dark sea is another
> ship passing in the night on the dark sea. The experience produces a fair amount of wonder. Who is that? What are they
> doing? Is some dude over there playing banjo, writing, singing, or just looking over at us and wondering the same thing?
> Odd thought I guess. It's like a parallel universe theory or a
> rip in the time-space continuum.
>
> I will sit here for a bit, enjoy these precious moments that
> have been given to me, and say a prayer of appreciation to
> God for all these blessings. To Him I give all the glory.
>
> I'm not sure how long I will sit in this spot or how long I
> might dwell on the passing moments, but I'm quite certain
> it will be several hours. Then I will go to bed and sleep deep
> in the arms of the Mother Ocean that Jimmy Buffet sings
> about. I will quote my wife, Mary. One night, years ago, as

we cruised through the night on the Caribbean aboard the four-mast schooner *Windstar*, I said, "Man, that's a lot of water out there."

Her reply…"And that's just the top!"

We sing tomorrow!

JOE'S ROAD TIPS
FOR THE CONSTANT TRAVELER

- If you must fly, go Southwest. It may be a no-frills airline, but you will not have to pay for peanuts or baggage, especially if you're flying a bunch of stage gear.

- If your hotel advertises a full-service restaurant, it's probably closed all afternoon. Not good for a traveling minstrel.

- If you must pay for your hotel WiFi, good luck staying online.

- A Marriot Garden Inn always has the best breakfast if you can awaken in time for it!

- If your room number is just two digits, you're probably booked into a very historic and rustic motel. In other words, a *dump*!

- Most hotel housekeepers speak only Spanish now. Learn a few Spanish phrases, such as "Can I please have some extra towels?" or "My toilet just overflowed!"

- The true measure of big-time show business is represented inside truck-stop restrooms. Avoid reading the walls…or writing on them!

- Old, refurbished, downtown hotels in small towns are usually pretty cool. Usually!

- Even in a full-service resort hotel with room service, the person on the other end of the line will never know what the soup of the day is!

- If you are in a hotel in the middle of a field and the only place to eat is at a gas station...*don't*!

- The elevator at the Westin Peachtree Plaza in Atlanta takes 14 seconds to get to the fiftieth floor. The elevator at any Hampton Inn takes 14 *minutes* to get to the third floor!

- Some hotel room towels do *not* dry you off. I have no idea why!

- Most hotel chains are pretty clean as a rule, but a bed-bug watch is still useful. This is one reason I rarely sleep on a hotel bed. Only when I have to. Always place your bags on a hard surface. If I bring bed bugs home from the road...well, my wife has threatened to gut me and then kick me out of the house!

8

THE TOUR

"Ain't No Short Way Home"

BOB DIPIERO AND JIM PHOTOGLO

W e've had a plethora of tour names over the years, and our longtime fans and friends probably remember most of them.

Cookin'

American Made

Deliver

Hot Summer Nights

Highways, Hotels, and Late-Night Pizza

Front Row Seats

Boys Are Back

Boys Night Out

Christmas Time's A-Coming

The tour name changes every couple of years for marketing and promotion purposes. But in reality, the Oak Ridge Boys are always on the Never-Ending tour, and that's a fact.

We're often asked, "How many days a year do you play?" or "How long is the current tour?" or "Do you guys ever go home?"

We *are* a hardworking band and always have been. Many acts take a huge chunk of time off and then plan, say, a six-month tour. But we've always been comfortable doing shows off and on all year long. This way we keep all our road people working, and we keep a steady cash flow coming in to pay salaries and expenses for ourselves and our staff.

We've learned how to do this after decades on the road, and in these later years of touring, each year seems to play out pretty much the same. We play between 140 and 160 show dates each year. We always take about three weeks off in January and then work half a dozen dates or more at the end of the month.

We usually start the year in Texas. Then we have a busy February that includes a 12-day West Coast swing. March, April, and May are usually light tour months, but we manage to play enough dates to keep things working well.

June starts to heat up, and July and August are usually pretty full playing fairs and festivals. And *then*…September through Christmas, the dates come on like gangbusters. Our year is always back loaded, but we just gear up for it, saddle up, and take it on. Fairs, Branson shows, casinos, and the Christmas tour keep us as busy as we would ever want to be during those four months.

The days at home in the springtime, watching the flowers grow and the trees bloom, are a distant memory once we hit September, but again, we prepare mentally and physically for that full schedule. It's all very doable, and we feel blessed to have the datebook filled. Many touring bands envy the Oak Ridge Boys' schedule and would trade datebooks with us in a heartbeat, so we never take one opportunity for granted. Singing is what we are about, and taking our music to the live stage is what we love.

✶ ✶ ✶

All the Oak Ridge Boys' dates are booked through the William Morris Endeavor Agency in Nashville. Our responsible agent for many years was Paul Moore, who retired last year, and our booking accounts are now in the capable hands of Barry Jeffrey and his excellent staff.

Our operations manager, who has been with us for 40 years, Jon Mir, works closely with the agency on every date that comes through.

About 50 percent of the dates need our approval. We work most dates on a flat rate, but we've always kept our price reasonable. We're willing to work with a promoter in every way to make sure a date is as successful as it can possibly be, whether it's a casino, a performing arts center, or a fair.

With some promoters, such as Al and Chris Zar, who have promoted us for years, we work a percentage split. That's always taking a chance because if the date doesn't succeed, nobody makes any money. But our track record with the Zars and several other top-tier show promoters is really quite good, especially during the Christmas tour.

We don't have to approve every date. The agency and Jon know full well if every base on a certain contract is covered to our liking. As an example, Jon may contact us with an offer for a stand-alone date with good money but almost impossible logistics and awful routing. We then have to decide if the bottom line is worth the effort and the wear and tear on our bodies. We usually say yes, especially if Barry and Jon feel they can book some quality dates around it. Many times this is how a six- to ten-day trip is created. Sometimes the money isn't what we usually expect, but if the date routes well and fills a night off on the road, we'll weigh the options and decide whether or not to play it. There is much consideration given for what we call a lowball money date.

Agreeing to sign a contract and book a particular date is only the beginning of the process. Now the whole team must kick into gear. Jon Mir has worked out all the details with William Morris Endeavor. Next our tour director (Darrick Kinslow) and production manager (Jeffery Douglas) jump onboard. Both men will be in close touch with the promoter and the venue to make sure there are no surprises or irregularities with logistics and production. We have a specially coded website with all our stage plots, lighting designs, and catering needs. They're all easy to navigate, and DK, Jeff, and our longtime lighting director, David Boots, are always on call to answer any questions that might come up.

At the same time, our travel girl, Janet Kinslow, is working with the promoter or venue to figure out where the best place might be to stay in that town, and she makes sure all the hotel reservations are set well in advance of our arrival.

We have a great promotional team as well. It starts with our marketing director, Kathy Harris, and extends to three public-relations professionals—Sandy Brokaw of the Brokaw Company in Los Angeles, the great Kirt Webster of Webster and Associates in Nashville, and Billy Glass of Glass Onion (Billy works with Cleopatra Records). Sandy Brokaw's job is to get major press in the town we're coming to. He secures local radio interviews and newspaper features, usually giving those interviews to Richard Sterban. We call them "phoners," and Richared uses his bass voice to do two to five interviews per show, depending of course on the size of the town and the type of event we're playing.

As a date gets closer, all the info goes up at oakridgeboys.com/tour, and each of us goes to work personally on Twitter and Facebook. Jon Mir and a company called Digital Dreamz in Nashville provide social-network aid and assistance.

If this date happens to be a fly date, all kinds of extra logistics need to be addressed, and Darrick handles almost all of this. Airline arrangements; transportation to and from the airport for Boys, band, and crew; and so forth. However, these fly dates occupy only a small part of our yearly schedule, as we're on our tour buses 90 percent of the time.

Multiply this by 150 or so dates, and you can see how much our team does over the course of a year. It's a good thing we have a loyal and long-serving organization, such as our receptionist, Carrie Ann Porter, who handles the comp ticket requests for every show, and Karin Warf, our longtime bookkeeper and comptroller (with us for 43 years!). Karin keeps a steady hand on the finances and payroll. In addition to Carrie and Karin, our office staff includes our marketing director, Kathy Harris (more than 40 years!), Jon Mir, as well as our tour director, Darrick Kinslow (who puts in a lot of office time when we are home). These great people have a combined 140 years with the Oak Ridge Boys! Besides the office staff, our front-of-house audio engineer, Marko Hunt, has been our knob dragon for 40 years. Our lighting director, Dave Boots, has been lighting us up for more than 21 years. Our production manager, Jeffery Douglas, has also been here for 21 years.

Quite the team, huh? You can see that nothing just happens. Now you know that when the house lights dim, the stage lights swell, and the Boys and band hit the stage in your town, a lot of people have worked very hard to make sure it all came off as smooth and as seamless as possible. We have dotted all the i's and crossed all the t's, so all we have to worry about on show night is singing our songs and enjoying the moment.

✳ ✳ ✳

In my previous book, *An American Journey,* I wrote this about the Cookin' tour.

> It is hard to explain the sheer energy of playing a major coliseum where every seat is sold and all ticket holders are on their feet screaming. The house lights go dim and the elaborate stage lighting truss begins to flash every color of the rainbow utilizing the highest technology of the day. Laser beams pierce the air and smoke rises up from the stage in a cloud as the band begins to play. Then, with an explosion of pyrotechnic fireworks from each side of the stage, "the act" suddenly appears onstage and there is pandemonium in the audience as they begin to sing hit after hit.
>
> The elaborate stage encompasses a walk around ramp so the act can run up and over the drums, performing to the crowd that is seated behind the stage. There is also a platform on each side so that individual members can climb up and sing right into the faces of those who sit to the left and to the right.
>
> Before the show, there were literally hundreds of people backstage to wade through—press, record label executives, radio disc jockeys from several stations, contest winners, local VIPs including politicians from both parties, friends of friends of friends who claim to know someone in the entourage, as well as TV crews from all the local TV stations wanting a sound bite from the act.
>
> For the performers, hitting the stage is actually a relief, because they have dealt with a crowd most of the day. When the buses and semis pulled into town early that morning,

there were several hundred people holding up welcome signs in the hotel parking lot. These folks had to be greeted before the performers could even get to their rooms and have some morning coffee. Then, more than likely, there would be an afternoon press conference, phone interviews, and a few big decisions to be made—and all that might take place long before sound check.

But, ah, that moment. Hitting that stage. What a rush. This is the stuff that dreams are made of. Little kids lie in the darkness of their rooms at night and wonder if something like this could ever happen to them. They sing in front of a mirror using a dust mop as a microphone stand—and a small oblong lamp shade as a mike as they picture themselves singing on a stage like this. Big sound, lights swirling, people cheering, yelling, and lighting their lighters [today it's their iPhones]—holding them up high above their heads—all for you and your singing partners and brothers!

I could be describing the Rolling Stones, Bruce Springsteen, or Garth Brooks. But this narrative is all about the Oak Ridge Boys in the early '80s when for three straight years, be it a state fair or a major coliseum, we never performed to an empty seat. This was the Cookin' tour!

Yes, in 1982, the Oak Ridge Boys' Cookin' tour was the stuff of legend! Sometimes at a show today we may still see a vintage Cookin' tour T-shirt or two in the audience. It always makes me smile. Back then I was young and strong, running with the wind at my back. I could prance around those ramps and sing "Dancin' the Night Away" like an athlete in his prime.

In many ways, the Joe Bonsall of today isn't much different from the Joe Bonsall of 1982, and I believe I can say the same of the Ace, William Lee, and Richard. We're all just a bit older, but I'll tell you, when I look out over my microphone and sing today, I feel no different. Everything seems the same as it did 30 years ago…until I walk by a mirror and think, *Wow…what happened? Who's the old guy?*

When the really huge years wore down, as they do for everyone eventually, and the big coliseums weren't quite as full as they had been in the past, I came up with a great idea for a tour name—the Good Seats Still Available tour!

Management voted it down.

My favorite tour name ever was the Highways, Hotels, and Late Night Pizza tour. Totino's Pizza sponsored the tour, we had a pizza party as a meet-and-greet every night, and it was a lot of fun. I even wrote a song by that name, but to be honest it wasn't very good.

For all my reminiscing, I don't really miss those days because I'm happy in my own skin today. But I do have fond memories. When I see young acts up on the big stage today, I'm happy for them. I know what they're feeling. There's nothing like the energy of 18,000 people in a huge arena, all there for one purpose—to see and hear *you*! They've planned this night for months, bought tickets in advance, and arrived early to party and buy a T-shirt.

Now the lights dim and…boom! We hit that stage and sing our hearts out for these wonderful people who have put down hard-earned dollars and used up a chunk of valuable personal time to be with the Oak Ridge Boys that night. My feeling as a performer has never really changed. I may not be able to jump quite as high as I once did, and I spot weld the energy a bit more than when I was younger, but I still feel the same way inside. I'm thankful that God has enabled me and my singing partners to still be singing well enough to warrant a spot on that stage and a crowd to sing for! We never take this for granted—not for a moment.

* * *

In addition to our normal tours, we sing at Special Olympics events, visit children's hospitals, and support Make a Wish Kids, Ronald McDonald Houses, Feed the Children, Save the Children, Compassion International, St. Jude Children's Research Hospital, and George Bush's Thousand Points of Light.

One of our biggest blessings over the years has been to see the way our music has affected special-needs children. I really don't have the words to describe the warmth in our hearts when we hear a mother say her autistic son responds only to the Oak Ridge Boys.

"He knows all your names and sings every word to 'Elvira' but says absolutely nothing else."

Over and over again this kind of thing happens, and it's usually quite overwhelming. To be a blessing along the way as individuals and as a group has always been our goal. The Oak Ridge Boys experience has allowed us to really make a difference from time to time, and we are thankful for this. Songs like "Elvira" and "Thank God for Kids" have played a big role in this endeavor.

For five straight years, the Oak Ridge Boys hosted Stars for Children benefit shows in the Dallas/Fort Worth area. Dozens of music stars, from Alabama to the Commodores and such local celebrities as the Dallas Cowboys cheerleaders joined us in raising money for the National Exchange Club's Suspected Child Abuse and Neglect charities. We were able to raise enough money to build several child-abuse centers in both host cites and in Houston.

Our participation in these events led to being asked to be honorary chairmen for the National Committee for the Prevention of Child Abuse. We served there with honor for several years. As a side note, Stars for Children was the first concert ever held in the Reunion Arena in Dallas, which is now also gone.

These events have all been so meaningful to us and have given us even more great memories and great stories. The problem is that when we talk about opportunities like these, we might sound as if we're blowing our own horn, and that would be the absolute last impression I would want to give. So I just thank God for putting us in a place where the way we live our lives and sing our songs sometimes gives us a chance to shed some needed light into the darkness, especially where special children are involved.

Sometimes making kids a priority has meant saying no. Right around 1983, a major cigarette company offered us a huge amount of tour sponsorship money. We turned it down. We just didn't feel as if we could do this while serving as spokesmen for child-abuse prevention and the Boy Scouts, and I have always believed we made the right decision. You can't sing "Thank God for Kids" and "Check Out the Boy Scouts" in front of a cigarette poster, and if it doesn't feel right, it's *not* right!

> The King will say to those on his right, "Come, you who are blessed by my Father, inherit the kingdom prepared for you from the foundation of the world. For I was hungry and you gave me food, I was thirsty and you gave me drink, I was a stranger and you welcomed me, I was naked and you clothed me, I was sick and you visited me, I was in prison and you came to me." Then the righteous will answer him, saying, "Lord, when did we see you hungry and feed you, or thirsty and give you drink? And when did we see you a stranger and welcome you, or naked and clothe you? And when did we see you sick or in prison and visit you?" And the King will answer them, "Truly, I say to you, as you did it to one of the least of these my brothers, you did it to me" (Matthew 25:34-40).

As a final thought on our music's amazing effect on special-needs children, here is an incredible excerpt from a wonderful book by Sharon M. Draper called *Out of My Mind* (Atheneum Books for Young Readers, 2010). The book is written from the standpoint of the child, and when someone shared this book with the Boys...well, grown men were in tears.

> For some reason, I've always loved country music—loud, guitar-strumming, broken-heart music. Country is lemons—not sour, but sugar sweet and tangy. Lemon cake icing, cool, fresh lemonade! Lemon, lemon, lemon! Love it.
>
> When I was really little, I remember sitting in our kitchen, being fed breakfast by Mom, and a song came on the radio that made me screech with joy...
>
> How did I already know the words and the rhythms to that song? I have no idea. It must have seeped into my memory somehow—maybe from a radio or TV program. Anyway, I almost fell out of my chair. I scrunched up my

face and jerked and twitched as I tried to point to the radio. I wanted to hear the song again. But Mom just looked at me like I was nuts.

How could she understand that I loved the song "Elvira" by the Oak Ridge Boys when I barely understood it myself? I had no way to explain how I could smell freshly sliced lemons and see citrus-toned musical notes in my mind as it played.

"SQUEAT"

Our group meal every night usually takes place around five o'clock. It gives us a chance to bond together in a special way before a show. Band and crew and the Boys usually laugh and catch up on personal friendships as we eat. Most of the day has been spent working or alone, and now all the players are gathered together. This is a special time for a touring band such as us. It's almost sacred.

This group meal is called "squeat."

Say this as fast as you can: "Let's go eat." Say it even faster. Pretty soon it sounds like "squeat."

"So what time is squeat tonight?"

"What are we squeating tonight?"

"There's a squeat room right under the grandstand."

"They're all at squeat!"

You get the picture.

9

THE CHRISTMAS TOUR

"Jesus Is Born Today"
VELTON RAY BUNCH

For the past 26 years, the Oak Ridge Boys have put together a hugely successful, full-production Christmas tour. This tour has become such a huge part of our year that we Boys are thinking about Christmas all year long. It could be May, and my mind will wander through the set list from last Christmas, wondering how we can make this year's show even better.

We start rehearsing Christmas songs in mid-September, and usually by November we have the show just about ready to go, complete with production and props. It takes a huge effort by everyone to pull this off year after year, and our band, staff, and crew put in a ton of extra hours getting ready.

If you've ever been to an Oaks' Christmas show, you know how much Christmas and Christmas music mean to the Boys. From small arenas to the most stunning performing-arts centers and theaters, our Christmas show has become a tradition for the entire family. We usually play 30 to 35 cities every year, and the turnout is always wonderful. It means the world to us to see these venues being sold out night after night.

We start the show with about 40 minutes of familiar Oaks songs. Yes, we still *must* sing "Elvira"! Then we take a 20-minute intermission, and when we resume, it's Christmastime for about 75 minutes. We cover a lot of Christmas ground too. We sing about snow, Santa Claus, romance, and cookies. We sing familiar songs as well as a smattering of new songs, all gleaned from the Christmas albums we've recorded over the years. We have a special time called the "rocking chair" segment, when we all sit before a stunning fireplace scene and rock our Cracker Barrel rocking chairs, tell stories, and sing songs from our childhoods. This part of the evening has become a real fan favorite over the past several years.

We always end the show by paying tribute to the birth of our Lord and Savior, Jesus Christ. We string four or five songs together in such a way that by the time the audience leaves, they're well aware that we weren't in their town for a *holiday* show. We were there for a *Christmas* show!

In this politically correct day and age, when many loud voices speak out against the very word "Christmas," we're honored to unashamedly stand tall, proclaim the gospel, and sing about the birth of Jesus Christ, the Lamb of God, our Lord and Savior. Songwriter Carl Cartee calls it "The Glorious Impossible."

When the concert is over, we come off the stage so charged and blessed that it's hard to wait for the next night to do it all over again. Of course, every show all year long is important. Playing the big fairs and festivals and such all summer long is exciting and fun, but when it's time to embark on the Christmas tour, I must admit, the energy level goes up a notch. Just seeing the trees and the lights and the fireplace and the reindeer and the sleigh being loaded into the truck in mid-November is downright exhilarating.

I'll also admit that by the time the tour ends, usually around December 22 or 23, we're pretty worn out and ready to get home to our own families and our own trees and dinner tables—and presents!

So how did this Christmas tour idea begin? With Kenny Rogers!

Kenny was doing Christmas tours a few years before we ever thought about it, and in the late 1980s, he asked us if we would like to join him on some dates. You already know that our friendship with Kenny went back to the days when he, Dottie West, and the Oaks were all a part of the history-making Full House tour. And man, it was just that.

Ninety arenas in 90 cities were packed! Kenny was riding "Lucille" and "The Gambler," and he and Dottie were having big duet hits together. We were the young guns, having big hits and winning awards.

It was something to behold, and we learned so much from Kenny. Then a few years later, in 1984 and 1985, we got together again for a reunion tour, and the success was there all over again.

So when Kenny asked us to join him on a Christmas swing out West and then another swing through the Northeast, we were honored to do it. Besides, we had two very successful Christmas albums on MCA Records at the time. *Christmas* included the megahit "Thank God for Kids," and *Christmas Again* was chock full of great songs as well. We had also been on three Minnie Pearl Christmas Party specials on CBS, so our Christmas persona was definitely in full gear. I think Kenny knew that going in.

I might add that the opening act on these shows was a young kid from Oklahoma named Garth Brooks. Garth was the most mannerly and polite young man I've ever met. He called us Mr. Bonsall, Mr. Allen, and so on, and the guy stood offstage every night and just studied the Boys and Kenny. He seemed to get better every night as well. What sincerity and raw energy Garth possessed—and still possesses today. Perhaps that's why he continues to be one of the most successful country artists in history.

One night at the Universal Amphitheater in Los Angeles, we were all onstage together for the grand finale song, "Carol of the Bells." Kenny and Garth and the Oaks were blasting away as fake snow fell from the ceiling. To be honest, I never got my harmony parts right on that song. I just ding-dingy-donged my way into just moving my mouth, pretending I was singing. Kenny would glare at me too. It's hard to put one over on the Sweet Music Man.

I remember taking a final bow that night and thinking, *We could do this. We could do a Christmas tour.* I was visualizing Santa and elves and scrims and trees, and within the next six months we were hammering out plans for our own Christmas tour. We were like little kids preparing a play for their parents. We had plenty of songs to sing, and ideas and input were coming in from everyone. We asked Marie Osmond to join us that first year, and the tour was called "The Magic of Christmas." It played about 15 dates, mostly in the Midwest, and it was wonderful. We even sold out the Palace in Detroit!

Over the next several tours, Brenda Lee joined us, and we even had the singing Chipmunks out with us for a few years. These were actually young dancing girls who, once they put on the Chipmunk heads, weren't allowed to speak—and they never did, no matter how hard we tried to get them to break protocol. If they had spoken while in the suit and the Chipmunk association had heard about it, they would have been fired on the spot, and a new Alvin or Theodore or Simon would have been flown in immediately.

As years went by, the show eventually morphed into being just the Oak Ridge Boys doing the whole show, and that has worked out wonderfully.

As December approaches each year, almost every act in the business is home, and their buses are parked. Only a few schedule Christmas tours, something the Oak Ridge Boys and Kenny Rogers have been doing for years.

One of the advantages of doing a Christmas show each year is that we have a lot of material to draw from. We've done six Christmas albums. The first was *Christmas*, released in 1982. The album was hugely successful and achieved Gold status for several good reasons. It was a great project produced by Ron Chancey, it had a strong mix of familiar songs as well as some awesome new songs, we were the hottest act in country music in 1982, and "Thank God for Kids" was on it! To this day people talk about growing up with that album. Overall sales has to be close to a million by now.

Our next Christmas project was called *Christmas Again*. (Clever, huh?) It was also produced by Ron and released on MCA Records. I wrote two songs on that album, "First Christmas Day" and "It's Christmas Time Once Again." But the flagship song on this project was "New Kid in Town."

I remember the first time we heard the song. We were doing a big show in Portland, Oregon, and Exile was our supporting act. During the sound check, someone (and I really don't remember who—probably Duane), played Keith Whitley's demo of the song through the house speakers. We were blown away. Truth be known, this one song was responsible for us wanting to do another Christmas album.

Keith was one of the writers on this song, and we have a vivid recollection of him coming by the studio the night we recorded it. He was so happy that the Boys were cutting his tune. Not terribly long after that we lost Keith. He was a great talent, and everyone still talks about his contributions to country music today. He is greatly missed!

Our third Christmas album was called *Country Christmas Eve* and was produced by Richard Landis for Capitol Records. I also wrote a song for that album that's one of my favorites. It's called "Daddy's Christmas Eve." But it was Duane singing "Mrs. Santa Claus" that really stuck out on this one.

Next came three incredible Christmas projects released by Spring Hill Records. The first was *An Inconvenient Christmas*, produced by Michael Sykes and Duane Allen. The title came from a terrific song called "The Most Inconvenient Christmas," written by contemporary Christian artist Kyle Matthews.

In fact, I wrote a children's book based on the song that was published by New Leaf Press. Some folks believe this project may be the best of the Oaks' Christmas albums. The fresh, crisp sound and the well-written songs all came together nicely on this one. I think of "Beneath the Christmas Tree" and Randy Van Warmer's "Just a Simple Christmas Song" as prime examples. We even managed to record the Hallelujah chorus from Handel's "Messiah." We worked off the men's choral arrangement and will admit that we recorded it one Boy at a time, one line at a time. A vocal coach named David Ponder worked with us on the parts and almost killed himself in the process, but it came out great. Every year we talk about doing it onstage, and we all go, *Nah*! Instead we play it over the sound system as people are leaving the Christmas show. (You can see it on YouTube, however.)

One music reviewer wrote, "The grand finale of the album is the 'Hallelujah' chorus. I say grand finale, because that is exactly what it is. It is like when you watch the Fourth of July fireworks. The whole show is great, but the ending is always extra special! The group arranged the music for this song and there are no words to properly describe it."

One more special song to talk about from this project is "My Son." A wonderful songwriter named Dorothy Moore dreamed one night that she witnessed the life of Christ through the eyes of His mother, Mary. She felt every emotion that Mary must have felt from His birth until His death on the cross. In the dream, she actually saw the crucifixion from Mary's view. When she awakened, she immediately called a songwriter friend, John McElroy, and together they sat down and wrote this blessed song. I had the privilege of singing the lead vocal on "My Son," and I have never performed this song without feeling the anguish and love of Mary and the very presence of her Son, Jesus Christ. Very few songs can do that every time I sing them. I truly believe God gave Dorothy that song.

Next came *Christmas Cookies*, also produced my Michael Sykes and our Duane Allen. This was really a fun project, chock full of great songs. An Amazon review reads in part, "Just when you thought the Oak Ridge Boys were all out of acorns, something whimsical and significant this way comes!"

The title song as well as my own "Uncle Luther Made the Stuffin'," "Little Annie's Christmas Wish," and "Hay Baby" were all about whimsy I guess. But if you keep listening, you'll also hear "Ordinary Days" and the real sleeper on the album, "From Love to Love," which is a masterpiece of a song as performed by Duane.

Richard's romantic "The Warmest Night of the Year" also makes a heart melt at Christmastime. I'll tell you, the *Christmas Cookies* album sure spiced up our Christmas show.

A funny aside to all of this is that on the Christmas Cookies tour, when William Lee would sing the title song, folks would run to the stage with boxes and boxes of cookies! I can't begin to tell you how many cookies we ate on our bus during those tours.

Christmas Time's A-Coming, on the Gaither Music label and produced by Ben Isaacs and Duane Allen, went more acoustic than all our previous Christmas efforts. If you're not going to take some different creative roads once in a while, there's no sense in recording a new Christmas album, and we used that new creativity to give this one a different blush and feel than the others. And it worked!

I give Ben Isaacs a ton of credit for coming up with a fresh approach to recording Christmas songs. Along with the Bill Monroe classic bluegrass title song, we recorded a fun song called "Peterbilt Sleigh" that resulted in us having one built for the show that delivered Santa to every performance. That's a pretty cool piece of show business right there, and we're always grateful to Santa Claus for taking time out of his busiest part of the year to join the Oak Ridge Boys onstage every night!

Not since a song I wrote on the first Christmas album called "Santa's Song" have I seen children react to an Oaks' song as they do to "Peterbilt Sleigh." We hear from parents all the time about it, and it's quite heartwarming.

Richard goes romantic again for "All I Want for Christmas Is You," and there are some cool, classic arrangements of favorites like "Let It Snow" as well. Then there are the four songs that I call the "final four"—they have closed our last several Christmas tours with the gospel of Jesus Christ. These four songs fit together perfectly in telling the story of events leading up to His miraculous birth and the birth itself.

First Duane sings "Getting Ready for a Baby." This is one of the best songs you will ever hear, and that's a fact. Next I get to sing "Mary Had a Little Lamb"—a beautifully woven parody of the old children's nursery rhyme with a healthy dose of meat and potatoes added. Then it gets even better as William Lee pours his heart and soul into the Mark Lowry–Buddy Greene masterpiece "Mary Did You Know?" which sets the stage for Duane Allen and the heart-soaring Carl Cartee song "Glorious Impossible." These four songs alone make the *Christmas Time's A-Coming* album a very special project.

There's a story behind "Glorious Impossible." I first heard this song as recorded by our friends the Gaither Vocal Band. I remember listening to the song on my iPod for the first time and being moved to tears by the lyrics and the incredible hook that described the birth of Christ as a glorious impossibility. But several years went by before I thought of it as an Oak Ridge Boys song.

Fast-forward to a plane ride from the West Coast to Nashville, when a very funny event took place that would become meaningful later on. A pretty blonde woman was sitting by the window across the aisle from where I was sitting. She was cleaning and sanitizing everything around her. The seat, the window, the countertop, and even the seat in front of her received a good spray and a wipe. It struck me as practical and yet rolling-on-the-floor funny at the same time. I instantly tweeted about it before we took off and called her Mrs. Clean as she sprayed Lysol everywhere around her.

As it turned out, she was part of the husband-and-wife contemporary Christian music group FFH (it stands for Far From Home). When Richard Sterban saw my tweet on his iPhone, he laughed and showed it to her and her husband.

Oops...busted by the bass singer!

Thankfully, Jeromy and Mrs. Clean—er, Jennifer Deibler— thought it all to be very funny, and we became good friends. Then last fall she sent me a copy of their new Christmas album, *One Silent Night*, and on it was a more laid-back but still very powerful version of "Glorious Impossible."

So one day on our 201† Christmas tour, I started to research the song and found out that it was written by a great contemporary Christian music artist by the name of Carl Cartee. I looked up his version on iTunes, found it, downloaded it, and compared all three versions.

With due respect, because I love them, I wasn't as fond of the Gaither version after hearing the more laid-back versions. I felt the song needed a big feel to it and although the Gaither Vocal Band rendition brought in girls' voices and more and more instrumentation at the end, and although very soaring and moving, I couldn't hear the Oaks doing that.

Yes, I was starting to hear it as an Oaks song. That is, if we were to ever record a new Christmas album—and I was seriously hoping we would do that because new songs always freshen up our big Christmas tour.

The Deibler's FFH version showed me how beautiful and tender this song can be, and the Cartee version came out right in the middle somewhere. Being the writer of the song made his version seem fresh and emotional. Let's face it—nobody feels a song quite like the songwriter.

Then it was December, and we Oaks were eating at our favorite Italian restaurant in Merrillville, Indiana, after our matinee at the Star Plaza. We were well into our dessert when I made my pitch. (I'd come to dinner armed with all three versions of the song on my iPhone.)

Over the clinking of dishes, I began. "We've been closing our Christmas show with 'Jesus Is Born Today' for decades, and if we ever do another Christmas album, this could be the song to take its place." I then proceeded to play "Glorious Impossible" in every possible way and as loud as I could.

Everyone loved it and agreed on the spot. *Whew*!

At that time, Duane was talking to Bill Gaither about us recording a new Christmas project, and the end result was *Christmas Time's A-Coming*. That project did indeed freshen up our lives—as well as our Christmas show—with new music.

So we did record "Glorious Impossible," and it closes our Christmas show with a great message, so well written by Carl Cartee, Joe Beck, and Wendy Wills.

So when you hear the Oak Ridge Boys' rendition of this wonderful song, just remember…every song, like every life, is a story and a journey.

That's it for Christmas…got the tree decorated yet?

SONGWRITER CARL CARTEE ON "GLORIOUS IMPOSSIBLE"

I guess stuff hits people in various ways...especially poetry, which is what "Glorious Impossible" is.

Nothing is impossible with God, that's true, but the song is intended to be a celebration of God stepping into what was impossible for us and making it glorious through His overcoming power. The verses try to set up pictures of things that seem impossible for us—the incarnation, walking on water, the resurrection—and then invite us to believe beyond ourselves and look for miracles that move us to worship.

Poetically, using two words that don't really go together normally, it sets the listener up to have one word redeem the other. Other songs that do that are "Beautiful Mess" by Diamond Rio or "Broken and Beautiful" by Mark Schultz. Without the verses, the chorus does not make sense or stand alone. The phrase "Glorious Impossible" is a response to the truth in the verses. Full context is best and especially important for this song.

10

THE GRAND OLE OPRY BOYS

"Howww-deee!"

MINNIE PEARL

On July 8, 2011, on the legendary stage of the Grand Ole Opry, in between "Y'all Come Back Saloon" and "Elvira," history was made. The oldest living Opry star, Little Jimmy Dickens, strode onto the stage dressed as William Lee Golden and surprised us all by announcing that the Oak Ridge Boys were to become the newest members of the prestigious brotherhood and sisterhood known by folks everywhere as the Grand Ole Opry! That night is now etched in music and Oaks' history.

We should have known something was afoot when so many friends showed up for what was to be just a quick Friday night Opry appearance. But as usual, we were pounding out a huge schedule, which included a ton of studio time. We were a bit tired and totally caught off guard when Dickens appeared behind us, dressed in a full, fake beard, a cowboy hat, and dark shades. Then he said, "I've always wanted to be a little bitty Oak Ridge Boy. You don't know this, but on August 6, I will become the newest member of the Oak Ridge Boys, and you all will become the next members of the Grand Ole Opry."

As Duane would say, "Holy moley!"

What an emotional night. We came offstage to face a ton of cameras and press from newspapers and TV stations, all the while trying to process this astounding honor. The *wow* factor was overwhelming. We did not see this coming!

For the next several days the accolades and congratulations continued to pour in, literally from around the world. There were tweets, Facebook posts, texts, and emails—all testimonies to the power of this great tradition in country music.

Many friends and peers expressed surprise that we weren't members sooner. Others thought we *were* members. The timing really didn't matter to me. The result was what counted.

In my humble opinion (or as my granddaughter might say, IMHO), there may be several reasons why the time came when it did and not earlier. In the late 1970s and early '80's, when the Oak Ridge Boys were topping the charts and selling out coliseums, the Opry was very different than it is now. Many of the older stars back then didn't seem to embrace the newer acts as much as they do today.

The Grand Ole Opry is bigger than it has ever been, and I believe that the cutting-edge leadership of Colin Reed, Steve Buchanan, Pete Fisher, and their associates, including Gina Keltner, has everything to do with it. They work hard to maintain the tradition of the great older acts and also bring in a healthy mix of the young stars, the likes of which are lifting country music to newer heights with every passing year.

Bring into the fold folks like Trace

★ ★ ★

"When you look back over the years and take note of all the good things that have happened to us, getting inducted into the Grand Ole Opry comes right at the top of that list. All of us have a hard time finding words to describe the feeling we get when we walk into that building. We feel like we belong, like we're part of the family...you really can't put a price on that! There's a circle in the center of the stage made from the floor of the old Ryman auditorium...All of us always touch that circle because it is just so great to be a part of all this history."

RICHARD STERBAN,
in an interview with
Cameron Dole for
KWHW radio

and Carrie and Brad and Dierks and Blake and Josh. As they join Bill Anderson, Jim Ed Brown, Jeannie Seely, and such, the Opry becomes a winning situation, making people of all ages happy they bought tickets. The Opry has also expanded to Tuesdays and Fridays and has added special events, such as classic country nights and a bluegrass series.

As years went by and the Oak Ridge Boys continued to pound away at our blessed career, I had thought our time to join the Opry might have passed us by. Although I felt their love and respect, I always figured we had gotten lost in the passing of time and the Opry membership boat had sailed away without us. That's why tears were shed when it was finally announced. What an honor!

Through the years, the Oaks have always been happy to sing a few songs on the hallowed Opry stage when asked, and in so doing, we've always felt we were a small part of the magic that is the Grand Ole Opry. But it's different now. As of August 6, 2011, we've been able to call ourselves Opry stars!

The best way I can explain it is to say it's as if a bunch of friends have been asking us over for dinner for years, but this time they said, "Hey, boys, pack a bag…you're moving in now. This is home!" Home at last… to the Grand Ole Opry.

If I have one regret, it's that some of our old Opry friends weren't still around to witness that night. So many of the older Opry legends have gone home, and I miss them all. But there was one I especially loved, and I know you did too. That was Minnie Pearl. I just loved Mrs. Sarah Cannon and continue to miss her. The huge picture of her backstage at the Opry House gives me goose bumps. Every time we play the Opry, I take some time to stand before it and pay homage to Miss Minnie.

Howww-deee! I can still hear it!

Another great friend from the Opry passed on more recently. That was our friend George Jones.

Here's a great George Jones story. The year was 1979, and the

Possum—as George was known by friends and fans like—and Tammy Wynette were to open for us at the DuQuoin State Fair in Illinois. Old "No-Show" Jones lived up to his reputation that night. He got into an argument with a few folks and took a five-hour taxi ride back to Nashville without performing that night. But my story is about what happened about two hours before showtime, when George boarded our bus. After some laughter and a few stories, George took his guitar out of its case, told us he had just recorded a wonderful song, and asked if we would like to hear it. Sitting there on our bus, George began to strum and sing "He Stopped Loving Her Today." Before the rest of world ever heard it, the four Oak Ridge Boys were stunned into submission by perhaps the greatest country song of all time. We have never forgotten this precious memory, and I'm thrilled to be sharing it now. The song was released in 1980, and the rest is history.

One of our greatest and most memorable moments on the Grand Ole Opry stage came in 2011 on the night George Jones was honored on his eightieth birthday. One artist after another crossed the stage and sang a George Jones song as George and his wife, Nancy, looked on and smiled and applauded from the front row. We were honored to sing "Same Ole Me" that night. We had recorded that song with George in 1982, and it was a number one country smash.

✱ ★ ✱

"You know how cool it is for an act like us, at our age, to walk out there on to the stage of the Grand Ole Opry? I mean, just look at it from our standpoint. Here are some of the biggest stars of the day on the show, the place is totally sold out, and we tore it down. Do you know how good that feels? I mean this in all humility. To go out there and receive *that* kind of acceptance from the people backstage as well as the people in the front of the stage... well, it's pretty meaningful. It kind of shows that we have done some things right over all of these years, and that's a nice feeling to go to bed on!"

JOE BONSALL, IN AN INTERVIEW WITH CAMERON DOLE FOR KWHW RADIO

THE GRAND OLE OPRY BOYS ✸ 109

Over the years we performed the song with George many times, but singing it *for* him on that Opry stage and on that night was very special.

After we finished singing, George came up onstage and hugged us and told us he loved us. It meant the world. How could we have known that George would leave us so soon after that unforgettable event? Since that night, we've performed "Same Ole Me" many times in his honor and in his memory. At his funeral in 2013, right there in the Grand Ole Opry House, we sang "Farther Along." George would have loved that. Rest easy, Possum!

The Oak Ridge Boys' association with the Opry reaches back for decades. In the late 1940s and early '50s, after the war, the Oak Ridge Boys with Wally Fowler moved to Nashville from Oak Ridge and hosted the Friday All Night Singing Convention at the Ryman. The shows were all carried live on WSM radio. The early Oaks played the Opry stage many times in those days.

✸ ✸ ✸

We were sorry to hear that we also lost Little Jimmy Dickens on January 2, 2015, at age 94. He had just performed on the Opry stage on December 20. He was one of a kind, and he will be missed by everyone.

To me, Little Jimmy Dickens was *the* ambassador for, and the face of, the Grand Ole Opry. With Minnie and Roy and Porter and so many of the old guard passing on, Jimmy stood tall in their place. Jimmy invited and then welcomed the Oak Ridge Boys into the Opry family, and we will never forget him for this honor and for his meaningful friendship. He was always there for everyone who graced the magic circle, whether as a family member or a guest, and his blessings mattered to every artist regardless of their style or level of success. Everyone sought him out. Everyone wanted a picture taken with this energetic legend. Selfies and photobombs were in abundant supply backstage around Jimmy Dickens.

We know that we all have appointments to one day pass from this earth into glory, yet there are those who seem as if they will always be here with us. Jimmy was one of those.

Not long ago I met a lady at the market who told me she was singing along with Jimmy Dickens when she was just ten years old, and now she was seventy-six. What a legacy!

Winston Churchill once said, "The longer you can look back, the farther you can look forward." So we look back over 94 years of fun and music and laughs and friendship and love and magical, memorable moments that Jimmy gave us all so unselfishly. Looking forward, we realize that the Opry and country music will certainly survive and even continue to thrive without Little Jimmy Dickens. But it will not be the same. It can never be the same. The only consolation is that we will see him again one day, and for this we rejoice. Right now, though, I dread the empty feeling of being backstage at the Opry without the "Tater."

★ ★ ★

In 2010 we had a horrible and historic flood in Nashville. A huge rain front stalled over middle Tennessee in early May, and it didn't stop raining for days. In fact, 17 inches of rain fell in just 36 hours. The damage was incredible. The Cumberland River rose 12 feet above flood stage, flooding the Grand Ole Opry House itself. The entire floor, the stage, and the dressing rooms were ruined.

The middle of the Opry stage had always included a famous circle made of wood from the original Ryman Auditorium, which once housed the Opry. When a solo artist performs, he or she stands right inside the circle. But because we're a four-part group, the guys on the end, Richard and I, have to make a conscious effort to step inside the circle as we sing—and we always do!

Well, when the flood hit, workers were able to remove that circle before the stage went underwater. Then, when the stage was rebuilt, a wonderful ceremony commemorated the reinstallation of the circle. It was beautiful. The Grand Ole Opry House is better now than it ever was, but to see that plaque showing the high-water mark backstage really makes us thankful that this historic country-music mecca is once again on solid ground.

11

THE ORB DOCTRINE

"He's Gonna Smile on Me"
THOMAS CAIN AND CLIFFORD CURRY

The music business is as easy or as difficult as you want to make it. I'm pretty certain that's true with most vocations in which relationships with people are vital. The Oak Ridge Boys live by the unwritten and mostly unspoken rule that I'll call the ORB Doctrine. It's not *the* blueprint for longevity, but in my opinion it's a big part of the secret to our long-term success.

How many times have you heard about someone who, after achieving a certain amount of success, became arrogant and self-centered? A few hit records and a few sold-out shows have changed this guy into a supreme being who mistreats people, flaunts his ego, and has become difficult to be around.

In reality, this person may have always been a jerk—on his school campus, in his neighborhood, and around his own family dinner table—long before he ever heard his own voice on the radio. Success can change a person, but more often than not, it makes people more modest, not more prideful. When most people are successful, whether in music or any other vocation, they are humbled and honored to succeed, and they try their best every day to earn their notoriety.

But then there are those very few whose jerkiness follows them into their success.

I can't tell you how many times over the years we've performed at, say, a state fair where everyone was talking bad about the act that played the night before. The fair board, the promoter, the stagehands, and the radio dudes were all glad to see this act's entourage pack up and depart the premises. The artist, his tour director, his band, and his crew were obnoxious to everyone and were not likely to be invited back.

On the other hand, the Oaks have been invited to the Kentucky State Fair 40 times, and we've always been welcomed with open arms by everyone associated with the event.

Why? I believe it's the ORB Doctrine.

As I wrote in an earlier chapter, when the Oaks book a concert, we promote the date by doing print and radio interviews. We tweet the show info on Twitter and post it on our website. Darrick Kinslow and Jeffery Douglas work out every detail with the promoter long before we arrive. Every base is covered—catering, meet-and-greet requests, expected show length, and more. The relationship is on a positive track long before we arrive. There are no surprises of any kind for anyone involved in the production or the preparation for the show.

Our crew and gear arrive on show day, and the crew sets up the stage while treating everyone there with respect. Later, when the Oak Ridge Boys arrive, we are nice to everyone, shake hands, smile, put on a big show, say thank you, and get back on the bus. The entire process can be just that easy. Keep the egos in check, make few if any demands, treat people right, and leave everyone happy with every part of the experience.

Now, don't get me wrong. The Oaks are far from perfect! We've made our share of mistakes over the years, but our batting average is pretty darn good, and every year our datebook is full of repeat business. Promoters and event planners are always glad to see the Oak Ridge Boys' tour buses pull up to their venue. They know that this will be a trouble-free day, and when the buses depart, we will leave behind some wonderful friendships and warm feelings. Did I mention treating people right? You bet I did! I'm proud of this legacy, and the credit goes to everyone in our organization. But as always, it starts with the top.

The four Oak Ridge Boys were all brought up in good, hardworking American families. We were taught to be honest, to honor God in our lives, to treat people the way we want to be treated, and to work hard every day. My mom, Lillie, assured me every single day she was alive that if I did these things, good things could and would happen in my life. My singing partners were all brought up the same way, and it shines through in our work ethic and may very well be the single biggest reason why we're still around today.

Success is dressed in coveralls and looks a lot like *work*. Too many people think that every good thing in life is owed to them for some reason, and they keep waiting for their limo to show up. Well, they can keep on waiting because that's not how it works.

But the catch is, you have to be willing! Willing to sacrifice much of your personal life for the cause of something greater than yourself. Each of the Oak Ridge Boys realizes that he is just a spoke in the wheel and that the big picture is way more important than his own contribution. This is the joy of being in a group that is much bigger than each individual's talent. The sum of the parts is what matters the most. I suppose being a big solo act would be cool, but all four of us Oaks are *group* men! We need each other, love each other, and respect each other. Each of us feels fortunate and blessed to be one of the Oak Ridge Boys, and we never take it for granted.

Duane Allen is a kind and generous man. If I had a serious problem in my life, he would be the first one I would call. He cares about people. He cares about everyone who works at ORB Inc. and is well loved in return by everyone.

William Lee Golden can rear up like any other Alabama country boy, but for the most part he's a gentle giant. He just may be the most

"The Oak Ridge Boys? Well, I feel that we're all fortunate to be a part of the group because we all bring something different to the group, and that's what makes up the mix that the people respond to. It electrifies us, and it electrifies the people out there, so it's a contagious thing, you know, and to be a part of it...it's something we don't take lightly."

WILLIAM LEE GOLDEN

popular Oak of all, and it goes beyond his mountain-man persona. Just look into those eyes and you'll see the gentle spirit and artistic vision in his heart and soul.

Richard Sterban is honest and true. He's as steady as a rock and always ready to go the last mile for the group. His bass voice provides the solid sound of our group, and his life and example provide the solid foundation of our way of life. He doesn't say much, but I assure you that when he speaks, it's always relevant and well worth listening to.

As for Joe Bonsall…I just try to live my life the way my mom taught me. I'm pretty consistent. What you see out of me today is pretty much what you will see tomorrow and exactly what you saw yesterday. I'm a good friend, and like my three partners, I'm not afraid of hard work.

Now, can I give you some examples of how the ORB Doctrine works out in real life?

The Oak Ridge Boys have always gone the extra mile to fulfill all our obligations, and we try our best to never allow a promoter to lose a ton of money on an Oaks' show. If a promoter has done his job well and a date fails for some reason, we're always willing to negotiate and make adjustments so he or she comes out okay. This is still a people business, and good relationships and good deeds always pay off in the long run. The guy you helped out today may be helping you a year from now. Now, if a promoter is a jerk—if he didn't work well with our marketing, operations, and advance people and didn't promote the date so it would succeed—we will take the arranged fee (and probably his first-born and his cat). But this has rarely happened over the years. For the most part we've always worked with good people who possess a keen work ethic, strong values, and a sense of integrity. This is how we do business. We expect the same from promoters and event managers, and we're rarely let down.

★ ★ ★

We've had a decades-long relationship with promoter Dave Snowden and his Triangle Talent Company. Dave books us not only at the Kentucky State Fair every year but also at 15 to 20 other fairs and venues around the country, so we have years and miles of friendship between us. Of course, that kind of relationship can also result in a little fun too. I remember calling Dave on the afternoon of a sold-out show in Louisville and telling him that everyone in the group was sick and had no voice—except me. He was so upset.

"What are we going to do?" he yelled into the phone. "How can you handle a show by yourself to a sold-out coliseum at the Kentucky State fair?" He was nearly in tears. I assured him that I could sing most of the songs by myself and do some stand-up comedy as well. I could even do some Elvis songs.

He actually started to cry, so I told him I was just kidding, we were all on the bus feeling fine, and we were almost to Louisville. I can't write the words that he said next, but man, we were all on the floor laughing.

But Dave had the last laugh. When we arrived at the Kentucky State Fair entrance, the huge computer sign read, APPEARING TONIGHT—THE STATLER BROTHERS.

One more Dave Snowden story. This time we were *not* kidding around. For some reason, we had booked the Idaho State Fair the night before the Kentucky State Fair. We had it all figured out. The buses would head out of Boise and would drop us off early in the morning in Salt Lake City, Utah, where we had flights booked into Louisville. Well, you guessed it. All of our flights were canceled. We tried everything we could, but we could not make it happen. Snowden was apoplectic. We just knew he might pass away on account of us.

At first, as you can imagine from my story above, he thought we were kidding again. But soon he realized we really were stuck in Salt Lake City. We urged him not to worry—somehow we would make it work. We hired two private jets to take us and our band and crew and a bunch of gear from Salt Lake City to Louisville. We got there two hours before showtime, set up, and did the show while a leased bus came up from Nashville to take us home. It cost us three times what we were paid that night to play the date, but we pulled it off.

Dave hugged our necks and said he owed us one, but in our minds, he owed us nothing.

A week later, a big corporation called Dave, asking for a major

Nashville act to come play for them the next month. Dave suggested the Oaks, we played the private gig, and the corporation paid us enough money to make up for the private jets to Louisville and then some!

★ ★ ★

In 1981, "Elvira" was hitting, and we were doing huge business everywhere. A small, family owned and operated country music park in Virginia had secured the Oaks for a show almost two years earlier. It so happens that this park was deep in the red, and the man and wife who owned the park were approaching bankruptcy—until thousands of fans showed up to hear the Oak Ridge Boys that night. There were people as far as we could see, and we gave them a big-time show. The contract negotiated two years earlier was for just $7500. The man was in tears after the concert and insisted that he pay us a lot more. We were, after all the hottest act in the business at the time, and our box-office receipts that night bailed out the park—and more importantly, this man's family. Of course, we wouldn't take any more. A deal is a deal.

"A music entity like the Oaks has a chance to affect people in one of three ways... positively, negatively, or not at all! We always strive for the positive."

DUANE ALLEN

The man followed our buses and trucks about 20 miles out of town, and while we were filling our tanks, he ran in to the truck stop and paid our fuel bill. He got away before we could catch him. Later on that man, Joe Harris, became a top Nashville booking agent, and we actually worked with him for several years. He put quite a few dates in our book too—dates that paid a whole lot more than $7500.

The ORB Doctrine again paid off! Do unto others! Thank You, Jesus!

Last summer we were booked on a big festival in Iowa promoted by a casino, but just before we were about to hit the stage, a huge front passed through and dumped enough rain on the whole place to cancel our show. This has only happened a few times in our entire career. When we found out about an hour later that many of the folks who had come to the show were gathered in a ballroom in the casino hotel, we arranged to go in and say hi to them all.

"We can't do anything about the weather, but we thank you for coming out!" we said. We stayed for more than an hour and held an impromptu meet-and-greet.

Taking pictures with hundreds of wet people was a nice thing to do, but singing to them is easier. When the idea came up to do this, all four Boys said yes. A little extra time taken sure made a lot of disappointed people happy!

The Clinton, Iowa, *Herald* newspaper heralded us for taking the time to do this, and that was very nice of them. They also called us the Soak Ridge Boys! We have actually been called that many times. It rained on us so often one summer that some county fairs were calling to book us in hopes that we might end a drought. It's amazing that most of these rainy-day shows still went on! (And yes, we always open a rain-soaked show with…you guessed it…"It Takes a Little Rain").

So you see, the ORB Doctrine is quite simple: four talented and good-hearted men, surrounded by a great team of like minds, working hard every day to make the right decisions and to keep everything and everyone on a positive and even keel, singing our songs every night to the best of our ability, all the while leaning on the everlasting arms of Jesus! We've found that good works, honesty, and integrity always come back around to us with dividends always paid. Some might call it karma. I say it is friendships and relationships and doing things the way God would have you do them.

Yes, it all starts at the top—the *very* top!

12

THE COUNTRY MUSIC BIZ TODAY

"The Pendulum Swings"

*I*nterviewers love to ask veteran acts, "What do you think of country music today?" Then they sit back and salivate at the woeful answers they're anticipating—"Oh, these kids today aren't country! They're more rock and roll!"

I'm sure some old-time performers subscribe to the negative theory that country music has been a victim of "Murder on Music Row," as songwriter Larry Cordle put it, but not me. With all due respect to Larry, my friend and hero who wrote that monster hit recorded by none other than king George Strait and traditional master Alan Jackson, I disagree. I love that song and concur that the music has indeed changed over the years, but I don't think it's been for the worse.

I say change is good, and country music is now more popular than it's ever been, so someone is doing something right. I maintain that most of today's young stars are the ones responsible for this rise in popularity. The pendulum is always swinging—nothing stays the same, and that includes music of every kind. Years ago I never thought that videos of an angry person walking in a circle reciting poetry to a hip-hop beat would ever be more than just a fad, but whether I prefer it or not (and I really *don't*), rap is here to stay. Joey here prefers nice melodies and great lyrics, so it's not a genre of music for me, but it is for many others.

My point is simple. If you would rather hear Merle Haggard than Eric Church, Willie Nelson instead of Jason Aldean, or Tammy Wynette as opposed to Taylor Swift, this is why God and Steve Jobs gave us iPods and iTunes. It's why we have Spotify and Pandora and Reverb Nation for that matter. In this day and age we can listen to whatever we prefer.

In the late 1970s, when the Oak Ridge Boys were making our big move, people came down on us pretty hard for not being country enough. Now we're considered classic, but back then, we were as new as the kids are today. We were always thinking big. People may forget this now, but the Oaks were the first act to bring big lights and sound to the show. We had smoke and lasers and such long before anyone else. We were even the first to use walkie-talkies on tour!

Besides the rock group Genesis, who developed and own the rights to the computerized light system called Vari*Lite, which everyone uses today, the Oaks were the only act using such a lighting system. We were just trying to take our music to the masses, and we succeeded—but not without some controversy and nay-saying.

The difference back then was that to fill arenas, one had to have crossover airplay on pop radio. Kenny with "The Gambler" and "Lucille." Johnny with "Ring of Fire" and "I Walk the Line." Dolly with "Nine to Five." The Oaks with "Elvira" and "Bobbie Sue"…

But today? Young acts are filling arenas and stadiums all over the world on just country radio airplay, without the need for crossing over. Thanks to them, country music is now the new pop music, and I have no problem with that.

Times change…the pendulum swings! Cowboy hats turn into trucker's caps, and time marches on.

Our friend Larry Gatlin once said that most people think of the Green Bay Packers of the early '60s as the greatest football team of all time, but if the Packers of today could go back in time and play their earlier forbearers, they would win and win big because today's players are bigger and faster and stronger.

Brother Gatlin is correct, and the theory applies to country music today. These kids are younger and faster, and they should be commended for the job they're doing. I love and respect every single one of them, and I admire their accomplishments.

I'm happy to know that just as George Jones, Merle Haggard, Alabama, Randy Travis, Garth Brooks, and so many others have added some stones to that country-music mountain over the years, so have the Oak Ridge Boys. We're definitely not the new kids on the block anymore, but grizzled veterans of the road and stage. It's easy for us to look out over the big valley and see where the music has been and where it's going. It will surely change even more as the pendulum continues to swing.

Our own music changes over time as well. On one of our most recent albums and the first live recording of our big hits, *Boys Night Out*, you'll notice little changes here and there. These are updated, stage versions of our old songs as we perform them today. Some songs have become a little edgier over the years, and some of the instrumentation is newer and fresher. I read a review last year on the *Boys Night Out* project that said "Dream On" could have been a big-time arena love song. Well, that's exactly what it was from 1979 to around 1984. I don't think the young music scribe had any idea that the song had been around that long. "Dream On" was originally recorded by the Righteous Brothers with Bill Medley on the lead vocal, and we all felt it was a perfect song for our Richard Sterban. And we were right. It was a huge hit, and today it is still a fan favorite. Richard may even sing it better today than ever before.

Music is a living and breathing entity and is just as subject to change as we are. So overall, change is good as far as I'm concerned. Every day represents a new beginning. We should always keep our eyes and ears and hearts open to newer pathways.

It's important to note that many of the older acts are continuing to do just fine. George Strait and Dolly Parton are more popular than ever before and doing *huge* business. Acts like Charlie Daniels, Willie Nelson, the Bellamy Brothers, Merle Haggard, Kenny Rogers, and the Oak Ridge Boys are playing as many show dates per year as they desire to play and doing great business as well. As of this writing, Garth Brooks is about to tour again. Garth will sell out the entire world in about 47 minutes, and even the G-Man is worried that he will be perceived to be too old now. Garth should take us out on the tour. We'll make him look like Hunter Hayes!

I also sincerely believe that Miranda Lambert, Blake Shelton, Brad Paisley, and many other younger artists *do* care about the legacy of country music and work very hard to keep it alive. Every year Keith Urban hosts a huge benefit show in Nashville called "All for the Hall" that raises a ton of money for the Country Music Hall of Fame. Because of the efforts of Keith Urban and Vince Gill and a huge donation by Taylor Swift, the Country Music Hall of Fame has been able to grow and expand. The museum today is now greater than ever before, and much of it is due to the respect paid in so many ways by many of these newer artists.

When Duane was asked the very question that opened this chapter, he wisely replied, "These young acts of today are filling up stadiums, and that's phenomenal. I'm proud for these young people and happy they're taking up where pop music or rock and roll left a void…Rock and roll went to rap and hip-hop, and country music replaced it with *music*! It might not be your mom and dad's music or my music, but it's music and it's good and I'm proud for them!"

As always, the bottom line for me is a great song! All of the Oak Ridge Boys feel the same way. We just want to hear a great song. We really don't care who is singing it!

Now, where is my iPod?

ON MY IPOD

- Southern rock and roll, like the Charlie Daniels Band and the Allman Brothers Band

- big-time rock, like Bruce Springsteen and Bob Seger

- lots of bluegrass, such as Dailey and Vincent and Rhonda Vincent, as well as banjo by the likes of Jim Mills and Earl Scruggs
- today's country, such as Blake Shelton and Miranda Lambert
- pop country, like Lady Antebellum and Zac Brown Band
- traditional country, like Merle Haggard and Jamey Johnson
- singer-songwriters, like Slaid Cleaves and Patty Griffin
- soft jazz, like Sarah McLachlan, Norah Jones, Herbie Hancock, and Diana Krall
- new kids, like Mary Sarah and Kacey Musgraves
- lots of gospel music, such as the Gaither Vocal Band and Jason Crabb
- light opera, like Sarah Brightman and Andrea Bocelli
- broadway, like *The Lion King* and *Les Misérables*
- and finally, *everything* Emmylou Harris has ever recorded!

So you see? You can listen to whatever you want! Life would be pretty shallow without good music.

13

OLD FRIENDS

"Precious Memories"

J.B.F. WRIGHT

One night my Mary said with an emotional quiver, "You always seem to have an old person in your life. I always feel so sorry for you when they pass."

Mary was right. For some reason, I do always seem to have older people in my life. So when I call this chapter "old friends," I literally mean *old*. It all started when I was a little boy. Daddy was sick and Mommy was working two jobs, so they decided to rent out our upstairs back bedroom, and God sent an angel to our doorstep in the person of Gertrude Clark. We called her Nana right away, and for her room and board, she happily looked after and helped raise little Joey and my sister, Nancy. My mom and Nana Clark were the biggest influences on my boyhood years.

It didn't take long for her to grow to love me—and I loved her back with every fiber of my being. Nana taught me to love books, and for this I will always be grateful. Zane Grey, H.G. Wells, Jack London, Jules Verne, a heavy dose of the classics, and of course, the Bible... all these shaped the imagination of a little Philadelphia kid who was allowed to dream his dreams and sing his songs.

After Nancy got big enough to need a room of her own, Nana moved to an apartment in west Philadelphia. I was about 12 years old, and almost every weekend I took two buses and a subway to get to

Upland Street in west Philly, where I visited with Nana. I gladly gave up hanging with friends or playing baseball to go see her.

Her little first-floor space had a nice bedroom and a kitchenette and a very small bathroom. Under her bed she kept an army cot and a quilt for Joey. I would lie on my army cot at night right next to her bed and listen to her tell stories until we would both fall asleep. I shared every moment of my life with her as well. She was always interested in me, and her input was always memorable and useful. We would pray together, and then I would try hard to get to sleep first. Her cancer was making her frailer by the month, but the old woman could snore like a jackhammer!

Like my mom, Nana always encouraged me to do and to be my very best and to put God first in my life. She died as I turned 14. I visited her in her room at the Philadelphia General Hospital and spent several hours with her before she left us. A very small and thin Nana Clark told me things that day I've never forgotten.

"Don't be so hard on your daddy, Joey," she said. "The drinking and his rage at times are all because of that war. Not that that's an excuse, mind you, but it *is* a reason. Your dad loves you, Joey, and he needs you now more than ever. Your mother is the most special woman I have ever known. She is full of nothing but love, and you must always look after her and your sister as well. You, my sweet boy, are also so very special. You worry about things too much, and that's why that asthma of yours kicks up like it does. You need not worry about anything, Joey, because you are going to live a long and wonderful life. You know why? Because I will always be looking after you."

In less than a year my daddy would suffer the stroke that disabled him for the rest of his life. He *would* need me more than ever, and I grew to love him more and more as the years passed.

Nana's last words to me were, "I will always love you, and I promise I will throw you a star!" I assure you that she has indeed thrown many a star my way. I might add that after she passed I never again suffered from the asthma attacks I had in my youth.

✦ ✦ ✦

Another of my "old" friends was Addaline Huff. We were playing at a beautiful casino resort on the north Oregon Coast, and about two hours before the show I received word that a woman in the building who was celebrating her hundredth birthday was a huge fan of the Oak Ridge Boys—and me in particular. Her friends asked if I would mind spending a few moments with her.

I gathered up a bouquet of flowers from our dressing room and took them to where she was waiting in her wheelchair in the back of the showroom. With her was a camera crew from a Portland television station to chronicle the event.

She was a stunning and beautiful woman, and even at the age of 100 she seemed to be a real presence. I gave her the flowers, and to the delight of the young reporter, she hugged me and kissed me on the cheek. Then we sat together and did an interview that was thoroughly enjoyable because she was so articulate and fun to talk to. During the concert that night, I wished her a happy hundredth birthday, and she received a standing ovation—all of which was captured by the news camera for a piece on Mrs. Huff that would show on the Portland station.

When the show was over, I had the casino manager bring Addaline backstage to meet all the Boys. When that was over, we sat and chatted for two more hours. She told me all about growing up on the Oregon Coast and about her husband, who was a successful businessman and had built her a beautiful home not far from where she grew up in McMinnville, Oregon.

She had seen much of the world as a younger woman. She loved flowers, the ocean, Jesus Christ, and the Oak Ridge Boys. We promised to stay in touch, and for the next year we wrote back and forth. I would call her on occasion, and we would talk for a long time. I so enjoyed listening to her stories about growing up on the coast.

During the next year she finally had to leave her ocean home and move inland to an assisted-living facility. She still wrote poems and drew beautiful full-color pictures of flowers and the ocean and sent them to me. Receiving a letter or a package from Addaline always meant the world to me, and I in turn sent her Oak Ridge Boys CDs and pictures of my granddaughter, Breanne. She especially seemed to love those.

I called her during the early summer of 1997, and she told me that it was time to go home to Jesus now because for the first time in her life she could no longer hear the ocean. Going to sleep at night without the sound of the sea was just such an empty feeling to her, and she absolutely hated it. She passed very soon after that.

In her last letter to me, dated July 23, 1997, she wrote this.

> The greatest gift I received on my hundredth birthday was you! I don't think I ever told you how flattered I was over all of the television attention you gave to me. Please give my love to your beautiful wife, Mary, and your daughters and of course Breanne. I am so proud that you are my friend. I will see you in heaven. Super good wishes to you and all the Boys...I so love to hear you all sing.
>
> Addaline Huff

There was also a small drawing of her favorite flower, the Oregon Coast Black Lily.

I sure hope she can hear ocean sounds in heaven. I'll bet she can!

Another fan the Boys came to love was Aunt Una Reeks. We first met her around 1977 at Busch Gardens in Williamsburg, Virginia, in an unusual way. Right before the show, we received word that the drummer's Aunt Una was at the backstage door and wanted very much to see him.

Our drummer in those years was Mark Ellerbee, who was a great story in his own right. Mark was a Vietnam veteran—a medic—and was known as the first rock and roll drummer in the history of southern gospel music. The guy was a trendsetter, and everyone loved him. Mark was also somewhat of a hippie. He wouldn't have looked out of place at Woodstock but *would* have looked totally out of place working at a Wall Street investment firm.

On stage
singing.
Our favorite
time of
the day.

We did three Minnie Pearl Christmas specials for CBS.
Can anyone say "HOOOOWWWWWDEEEE?"

TOP: Leon Volskis BOTTOM: © Alan Messer (alanmesser.com)

An early Christmas with Mom and Dad (before his disability) and my sister, Nancy. Also pictured are Patty Playpal and Lucky the Puppy.

We love to perform with other noted artists. This was a great night when we shared the stage with Kenny Rogers, Dottie West, and the legendary Ray Charles.

In his heyday, Mike Douglas was a "must" for afternoon TV viewers. He loved the Oaks!

TOP: Bonsall Family Photo MIDDLE: © Alan Messer (alanmesser.com) BOTTOM: Kathy Gangwisch

One of our greatest honors was being spokesmen for the Boy Scouts of America.

All four Oaks love baseball. It's a treat when we get to meet great players like Reggie Jackson.

We do a lot of pre-show publicity, including radio interviews.

Here are four great poses from the past of us "Boys."

Richard Sterban

Joe Bonsall

William Lee Golden

Duane Allen

We never tire of playing the Opry!

The night we were inducted into the Grand Ole Opry was one of the best honors we've ever received.

Over 41 million sold! Wow. The number's even higher now. Here we are with popular daytime TV host Wendy Williams.

We loved the great George Jones and were honored to be part of his eightieth birthday celebration at the Opry.

Backstage at the Opry with our manager, Jim Halsey; Steve Buchanan, president, Opry Entertainment Group; Sherman Halsey; and Del Bryant, former president and CEO of BMI.

Here's Duane with Dallas Frazier, the talented songwriter who wrote our colossal hit "Elvira." Dallas also scored big with his novelty song "Alley Oop" by the Hollywood Argyles in 1960.

Many great concerts have been held in the theater bearing our name in Branson.

We're the "Anthem Singers" for sure. I can't count the number of games and events we've been asked to sing "The Star-Spangled Banner." This performance at Lucas Oil Field was at the invitation of the Indianapolis Colts.

TOP: Mark Parham   BOTTOM: Darrick Kinslow

Our annual Christmas tour is always a highlight of the year for all of us. We start to plan in September and we usually perform right up until a few days before Christmas. We've been doing this special tour for a quarter of a century now. No, we're not tired of it. Never!

Cracker Barrel is one of our favorite places—especially around Christmas time. We did an album sold exclusively through Cracker Barrel. Good food, good people!

We love the Rocking Chair segment of our Christmas tour. It's popular with fans and a great time for us Boys to reminisce.

Our faithful bus taking a well-earned rest after traveling many snowy miles during our Christmas 2013 tour.

TOP & MIDDLE: Jon Mir BOTTOM: Chris Demonbreun

We remember young Garth Brooks just starting out. I was "Mr. Bonsall" to him back then.

We love what's happening in country music today. Here we are with Taylor Swift, Dr. John Mahlmann and Earl Hurrey of the MENC, and Jim Halsey.

TOP: Jon Mir BOTTOM: Darrick Kinslow

On the night George H.W. Bush lost his reelection campaign to Bill Clinton, we sang "Amazing Grace" to the President aboard Air Force One. We love the Bushes!

Barbara Bush has been a fan of ours for many years—as have all the Bush family. We're great fans of theirs too.

TOP & BOTTOM: Darrick Kinslow

We'd be lost without our Mighty Oaks Band. *Left to right:* Jeff Douglas, Rex Wiseman, Ron Fairchild, Roger Eaton, David Northrup, and Scotty Simpson.

Here we are at Café Rakka across the street from our office with famous chef Guy Fieri of "Diners, Drive-Ins & Dives."

While the bus is rolling, Darrick Kinslow, our tour director, stays on top of things.

Vivian Abalon remembered my mom from her World War II days. How I connected with Vivian is nothing short of a miracle!

LoDee, one of our fans I'll never forget. I treasured my friendship with Miss LoDee. She was a second mother to me.

A selfie with my beautiful wife, Mary Ann.

Ban-Joey pickin' on the farm!

TOP LEFT & RIGHT: Darrick Kinslow   MIDDLE: Joe Bonsall   BOTTOM: Mary Bonsall

THE OAK RIDGE BOYS®

keep on keepin' on!

Forty more years?!

★ ★ ★

PHOTOS: Daniel Tommasino

Well, Mark didn't have any idea whether he actually had an Aunt Una, but he told the security guards to allow her backstage. The two of them hugged and laughed like old friends. Mark introduced her to everyone, and we put a seat on the side of the stage where she could comfortably watch and enjoy the show.

Fact is, it was all a ruse. It turns out that this woman, who was well into her seventies, was a big fan of the Oaks and just wanted to meet everybody. Mark just shrugged it all off, but I must tell you we all fell in love with this spunky woman, and we proceeded to let her come and visit us until the day she died at the ripe old age of 104!

Aunt Una would show up most anywhere, and when she did we always made a fuss over her. When she came to shows at more than 100 years old, we introduced her as our oldest fan. Audiences gave her a bigger ovation than they gave for "Elvira." Everyone loved Aunt Una. In her day, she was the chair of the Republican Party in the state of Virginia. If you really wanted to get her going, you could just tell her you were a Democrat!

When I was first learning to play the banjo, I was sitting with Aunt Una backstage in Huntsville, Alabama. She was in a wheelchair beside me, and I was picking a few simple banjo tunes for her. She was quiet for a while and then seriously looked up at me and said, "Someday you might get really good at playing that thing, but it won't be today!"

School was out.

Once at a fair in South Carolina, a car full of folks pulled up beside the bus. When I saw Aunt Una in the backseat, I ran over to the car, and we chatted and laughed for several minutes. As I was walking back toward the tour bus, I heard Aunt Una say, "Now, who was that?"

I stopped in my tracks and turned. I was really sad there for a minute until she said, "Ha ha—just kidding, Joe, just kidding. What a face!"

She was 101 then, and I figured…well, you know.

Aunt Una's daughter, Mary, looked after her and always brought her to the shows. And when Aunt Una passed, Mary took up the mantle.

Mary Wheat is now well into her eighties and has become an even bigger part of our lives than her mother, if that's possible. Every close friend and fan of the Oak Ridge Boys knows and loves Mary. The woman is such a character, and her energy is amazing.

Mary just might show up anywhere in the country to see a show, and I mean *anywhere*. She may be on the front row of the Opry or in the third row in Las Vegas. She never lets us know when she's coming. We could be most anywhere, and after a few songs it's entirely possible to see her out there in the audience smiling and waving. She always brings us gifts too, like stuffed animals, Virginia peanuts, and such. I might come home from a road trip and say to my wife, "I saw Mary Wheat on this trip."

Mary will answer, "Peanuts?"

Once while in Branson we got word that Mary Wheat had ridden a zip line, and that scared us all to death. The visual of Mary hanging there and zipping down the side of a cliff far above the trees was bad enough, but when she showed up at the hotel in a body cast and bandages we were petrified. To make matters worse, she seemed to lose her mind and began tearing the cast off. It turns out that she did ride a zip line through the Ozark Mountains and had a blast. It also turns out that she was never hurt at all. It was all faked for our benefit. I have never seen a woman laugh so hard. Yep, she got us good. The Mary apple didn't fall far from the Aunt Una tree.

We have taken three big Caribbean cruises with about 600 of our fans. We do a lot of singing and have a lot of fun with the people who join us on these trips. Mary Wheat has been on two of the cruises, and as you might imagine, she was the star of the ship.

One night I had retired to my cabin and was sitting on my deck watching the sea go by when my phone rang. It was our tour director, Darrick Kinslow.

"Hey, man, do you know where that disco club bar thing is on the fifth floor aft"?

I told him I thought I did.

"You need to get down here and see this!" I could hear him laughing as he was hanging up.

I made my way there to find about seven of our bunch sitting in a booth in the corner. Down on the dance floor was a competition of sorts. People were dancing up a storm in couples or by themselves while the Bee Gees were blasting loudly over the sound system. You couldn't even talk in there because "You Should Be Dancing" was playing so loudly. Well, right there in the middle of the dance floor was what I was summoned to see. One old woman in a scooter, turning circles and doing wheelies while the other dancers cheered. Mary Wheat was now a disco queen!

One of the funniest things Mary ever did was to bring us a little lamb…a homemade, stuffed little lamb. She thought that since we had a Christmas song called "Mary Had a Little Lamb," surely a stuffed lamb should become a part of our Christmas set.

So the night she brought it, the lamb was displayed right by the keyboards for all to see. I hate that she will read this, but the knitted lamb was not really very attractive, so the next night it stayed in the truck.

Then the lamb started to appear on the stage again, but only in places where only the Boys or the band could see it, not the audience. Hiding in a fake snowbank, concealed behind a speaker, peeking around a corner, nestled inside a Christmas tree…I swear we got a ton of laughs over where that lamb might appear or not appear on any given show.

One night it just vanished forever. I think it got left somewhere on purpose after a Christmas show load out, or maybe someone stole it. But that's very doubtful. The little lamb is probably still backstage somewhere in Iowa, stuffed into a corner.

Yes, like Aunt Una, Mary has become a huge part of our lives, and we love her dearly. And to no one's surprise, her daughter Myra now brings Mary to the shows. Maybe someday Myra, who is now in her fifties, will be the new Aunt Una or Mary Wheat, traveling the world to hear the Oak Ridge Boys. I wonder how old we will all be when *that* happens!

✳ ✳ ✳

Ms. Lo-Dee Hammock may be the hardest of all our old friends to write about, but I will do my best. I guess if I could summon the strength to write an entire book about my mom, Lillie, I should be able to come up with a few pages for Lo-Dee. It's just difficult to fully explain the depth of my love and adoration for this remarkable woman.

I first met Ms. Lo-Dee in about 2000, when the Oaks were playing the Charlie Pride Theater in Branson. We always stayed at a place called the Foxboro Inn, and Lo-Dee was the housemother there. She not only provided a nice public-relations presence for the hotel by guiding the guests and helping them find the right places to visit and which shows to attend, but she also ran a very successful bus charter business.

It was always a joy to see her and to talk with her, and she just adored the Oak Ridge Boys. When we moved to the Grand Palace Theater several years later and started to stay at the Ramada, Lo-Dee moved to the Ramada herself and became housemother there.

I adored Lo-Dee, just as everyone else did, but our relationship and friendship accelerated one day in about 2004 when the Oak Ridge Boys' bus pulled into the Ramada parking lot early one morning and I received a message that Lo-Dee wanted to see me in her office as soon as possible.

I sheepishly knocked on her door, and when she answered, she put her arms around me and held on to me and wept. I was so moved. I had not been held in this way since my mom passed away, but I was also concerned for her. She quelled my fears almost immediately.

"I just read your book *G.I. Joe and Lillie*, and all I could think about was my husband and his experience in that war, and I had to see you to say thank you for letting me know through this wonderful story that I was not the only one to ever go through this."

Her husband had passed several years earlier in their hometown of Beaumont, Texas, and he fought that war until the day he died, much the same way my father did. Lo-Dee could easily identify with my mom, Lillie. In fact, she thought of Lillie as a kindred spirit and almost on the spot adopted me as her own.

From then on, whenever the Oaks played in Branson, I spent my time there with Ms. Lo-Dee. She in turn never missed an Oak Ridge Boys Show there—not one! We moved back to what was once called the Glen Campbell Theater for our 27 shows a year in Branson, and Lo-Dee was thrilled that the owners renamed it the Oak Ridge Boys

Theater. She had her own seat on the front row, and right up until she passed at the age of 94 a few years ago, she was still booking busloads of folks into town. An Oak Ridge Boys show was always on their tour schedule.

It's impossible to overstate my love for this woman. I am a better man and a better Christian because of Lo-Dee Hammock. Let me share just a bit of a piece I wrote in her honor after God took her home. Her son, Bill, had died of an illness about six months earlier.

> I shared my innermost thoughts and philosophies with her, and she with me. We laughed, we cried, we prayed, and then we laughed and cried some more. On some days, we ran errands, and I always loved doing that. Everyone we met along the way not only knew her but loved her as well.
>
> Such a funny woman she could be.
>
> Back when she was moving very slowly, I remember going around to her side of the car to position her wheelchair just right. She would try to turn and rise up from the car seat. We would count one…two…THREE, and sometimes when THREE wouldn't work we tried FOUR! and laughed so hard, that that didn't work either. A million memories of Ms. Lo-Dee, and not one of them bad!
>
> The things Ms. Lo-Dee and I shared together will stay private with me except for this one thing. I know that losing her own son was devastating to her. It broke her heart on many levels. Like my own mom, whatever Ms. Lo-Dee might have been, she was a mother first and foremost, and in my heart, I think her losing Bill was really the beginning of the end for her. She shed so many tears over this loss. Trembling, deep, shuddering tears that only those who have experienced such loss can fathom.
>
> One day she shared a dream. In this dream her son was leaning over her bedside and asked if she was ready to go home yet. She told me it was tempting to go because everything felt so very peaceful and serene around him, but she told him, "No! Not yet!"
>
> She told me she didn't know if that was the right

decision at the time, but as she woke up she heard him say, "When you are ready, Mom, I will be right here to help take you home!"

Eventually, she was ready, and I have no doubt that Bill was there to help.

She always told me that I was the best thing to ever happen to her. I'm not sure how that could be, but I assure you that Ms. Lo-Dee Hammock was an incredible blessing to Joe Bonsall and all the Oak Ridge Boys.

I will never forget her as long as I live. I only regret that the rest of my family never met her. My wife, Mary, did chat with her on the phone often, which was great because Lo-Dee loved Mary as well.

So, goodbye Dear One. I will see you on that golden shore that we once mused about, and we will rejoice and laugh and worship Jesus some more. In the meantime, I hope that, as you promised, you will have found my first mom, Lillie, and already gotten to know her. Just think... little Joey has *two* moms in heaven waiting for him now. How many guys can say that?

Lo-Dee once told me that I was the only one who ever listened to her because nobody really pays attention to old folks. Well, I do. I always have. There is so much to learn from those who have traveled the road ahead of us. Someday, if God allows me to grow much older as I travel here below, I hope someone takes the time to listen as I tell *my* little stories about a life full of songs and words and faith and love. Perhaps I can be a blessing to them just as the old friends in this chapter have been to me...God willing!

✦ ✦ ✦

Over the years, we have been honored to make friends with many wonderful veterans. This brings me to Mr. Sterling Lankford, from right here in our hometown of Hendersonville, Tennessee.

Duane met Mr. Lankford quite a few years ago during a workout at a local gym. When Sterling told Duane he was a Marine veteran of the Pacific Theater in World War II, Duane was very moved and honored to be in his presence. Over the years the friendship between these two men has grown, and we have all benefited by knowing this wonderful man.

Sterling has shared a lot of stories with Duane and just a few with me, and it's always an honor to listen to him. When we went with a military theme for our video for "Write Your Name Across My Heart" from our Grammy-nominated 2002 gospel album *From the Heart*, we called on Mr. Lankford to star in it, and he did a wonderful job. We included a few other veterans in the story line of the video as well. Check it out on YouTube!

A few years ago, I took part in a huge Veterans of Foreign Wars event right here in our hometown, and Sterling was there. He was the oldest vet in attendance, and the younger veterans all treated him like a superstar. This was a great thing to witness. Everyone wanted to shake his hand and have his or her picture taken with the old Marine who battled across the Marshall Islands to Iwo Jima.

I sat with him for a bit and asked him about Iwo Jima in particular. Being a World War II buff, I've always been moved by what our young boys accomplished in this horrific conflict, and Mr. Lankford was there for the whole incredible battle—from day one, when he hit the beach on February 19, 1945, to the final capture of Iwo and its three strategic airfields on March 26. The five-week operation comprised some of the most vicious and bloodiest battles in the history of warfare, with 24,000 American casualties. Mr. Lankford saw it all, and as he put it, "was dang lucky to have survived that mess!"

I had just seen the HBO series *The Pacific* and had studied the life of the only enlisted Marine in history to receive the Congressional Medal of Honor as well as the Navy Cross, USMC Gunnery Sergeant John Basilone. Sergeant Basilone earned the Medal of Honor after individually holding off 3000 Japanese when his unit was reduced to just two men on Guadalcanal. He was awarded the Navy Cross after his death, and his remains rest in Arlington National Cemetery. "Gunny" Basilone is also the only Marine in history to be awarded the Medal of Honor, reenlist, and then be killed in action.

That day at the VFW over a barbecue sandwich and some sweet tea, Sterling talked a bit about Iwo Jima, and I asked him about Basilone, who I thought was killed on the very first wave of attack.

"Yep, it happened the first day of battle there, not long after we hit the beach," said Mr. Lankford in a soft voice. "He was just ten or fifteen yards away from me at the time. They blew him all to pieces too. I remember us hunkering down and thinking that this could not have happened. We all thought Basilone was indestructible after what he did at Guadalcanal…well, he wasn't."

The Oak Ridge Boys' friendship with Sterling Lankford is one of our most cherished. Duane and Sterling still see each other frequently, and Duane has heard many more stories than I have. The Ace could probably write a book on Sterling Lankford and his service all over the Marshall Islands in those days of that horrible war with Imperial Japan.

As of this writing, Mr. Lankford is about to turn 90. After looking after a sick wife for more than a decade, he laid her to rest six years ago. He now lives alone, but he's still healthy and sharp as a tack. He told me recently, "I ain't a-jumping over no fences these days, but I'm still doing pretty dang good!"

I hope he does pretty dang good for many years to come. An old blood-and-guts Marine on every level, he's an American hero in my book.

Because of my book *G.I. Joe & Lillie*, I've been honored to meet and talk with many veterans, and many times these men have told me stories they had never shared—even with their own families. I'm always grateful for every time I've had an opportunity to hear and learn from these incredible heroes. We have such love and respect for all who have served and paid a price for our freedom in America. Yes, there is always a price, and we need to love these men and women and pray for them every day.

I have just one more older friend to write about here, and this is also a bit more personal than group related, but oh, how Vivian Abalon has affected my life. This story is incredible, so let me start at the beginning.

It so happens that a Mrs. Patrick and her husband run an air-conditioning company in central Florida. After a hard day of work, they decided to unwind a bit and dine out at the local Cracker Barrel. While Mrs. Patrick was perusing the Old Country Store, *G.I. Joe & Lillie* caught her eye. She is a patriot who has often said that if her life had taken a different turn, she would have loved to serve in the military. So a book about "love, loyalty, and service" appealed to her.

She bought a copy, took it home, and began to read it. Within three and a half hours, she read the book cover to cover, shed a few tears, and went to bed.

I'm not sure why Mrs. Patrick put the book in her car, but she did. Her husband had an appointment in a retirement village with a woman who needed a new air-conditioning unit, so she drove over there to meet her husband. The very vibrant and lovely resident of the home was 88 years old, and Mrs. Patrick took quick note of the World War II pictures and memorabilia on her mantle. Some showed a much younger version of this woman, dressed in the uniform of the Women's Army Corp.

The older woman introduced herself as Vivian Abalon and said that yes indeed, she had been a WAC and was darn proud of it.

Well now, didn't Mrs. Patrick have *the* must-read book for Vivian? She went out to her car, retrieved her copy of *G.I. Joe & Lillie*, and gave it to Mrs. Abalon.

After a few days, Mrs. Patrick's phone rang. A very emotional Vivian Abalon was on the line, and with much excitement she said, "I *knew* Lillie—we were friends! I've never forgotten her. We were WACs together! Please help me find this Joseph S. Bonsall, Lillie's son. I must talk to him. I have pictures of Lillie he'll want to have."

Well, Mrs. Patrick got in touch with the publisher, New Leaf Press. They in turn got in touch with Kathy Harris, our head of marketing, and Kathy called me. I called Mrs. Patrick, she gave me Mrs. Abalon's number, and then I called Vivian.

Mrs. Abalon told me she was so excited about my call that she had eaten a whole bag of caramel-centered candy while waiting for the phone to ring.

My first thought was, *Now THAT is a Lillie thing to have done for sure!*

Vivian Abalon was just wonderful. Allow me to use her words for a bit.

> I started to read, and the name Lillie Maude Collins hit me hard. I thought, oh my, this is she...I know Lillie. A few pages later I saw her picture and was so overcome I nearly fainted. On our first leave, I went home with her to the farm in Roanoke Rapids, North Carolina. That house was just as you described, and it was so cold there with that Congoleum floor and that awful outhouse. When we got back I had bronchitis. No wonder she wanted out of there. It's so hard to find women when you separate because they get married and change their name, so after the war I tried but I could never find her. And now after all these years I find her...and she is gone.
>
> I have changed names a few times. My first husband was a Hawthorne. He had a heart attack and died at age 37, but we had a daughter, Ann, who is 60 now. Then I married a Figlar, and darn if he didn't die too at age 47. We had a son, but he passed away at three days old. Well, I never did like the name Figlar, so I just went back to the name my daddy gave me—Abalon. I also thought it might make it easier for old war friends to find me, but there are not many of us around anymore.
>
> Every good friend I have ever had has passed. I am an active member of the woman's honor guard here. I am actually the *only* woman. I am at every military funeral. I read a poem. These funerals are so special. We have a bagpipe, a drum, a bugler, and of course, a gun salute. My poem has been used at other military funerals as well. Knowing you would be calling, I went to Walmart and had copies made of all the pictures I have of your mother. They are starting to fade a bit now, but I want you to have the originals, especially the one Lillie signed with her name and address on the back.

You get the idea. It was a wonderful moment for both of us, and I am so grateful to Mrs. Patrick for sharing the book and then getting the ball rolling. I am also grateful to my friends at Cracker Barrel for making my book a part of the Old Country Store patriotic celebration display. Every piece had to be in just the right place, so I must also thank my Lord for His part in this, for I believe *nothing* just happens. My life is all the better for knowing Vivian Abalon.

We've been writing to each other for two years now, and when the Oaks were in Plant City, Florida, for the annual Strawberry Festival last year, Vivian came to the show. All of the Boys treated her royally, and I was just blown away to meet her. She took my face into her hands, looked into my eyes, and said, "I see Lillie in there. Hello Lil'—I'll bet you are proud of this boy!"

Then we both cried. Vivian Abalon has just turned 90 as I write this page. God bless her.

✶ ✶ ✶

I must admit that as I write I'm finding that this chapter has become my favorite, for the people we meet and the friends we make along the journey are the most important puzzle pieces of all. God places people and events in our lives for certain reasons that perhaps never become quite clear until the whole picture is revealed.

I do know this much. My God knew just what He was doing when He placed these special people at these various crossroads, and each one in some way or another has illuminated me and helped define my purpose in being here.

I no sooner finished this chapter (I thought!) when all of a sudden I met another old friend. The Oak Ridge Boys were taping a segment of a Nashville TV show for the RFD Network called *Music City Tonight*. After an interview segment, we were getting ready to sing when Duane called to me. He was chatting with some folks on the front row and said this woman wanted very badly to meet me, so I went over and met Mildred Spethman, who came all the way from California to visit family and attend the taping.

She was about to turn 100 years old, and her presence was just angelic. I knelt down and took her hand, and she said, "I so wanted to meet you because I read your book about your mom. I just loved every page. I read it more than once too, and my whole family just loves the Oak Ridge Boys too."

My eyes filled with tears as she spoke. She was so sweet, so honest, and the love of Jesus just shone in her face. Her family was also teary-eyed, and I looked up and saw that Duane was wiping a tear as well. So I of course have her address and phone number, and I plan to stay in touch with her.

It's so like God to place folks like Mildred in my pathway. By the time this book drops into the marketplace, I hope that Mildred Spethman is still here, but if she is not, I assure you she will be resting on that beautiful heavenly shore with Nana Gertrude Clark, Aunt Una Reeks, Addaline Huff, Lo-Dee Hammock, and my mom, Lillie. Having one more guardian angel never hurts!

✱ ✱ ✱

Not all of my "old" friends were simply fans of the Oaks. Some were mentors. You may have seen the *Gaither Homecoming* videos. If you have, you probably recognize the names George Younce and Glen Payne. They're both gone now, but both men were old friends who dated way back to when I was just 18 and singing part-time with the Faith Four Quartet. My mom and I were huge fans in those days of our TV pastor, Reverend Rex Humbard of the Cathedral of Tomorrow. We watched his broadcast every Sunday morning before we went to our church. Mom would watch to hear Brother Humbard speak, but I would watch to hear the Cathedral Quartet. I had all of their albums and just loved their full and dynamic quartet sound. No other group was able to soften up and then go huge the way they did.

It was Bobby Clark singing tenor, Glen Payne on lead, George Younce singing bass, and Danny Koker on piano and singing baritone. I adored them so much that I stepped out big-time and actually booked them for a show in Pennsauken, New Jersey. I thought I could promote the show well enough to fill a small auditorium and make enough money to pay them. After all, my little Faith Four had sung in every little church in South Jersey, and I just knew that all my friends in these churches would allow me to put posters up, which they did.

I also bought some radio spots, made a ton of calls, and posted pictures of them all over the place. Their television exposure was obviously a big help as well, and on concert night a huge crowd came out to hear the Cathedrals. Bobby had just left the group, and a new, long, tall drink of water by the name of Mac Taunton was now singing tenor. He wasn't as smooth as Bobby Clark, but he had a cool charisma going for him, and he sang just fine. By the way, Bobby Clark once sang with the Oak Ridge Boys in the 1950s before Little Willie Wynn, the man I replaced.

After the show that night, they drove their big bus on into Philadelphia and right down my street. My mother had invited them for a meal after, but I really didn't think they would come. It would have been easy for them to say, "Sorry, but we have to get back to Akron."

My daddy had just gotten home from a stint in a Veterans Affairs hospital, and although he was much younger then, he was suffering from his stroke. But that didn't stop him from being totally stoked that these guys were in the house drinking iced tea and eating meatballs. I mean, he had seen them on *television*!

Then the unexpected happened. George said, "Before we go, guys, let's say a prayer for Mr. Bonsall and sing a song for him."

I nearly fainted when all four Cathedral Quartet members prayed for my father and proceeded to fill my little Philly row house with the great gospel song "I'm Nearer Home Than I Was Yesterday."

I never forgot that moment, and neither did the Cathedral Quartet. The next year I left my job at National Sugar Refining Company and joined Richard Sterban and the Keystones, and wouldn't you know we would work a ton of dates with the Cathedrals. They would make a few more vocal changes over the years, but Glen and George were always there, and they would forever be dear friends and mentors to Joe Bonsall.

I rode on their bus all the time, and George would counsel me on

how to sing properly. He would show me techniques on how to project and breathe and add notes to the top end of my vocal range. I still
utilize those techniques today. I can still hear him say, "The tone must
be green and bright, son, not blue and dark! You need to drill it into
the wall!"

As the years went by and I eventually joined the Oak Ridge Boys,
late-night calls from George Younce provided the encouragement I
needed to take on such a task. Even when the Oaks left gospel and so
many gospel singers of that day were putting us down for this or that,
George and Glen always held us high. They loved me very much, and
they also loved the Oak Ridge Boys. And more than anyone else in that
business during that time, they understood where we were and where
we wanted to go.

Somewhere along the line, the mighty Cathedrals turned older.
Danny Koker passed away first, and long after the demise of the big
church in Akron and the Humbards, Glen and George continued to
guide the Cathedrals on to become one of the most respected groups
in the history of gospel music.

When Bill Gaither filmed the Cathedrals' final concert on May 18,
1998 (my fiftieth birthday, by the way), the Oak Ridge Boys took part
in the evening by singing "Life's Railway to Heaven." This event was
held at the Ryman Auditorium in Nashville, and if you have ever seen
the Gaither Homecoming video *The Cathedrals: A Farewell Celebration*,
you will agree that it was an incredible evening.

George and Glen were singing better than ever, now surrounded
by the incredible talents of Ernie Haase on tenor and Scott Fowler on
baritone. Glen passed just six months later with a liver problem. I visited him at his home a few days before he left us. He told me he loved
me and that my mother had once made the best meatballs he had ever
eaten. I didn't have the heart to tell him that my mom couldn't have
made meatballs like that with a gun to her head. It was actually our
Italian neighbor, Marge Giarizzo, who made the meatballs. Once a few
years later on a late-night phone conversation with George, I told him
the meatball story. He laughed out loud for a long time. He said Glen
had bragged about those meatballs for years and years.

I once wrote a commentary about my love for the Cathedrals, and I just was thrilled to see that Glen had the piece framed and hanging on his living room wall. It made me cry.

The ultimate bass singer, George Younce, went on to glory in 2005, and over all of that time we remained very close. I would get home from a trip and Mary would say, "There are several messages from George Younce on the answering machine. You just *have* to hear them."

Sometimes Mary and George would chat for an hour, and I know she grew to love him too. But oh, were those messages always great! Sometimes all he would do was sing. Other times he would be spiritual and reflective, but most times he would have a joke or two for me. Always funny, always encouraging, always loving—I sure miss George. Even all of these years later, it seems like he's still here. Much of what and who I am today, I owe to George Younce and Glen Payne.

Duane Allen was also very close to Glen and George, and in George's later years he would call Duane up frequently as well. George was fighting kidney disease and was on dialysis once a week. He always seemed to call Duane after a dialysis trip, and with a body full of freshened blood, he always seemed more energetic than usual.

Duane loved these calls from George. He would say, "George Younce called me last night. He was feeling good. I heard some great jokes and stories!"

I know we both wish we could still get a call from George!

As I'm writing this piece, I've learned that Bobby Clark has passed away too. So now all of the Cathedral Quartet members, whom I so adored as a kid, are in heaven. Danny, Glen, George, and now Bobby—old friends.

"I'm Nearer Home Than I Was Yesterday." Yep!

14

GOSPEL MUSIC

"When I Sing for Him"

PORTER WAGONER

I've said many times that southern gospel quartet music is where the Oak Ridge Boys' heritage resides. I daresay that if not for the influence of the great gospel quartets during our younger years, each one of us Boys may have taken different pathways and never met. It's our love for gospel that brought us together, holds us together, and keeps us together.

My introduction to southern gospel music came about this way. I grew up in Philadelphia in the 1950s and '60s, when Philly was producing some of the great music kids everywhere were listening to. All the great doo-wop bands of the day seemed to come from Philly, as did some of the great black groups, like Sam and Dave. A little bit later on, there were groups like Hall and Oates and the Stylistics. Early on, South Philly High School had given us Fabian, Frankie Avalon, and Paul Anka—all teen idols.

The big rock radio stations in Philly were cool too, with guys like Joe "the Rockin' Bird" Niagara and Jerry Blavat. And just about every cool teenager in the nation tuned in every afternoon to *American Bandstand*, beamed from Philly. Years later I told Dick Clark about how a neighborhood girl, Kathy Stathias, and I would hop on the EL (Elevated Line rail system), get off at Sixty-Ninth and Market, and stand in line to try to get into *Bandstand*. Every once in a while, we got in, and we'd actually dance on the show, watching Chubby Checker lip-sync to his latest hit or something. And if we didn't get into the show, we got ourselves a hoagie, hopped back on the EL, and went back home.

When the Oaks became big in the 1980s, people started writing that I used to be a regular on *Bandstand*, but it's just not true. But I was good friends with Dick Clark back then, and I got to know him well. When Dick did his twenty-fifth-anniversary book, *The First 25 Years of Rock & Roll*, I wrote four pages about what it was like to go down there and stand in line, waiting to be let in. So *American Bandstand* was a huge influence on me musically—right there in Philadelphia.

Of course, this is also about the time a Mississippi boy by the name of Elvis Presley was hitting big. Like most everyone else my age, I was a huge Elvis fan. But I loved to sing. In my bedroom at night, I *was* Elvis Presley and put on some of the finest shows, sneering and shaking my behind in front of my full-length closet mirror, using a dust mop and a small lampshade as a microphone and stand.

By the time I was about 15, I found myself at a huge crossroads in my life. I was failing in school, hanging out with the wrong crowd, and lacking direction in my life (despite my mother's ongoing prayers). I was also oblivious to the fact that my father was about to have a debilitating stroke caused by a piece of shrapnel, courtesy of the battle for Saint-Lô, France, in July of 1944. A piece of shrapnel that would eventually lodge in his carotid artery.

I was working at a luncheonette, flipping burgers and making Philly cheesesteaks and pizza, while also holding down a job as a veterinarian's assistant. I made just enough money to buy some decent clothes, go to lots of movies, and chase girls (although I caught very few). The notorious K&A Gang of northeast Philly had a bunch of young wannabes, and I was one of them. I was sort of a hoodlum in waiting, so to speak. Thankfully, some of the kids from my church never gave up on me. They all belonged to a youth group called Christian Endeavor—a wonderful organization that continues to be a beacon for Christ for young people all over the world.

God placed these people in my life when I really needed them. They told me about a cool gospel group called the Couriers out of Harrisburg, Pennsylvania, who performed shows around the state. My friends invited me to go with them to the next concert and told me that if I didn't enjoy the show, they would never bother me again. Had I got on my tough-guy high horse and told them to kiss off and leave me alone, only God knows where I might be today. But instead, I said yes. Besides, Bunky Smulling drove a cool 1960 Buick convertible. It was white with a red interior, and I really wanted to ride in it, so I guess in some ways my life changed because of a Buick!

We drove out to Ardmore, Pennsylvania, and there in a high school auditorium, for the first time I heard the Blackwood Brothers and the Couriers sing live. Even though I had not yet entered into a real relationship with Jesus Christ, that Saturday night I knew in my heart that I would someday sing in a great quartet. My course was set, and I was about to set sail.

In 1963—a transitional year for me—God's direction for me was beginning to be clear. On a June night, I convinced my father, who never went anywhere but to the factory or the corner bar and back again, to drive me 90 miles to Harrisburg, Pennsylvania, to a big gospel quartet show at the Farm Show Arena. The Couriers promoted this event, which included nine groups on the program. That night was simply amazing to me. My father wasn't as enthused, but he had a pretty good time even though there was no beer for sale.

"This isn't Connie Mack Stadium, Dad," I told him, recalling the Phillies games we attended when I was younger. Sometimes I wondered how we ever got home without wrapping that old Chevy around a telephone pole, but Daddy kept his cool in Harrisburg, and he actually enjoyed the gospel music. Perhaps he knew something down deep. Perhaps God witnessed to him that night that his life would soon change forever.

That was the last time Daddy and I ever did anything together before the stroke. On the way home I remember telling him that I was going to sing in a group someday, and as I look back now, I think he was good with that. As I grew older and became a success with the Oak Ridge Boys, he was always proud of me. We had a lot of differences, but we grew closer in later years, and even though Daddy had very little speech and was crippled, he always let me know that Jesus mattered to him. I believe in my heart that it all began on that night in Harrisburg.

On that same night, a young bass singer onstage named Richard Sterban was singing with the original Keystone Quartet. Also that night I saw the Oak Ridge Boys for the first time. I thought their little blond-headed tenor, Willie Wynn, was the coolest thing ever. William Lee and Duane were still a few years away from joining the group, but I did love the Oaks! They were cool even way back in 1963!

I also saw the Statesmen Quartet, the Happy Goodman Family, and the Blackwood Brothers. I was thrilled that the Blackwoods' illustrious bass singer, J.D. Sumner, remembered a letter I had written to him. He had even answered it.

As fate would have it, that night I also met a young Philly kid named Ron Graef, who loved gospel music as much as I did. I found out that he lived just 20 blocks from my house, and we became best friends. A year later, Ronnie and I started the Faith Four Quartet.

What a night, right? I saw the Oak Ridge Boys, I saw Richard Sterban and the Keystones, J.D. Sumner remembered me, I met Ronnie Graef, and I bonded with my father for one of the few times in my young life. Richard would hire me at age 19 to sing full-time with the Keystones, he would leave the Keystones to sing with J.D. Sumner, I would one day buy a bus for the Keystones from J.D. Sumner, Richard would join the Oak Ridge Boys, and a year later I would replace a hero, Willie Wynn, and become an Oak Ridge Boy for most of my life. My first quartet would be formed with Ronnie Graef, who remains a good friend to this day, and my daddy is now in heaven! That night in Harrisburg was one huge turning point in so many ways.

I need to add that the Couriers have had a great impact on my life. Don Baldwin has since passed, but Duane Nicholson, Neil Enloe, and Dave Kyllonen continue to sing to this day. I loved this group, and I still do. Had they not promoted those shows and brought the big southern groups up north to sing…well, I guess I just don't have the answer to that one. They were always nice to me too. As a kid I bothered the heck out of them, but they were always thoughtful and encouraging. Just like the Cathedral Quartet—Bobby Clark, Glen Payne, Danny Koker, and George Younce—they took time with this strange, energetic little Philly boy who wanted to be just like them, and I am eternally grateful.

I'm certain that my three singing partners have similar stories about how God used gospel music to bring about this four-decade-long success story. Gospel music has had an indelible effect on each of our lives. I hope giving you this background shows just how deep this river runs.

✳ ✳ ✳

Because of that monumental night, the next year saw a lot of changes take place in my life. Most significantly, my father had the stroke, and I pretty much became sole support of the Bonsall family. But that year I also accepted Jesus Christ as my personal Savior at a Christian Endeavor camp meeting in Millville, New Jersey.

It happened one night around a campfire as my friends gathered around me and sang "Turn Your Eyes upon Jesus." I did just that. I have loved my Lord ever since, and I give Him the honor and praise for all things in my life.

Within that one year, from age 15 to 16, I went from being a street hood to being president of the Frankford High School Bible Club. I joined the Frankford High Ambassadors of Song and even toured Scandinavia with that renowned choir. I became a better son to my mom and a better brother to my sister, Nancy.

By age 17, I had made friends with the Couriers and groups like the Cathedrals. I got to know all the local part-time groups in the Delaware Valley and started up my own little group, the Faith Four Quartet. It was an amazing time to be a young, energetic Christian, and even though my mom was having a rough go with a disabled husband traveling from one Veterans Affairs hospital to another, she and I became closer than ever, and we supported each other in every way. At least Lillie Bonsall didn't have to worry about her son anymore. Instead of coming home bleeding from street fights, he was singing gospel songs and dreaming that the Statesmen Quartet would need a lead singer and call little Joey to fill the spot.

I started my own little gospel group, and one thing led to another. I had heard that Richard Sterban was selling clothes at Gimbels in northeast Philly, so I sought him out. He was the only other person I knew of in Philly who was such a gospel fan that he would go downtown to old record stores and search for old gospel group albums. It's no wonder we became good friends.

To be honest, my own little part-time group, the Faith Four Quartet, was pretty bad—but we really enjoyed singing. Richard and I became close friends, and he had started the Keystones. I joined with Richard and continued singing with the Keystones right up until I joined the Oak Ridge Boys. Ironically, as mentioned earlier, Richard left the Keystones to join J.D. Sumner and the Stamps in Nashville, backing up Elvis for two years before becoming an Oak.

During that time, I was living in Buffalo, New York, working with the Keystones and promoting gospel shows. I would bring the Oak Ridge Boys up there, and they'd bring the Keystones down south. We had a reciprocal agreement, and we did a lot of work together. Duane started producing Keystones albums, so he and I became friends. Eventually, as I related earlier, he and the other two Oak Ridge Boys offered me Willie Wynn's job as tenor. That gave me the opportunity to come to Nashville, sing again with Richard, and be with the mighty Oak Ridge Boys. At that time, we were pretty much riding the top of gospel music and had not yet started transitioning ourselves into a country band. That would happen in the later '70s.

So that's how a kid from the streets of Philly ended up singing in a gospel-country band. It was a long journey, but it's also a pretty cool story.

By the way, several years ago, I was inducted into the Philadelphia Music Alliance Hall of Fame. I'm still amazed that I'm there with all those acts I thought so much of growing up and have grown to love all these years.

✱ ✱ ✱

While I was going through those informative and transitional years, the Oak Ridge Boys were busy becoming the best group in the business in the late '60s and early '70s. The group consisted of Willie Wynn, Duane Allen, Bill Golden, and Noel Fox. These Boys took southern gospel to new levels by singing great songs, hiring a full band, growing their hair just a bit longer, and exhibiting a creativity of style and sound that had simply never existed in southern gospel music.

The group won critical acclaim for cutting-edge albums, including *It's Happening!*, *Thanks*, *Talk About the Good Times*, and the groundbreaking *Light* album, which won every award possible for a gospel act in those days. The goal of the Oak Ridge Boys was to make gospel music cool, and boy, did they ever! The Oaks began to interest a younger crowd than the stodgier and dyed-in-the-wool groups of the day. They looked cool, they sang cool, and they *were* cool! They were certainly accomplishing their goal of taking gospel music to a new level.

When Richard replaced Noel Fox in 1972, they kept the string of successes alive with an album called *Street Gospel*. Yes, the Oaks' shelves were alive with GMA Dove awards and Grammy awards long before I arrived on the scene. The Oaks in those days recorded gospel hit after hit, including "Jesus Is Coming Soon," "I Know," and the Del Delamont song "King Jesus." Duane was writing some of the most important gospel songs of the day as well. You can still find "He Did It All for Me" and other Ace-written songs in some church hymnals today.

In the late 1960s, when most popular music was revolving around the Vietnam war (protest songs) and the hippie movement, some of the rock-and-roll counterculture shook the foundation of Christian music. Christian rock bands and soloists were slowly emerging and forming a movement of "One Way" Christian rock that was both heralded and scolded. These early pioneers of praising Jesus with loud guitars and drums and edgy vocals were the early versions of today's contemporary Christian music.

In those days of assassinations, race riots, an unwanted war, and a new culture of drugs and free love, Christian young people rose up and demanded their own say in the matter. Some of the mad, hateful music of the day was replaced with the much-needed hope and faith and love of Jesus Christ in a new musical movement that spawned Christian music festivals as big as Woodstock. These kids plugged in and played loud with the same fervor as Jimi Hendrix, but they were rejoicing in the message of Jesus rather than spewing hatred for the establishment and letting sin fly.

The Oak Ridge Boys and some of their peers, such as the Imperials and André Crouch and the Disciples, could never have been compared to the Jesus rock bands of the late '60s. But their modern approach and style provided a nice alternative for clean-cut Christian youth who were still not into the heavier Jesus rock. But in these crazy days, church kids needed heroes too, and as I see it, the Oak Ridge Boys filled that gap, much to the chagrin of the older southern gospel music crowd, who simply could not understand why the Oaks had to look and sound the way they did. (God help those people if they ever ran into the All Saved Freak Band, who made the Oaks look like the Inspirations!)

On a gut level, though, the mission of the Oak Ridge Boys was simple. The Oaks just wanted gospel music to be as forward thinking and as popular and as well performed as any other kind of music— and why not? Shouldn't the message of Christ be presented in a fun and first-class way?

This philosophy has never changed, no matter how many missiles have been shot over our bow. The Oaks never did gospel like everyone else, and to this day the Oaks have never done country like everybody else. Musically and philosophically, the Oak Ridge Boys have always been an island unto ourselves, creatively speaking. It doesn't matter how this group or that group does things. What matters is how we do things, and history has proven that this philosophy has paid many dividends in longevity and respect.

✷ ✷ ✷

Over the years, people have been curious as to what it was like for us to move from gospel music to somewhere else. They ask us about the criticism we received from some traditional gospel fans and the business leaders of the day. The answer is simple. The Oaks took a *ton* of heat for being different long before deciding to leave the gospel music business. I say "business" because we never left the music. We just found it harder and harder to make a living at it.

By the time I joined the Oaks in 1973, they were already on the receiving end of a lot of resentment from a portion of the gospel music business establishment, and it was enough to make it very hard on us. The Oaks kept moving forward while many more of the more traditionally minded folks started moving backward. According to many of the gospel music powers that be, the Oak Ridge Boys didn't fit the image of what a gospel quartet was supposed to be.

I won't get into some of the petty bickering and such. It's insignificant now because it was a long time ago and many of those involved aren't even alive anymore. But I'll tell you this—to many people, we sinned greatly when we went to Las Vegas with Johnny and June Cash. It didn't matter that Johnny was helping us out by putting dates in our datebook, or that we also played other dates besides Las Vegas with John and June, or that we sang only gospel songs on the Cash stage. It only mattered that we had played Las Vegas!

"The Oaks have become a nightclub act!" people sneered. Once a group on a show before us proclaimed, "Turn those lights up—we aren't a nightclub act!" We were on next, and of course we turned the house lights off and the stage lighting up. We were, after all, now a nightclub act! I'm joking some, but the fact remained that for the most part, our datebook was empty and the money was running out. We knew we could no longer focus on gospel music when another group urged an audience to walk out on us when we came onstage—and several hundred folks did.

It wasn't goodbye to gospel music. It certainly wasn't goodbye to Jesus, because He stayed with us. But it was goodbye to trying to make a living in that business. It was as plain as that.

We were so thankful for all of the good that this group had accomplished throughout its long history, and we knew down deep that it wasn't over by a long shot. Soon after all this, we met our manager and godfather, Jim Halsey, and together we set a plan in motion to take the Oak Ridge Boys to the moon and beyond. We're still doing that together today.

We love gospel music more than ever, and we've never stopped singing gospel songs onstage or even on recordings. In fact, our biggest-selling album, *Fancy Free* (which includes "Elvira"), contains a kicking gospel song called "I Would Crawl All the Way to the River." And the *Bobbie Sue* album includes a tremendous song, loved by multitudes, called "Would They Love Him Down in Shreveport?"

Going back to 1980, the *Together* album featured a cool gospel song called "A Little More like Me," and it's impossible to not detect our heritage in hit songs such as "Everyday," "Touch a Hand, Make a Friend," "Dig a Little Deeper in the Well" and so many others. In fact, the very popular Triumphant Quartet made our "Everyday" into a number one gospel hit.

Over the past dozen years, we've actually recorded several gospel albums and have earned more Dove awards for our efforts. So although we're still not singing gospel music for a living, we've been able to dip back in and enjoy the fellowship and respect of today's gospel music artists from time to time. The music and the message are still very important parts of all we do. When we branched out into newer musical horizons in the mid-'70s, we had no idea that a legendary career lay ahead of us. But I assure you that Jesus Christ is still first and foremost in our lives, and we are thankful to Him for His constant blessings. We give Him the honor, praise, and glory in all things!

✳ ✳ ✳

I can't talk about the Oak Ridge Boys and gospel music without mentioning William J. Gaither. I believe Bill is the single biggest influence on southern gospel music today. I am blessed to call him a friend and a mentor. Over the past dozen years, Bill has brought us back into the fold with an open heart and open arms, and we love him and his wife, Gloria, dearly. We so appreciate all he has done, not only for the Oak Ridge Boys but also for gospel music, keeping it alive and vibrant and forward thinking today.

Bill and Gloria are the most celebrated and prolific songwriters in the history of the genre, and they have taken gospel music around the world through their enormously popular Gaither Homecoming television shows, video series, recordings, and live appearances. The Gaither Vocal Band is probably the best singing group alive today, and Bill is also the force behind the Gaither Music Company and the Spring Hill Music Group, which has released a lot of memorable and meaningful music by the Oak Ridge Boys over the past dozen years.

I remember the first time I saw a Gaither Homecoming video. I had arrived home on a red-eye flight from Los Angeles. It was a Sunday morning, and I had crawled into my wonderful bed at home right about the time my wife, Mary, was crawling out. I just wanted to sleep a little bit more, but instead I turned on the TV.

There before my tired, red eyes were my gospel heroes sitting in a semicircle—singing, crying, and having a great time in the Lord. My memory started doing cartwheels over several decades, darting back and forth from one all-night sing to another. I never did get to sleep that morning. I was so excited and blessed to be watching the Cathedrals, the Happy Goodman Family, and such legends as Jake Hess and James Blackwood. Many of the newer, younger artists were in the circle too, including Ivan Parker and the Isaacs. And there was Bill Gaither, leading everyone in prayer and song. I picked up the phone immediately and ordered a DVD. How could I have known that after making country music hits, the Oak Ridge Boys would once again become a small part of the southern gospel music world? And it's all because of Bill Gaither.

In 2000, the Oak Ridge Boys were inducted into the Gospel Music Hall of Fame. What a night that was! On that night we took every living member of previous Oaks into the Hall with us, including Willie Wynn, Gary McSpadden, Ron Page, Jim Hamill, and one Lon "Deacon" Freeman, who was the only living member of the original Georgia

Clodhopper/Oak Ridge Quartet. We lost the Deacon not long after that night.

About a year later, a late-night phone conversation between Bill and Duane would put into place a plan for the Oaks to record a brand-new gospel album and make an appearance in a Homecoming video. When we heard about it, we all latched on to the idea. Duane and Michael Sykes produced our first gospel album in decades—the Grammy-nominated *From the Heart*, for Spring Hill Music Group. The next thing you know we had a hit record on gospel radio again with a song called "I Know What Lies Ahead."

We also found ourselves in the big singing circle of a Homecoming video, surrounded by heroes and friends. It was a huge event, and the love and respect shown to the Oak Ridge Boys during that Homecoming taping was very moving and most appreciated by all of us.

On a personal note, when I was younger I just adored the Statesmen Quartet, out of Atlanta, Georgia. Sitting right nearby in the singing circle was the legendary Hovie Lister. It took all night long, but I finally summoned the courage to introduce myself to him. He was so gracious to me. We chatted for more than an hour after the taping was over, and he kept telling me old Statesmen road stories. Hovie mesmerized me. I kept flashing back to listening to *The Statesmen: Live* on RCA records in my bedroom in Philly and hearing Hovie say, "If it would *please* you, we'd be *pleased* to have each member of the Statesmen come up and sing his favorite hymn or spiritual song for you right now!"

I loved that album, and I loved the Statesmen. And here I was, actually talking to Hovie. I was a friend of presidents and rock and country legends, but this was *Hovie Lister*!

I'll stop now, but trust me—I could go on and on about that night in Indianapolis. A night that set the peg for many more Homecoming video appearances and several more gospel, country, and Christmas projects released by the Gaither Music group.

There have been so many wonderful and memorable experiences in the past decade or more for the Oak Ridge Boys, and all because of Bill Gaither.

* * *

In 2007, we were invited by Teddy Gentry, of the group Alabama, to take part in a unique project in which country stars sang praise and worship music. It was called *Songs 4 Worship: Country* for Time Life records, and the Oaks' rendition of "Come, Now Is the Time to Worship" garnered a ton of attention. We certainly can't be compared to Third Day or Casting Crowns or Mercy Me, but this recording really came out well, and we enjoyed dipping into some Christian contemporary gospel creativity.

In 2009, Bill Gaither produced a Homecoming video on just the Oak Ridge Boys called *A Gospel Journey*, chronicling our years in gospel, the present-day influence of the genre, and the message for our lives today. It earned us a Gospel Music Association Dove award for Best Long Form Video.

The Oaks have been awarded nine Dove awards and four gospel Grammy awards over the years. The Christian Country Music Association gave us their Mainstream Artist of the Year Award in 2004, and the Southern Gospel Music Association awarded us the prestigious James D. Vaughan Impact Award in 2012.

We had come a long way—from folks walking out on us to now being included in a Gaither Homecoming video. Part of that is due to some changes I've seen in the gospel music world. Everyone seems to get along and be more supportive of each other's talents and success. Some narrow-mindedness undoubtedly still slips into the mix sometimes, but it's hard to imagine Michael Booth of the Booth Brothers fighting with Greater Vision's Gerald Wolfe over where to place a merchandise table. It's hard to imagine Sonya Isaacs pulling the plug on the Gold City Quartet because they were bringing the house down. I just can't see Rambo McGuire arguing with Jason Crabb as to whose sound system to use.

Thankfully, things seem much better in the land of southern gospel music these days than when four longhaired mavericks with an attitude and a swagger *and* a hippie drummer tried to change the world.

And I seriously think that Bill Gaither is the reason for all of this. God bless him for that.

As of this writing we're about to go into the recording studio with Duane Allen and Ben Isaacs coproducing an album of hymns for Gaither Music. The album release may coincide with this book release somewhat, so as you are reading you may be listening to the Oak Ridge Boys singing *The Old Story*.

Bill Gaither once said that gospel songs written by country music writers always seems to look through a different creative window than gospel songs written by gospel music writers, and I think a great example of this is our Grammy-winning performance of "The Baptism of Jesse Taylor," written by none other than Dallas Frazier, who also wrote "Elvira." We also have gospel music Grammy awards for our performances of "Where the Soul Never Dies" and "Just a Little Talk with Jesus."

★ ★ ★

I'm constantly amazed at the fortitude and sheer willpower of gospel music singers. Coming up in the music business by singing in churches is not as dangerous as getting hit by a flying beer bottle in a nightclub, but I'll tell you, quartet guys have a will and a spirit like no other on the pop music stage.

I have a good friend named David Sutton who sings tenor with the very popular Triumphant Quartet. He had a gallbladder removed on a Sunday and was singing by Wednesday. I've seen big-name acts cancel a week's worth of shows because they caught a cold. I've also seen our guys be so sick they could hardly get off the bus, but they still went onstage and did the job.

A few years ago our Richard Sterban walked off a curb the wrong way while on vacation and tore up his Achilles tendon big-time. After several operations and a ton of pain and discomfort, he was right there onstage singing bass. It was a tough time for him, but man, we would wheel him out there, sit him on a stool, and put a microphone in his hand, and he would do the rest.

Two years ago I caught something evil and was so sick before a Christmas tour that I was sure Wes Hampton of the Gaither Vocal Band might have to fill in for me, but I got on the bus anyway. Why? Because I asked God to help me sing, and I knew He would. I did not ask for healing—just for help to sing. The very next night, in South Dakota, I felt so bad I could hardly stand up, but I sang just fine.

So there's the answer. Faith in Jesus Christ—a childlike faith that can get you through most anything. I guess that is what gospel singers have that many others do not.

✳ ✳ ✳

It's impossible to write about the Oak Ridge Boys and southern gospel music without adding a few paragraphs about Rockland Road in Hendersonville, Tennessee. As I mentioned earlier, our Duane Allen recorded and produced many albums for my Keystones group in the late 1960s and early '70s, but this is only a small part of the history and legacy of all that went on at 329 Rockland Road.

Duane first opened a studio in the basement of his house. This is the same house where he raised his two children, Jamie and Dee, and the same house where Jamie and her husband, Paul Martin, are raising *their* four children. Paul also has a studio in the same basement. The Lion King would call this the Circle of Life.

Duane would eventually purchase a building on Rockland Road, and history would be made. He built an incredible studio there, and before long we would all buy in and expand the property to house all of the Oaks' offices and staff and warehousing needs. We worked out of that building for many years.

When I joined the Oaks in 1973, Duane had built Rockland Road into Superior Sound and even housed a state-of-the-art printing company. A small, part-time gospel music group could come into the studio and record an album with great musicians at a great price and walk away with custom albums, pressed and finished and ready to sell.

Duane would have the albums pressed in downtown Nashville while he printed the covers and liner notes in the back on huge printing presses.

This was a fun time for all of us. Young and talented studio musicians like Pete Cummings, John Rich, Tony Brown, Mark Ellerbee, Skip Mitchell, and Don Breland would all work very hard to make this a great experience for whoever came by the studio to record, and I even got to book and produce some of these custom projects. It was a learning experience and a building block for all of us, and as word spread, Rockland Road became a haven for gospel quartets, trios, and soloists from all over the country.

We still run into people today who once recorded at Superior, and they are always grateful for the experience. Some, like Woody Wright and many others, are very successful gospel singers to this day.

The Oaks even recorded the Grammy-winning gospel song "Where the Soul Never Dies" on Rockland Road, and we will never forget a young Charlie Daniels coming in to put some memorable slide guitar on the record.

Times change and years go by, but I'm happy to say that Ricky Skaggs and his Skaggs Family Records now own the complex, and Ricky has put a ton of money into the studio, which now focuses on bluegrass music. The studio is always busy, and we recorded our upcoming hymns album right there on Rockland Road. The circle of life again!

Yes, back in those days we were all young and willing and energetic long before the Oak Ridge Boys would hit it big, and God blessed us over and over for our work, just as He does to this day. Because of Duane's early vision, we were helping people with their music, publishing songs, and running a recording studio that would become legendary.

The Oak Ridge Boys and our band of that era made many memories and created a lot of blessed music on Rockland Road—and *that* is a fact!

15

PRESIDENTS

"An American Family"

BOB CORBIN

When we're asked about our most memorable moments as Oak Ridge Boys, we often recall the honor of singing in the White House and our friendships with several of our nation's presidents…and why not? It's simply the truth that these events have provided us with some of our greatest memories.

President Jimmy Carter and his wife hosted a country music celebration and dinner at the White House in the late 1970s. We performed there with quite a few other artists.

We sang several of our hit songs of the day, including "Y'all Come Back Saloon" and "You're the One." It was a great night, and eating dinner at the White House for the first time was astounding. There were no cell phones then, but we could use a few landlines. There were long lines behind every available telephone as guests wanted to phone home. Today, everyone would be taking selfies and tweeting them to the universe. "GUESS WHERE I AM, MOM?"

We have joined with President Jimmy Carter in his support for Habitat for Humanity several times over the years to help build homes for those in need. I once helped build an entire roof in eastern Kentucky. I wonder if it held up.

When President Reagan invited us to sing at the Congressional Barbecue on the White House lawn in 1983, we again performed our hits and added some gospel songs at his request. This event is held every year and is promoted as an opportunity for Republicans and Democrats to put aside partisan politics and gather on the White House lawn to eat picnic-style barbecue and listen to some good country music.

We would eventually perform at this event three times over the years for three different presidents. But we remember the Reagan event as the beginning of our longtime friendship with George H.W. Bush, then the vice president.

★ ★ ★

During our sound check that afternoon, Bush 41 came by to greet us on the White House lawn, and we hit it off big-time because he was such a fan of the Oak Ridge Boys. He explained that he couldn't come to the show that night because he was scheduled to leave for Africa, so we performed a special set of songs just for him while doing the sound check. We knew he was a real fan because he wanted to hear specific album cuts, songs most people would never have known about. He specifically asked for "Freckles" off the *Saloon* album, and that just blew us away.

After he became president, we sang for him many, many times, and we still sing for him today. In fact, he and Barbara Bush came to see us in Galveston, Texas, recently, and we had "An American Family" all ready for him. That song has always been a favorite of his.

Two events with President Bush are very memorable. Once, while he was president, we were in the Oval Office with him, and he said, "Hey, I have to show you where I listen to you fellows here. I have a new sound system that's just great."

He led us to a small, private, inner office right behind the Oval Office, and he turned on the sound set. Immediately "Dig a Little Deeper in the Well" blared out of the speakers, and we are all grooving and laughing when I noticed the red phone on the desk. I was thinking, *Boy, if this were to ring now, he'd never hear it!*

We actually spent the night in the White House once at the invitation of George and Barbara Bush. Mary and I slept in the Queen's Bedroom. Well, I never really slept. I remember being awake all night long, just pondering actually being *inside* the White House in the middle of the night with the president and First Lady actually sleeping right down the hall. It was all so humbling to be there.

Duane and his wife, Norah Lee, were right across the hall in the Lincoln Bedroom, and I don't think they slept either. The actual Gettysburg Address hangs on the wall in there! How could you sleep?

Early the next morning, President Bush knocked on our doors and urged us to get ready as quickly as possible, and of course we did. We were all invited to attend a private ceremony in the East Room that morning. On this day, President Bush would present the Presidential Medal of Freedom to President Ronald Reagan. We did *not* see this one coming. We got to shake the hands of Ronald and Nancy and, along with a very distinguished roomful of people that included the Reverend Billy Graham, we witnessed a piece of American history. We have experienced many wonderful things because of our friendship with 41, but this may have taken the cake. I will never forget it.

We once joined the president on Air Force One during the 1992 campaign. Everyone on the plane knew the election was lost and that the young governor of Arkansas, Bill Clinton, would be the next president. President Bush's son George W. Bush came back to where we were seated and spoke softly. "My dad really needs you guys right now...He's kind of down and really needs a lift."

He led us to the front of the plane to a version of the Oval Office, and there sat the president. We gathered around him and sang "Amazing Grace." Everyone onboard came up to the front of Air Force One as we sang, and there wasn't a dry eye. Another unforgettable moment.

George and Barbara Bush have invited the Oak Ridge Boys and our wives to their summer home on Walker's Point, their private peninsula in Kennebunkport, Maine, many times over the years. For us it's like staying at the world's greatest bed and breakfast...only much better! The historic vibes alone in this wonderful place are mesmerizing. World leaders of all kinds have met there, and to stand on the veranda and gaze out over the North Atlantic is always humbling and thought provoking.

We have put on some wonderful private shows for the Bush family and their friends there, and as a reward for singing, we eat great food and even get to go fishing way off the Maine Coast with 41 on his monster speedboat *Fidelity*.

Not long ago, the four of us were singing in New York State and made a quick swing over to Maine to share a bit of lobster with the Bushes at Walker's Point. Talk about old friends—these precious people are getting older now as well, and I dread the day when I will hear we have lost them. Some of the greatest memories I have during this life of singing songs are the results of our friendship with George and Barbara Bush.

Once while at Walker's Point, a bunch of those Segway Personal Transporters turned up. Everyone was freewheeling all around Walker's Point, and a secret service agent invited me to give it a try. I lost control immediately and went head over teakettle right into Barbara Bush's garden. I really made a mess too. I ran to my cabin to bandage up and hide from her for almost two hours.

In late 2013, we were told that CNN Films and the George Bush Presidential Library Foundation were putting together a documentary that would show right after President Bush's ninetieth birthday in June of 2014. A camera crew came to a show and filmed us sitting in a semicircle, telling stories. That night the crew also filmed us singing "Amazing Grace," and that was it.

Fast-forward to June 15, 2014. The film is called *41 on 41*. It's the complete story of the forty-first president of the United States as revealed through the storytelling of 41 friends. It was magnificent and very moving. I sat in front of my TV and took in every moment, but I'll tell you, as I witnessed the way the documentary flowed, I couldn't envision how the Oak Ridge Boys could fit in this tribute.

As the two-hour film entered the last half hour, I figured we had ended up on the editing room floor, and I was fine with it. I was so honored just to know this man, and I was deeply moved by the story of this great American. Then, with two minutes left, I heard my own voice saying, "Here is a song for our President George Herbert Walker Bush," and there I was up on the screen with all of the Boys.

We started to sing "Amazing Grace." A full panorama of the Oaks appeared, and the script underneath read, "The Oak Ridge Boys in a special performance."

Then the credits rolled as we continued to sing, and I was so overcome with emotion that I wept my eyes out right there on my couch! We were the only music act to appear on *41 on 41*, and we will forever be grateful to CNN Films and the George Bush Presidential Library Foundation for including us.

The reason for "Amazing Grace" is very poignant. President Bush 41 has wanted to hear this song at several meaningful and historic moments over the years. Aboard Air Force in 1992, as I mentioned earlier. During his eightieth and eighty-fifth birthday celebrations. In his living room in Kennebunkport, Maine, several times. And in early 2014 when he was ill, we called him on the phone and sang it as well. He was released from the hospital the very next day, and national news outlets gave us credit for helping to heal the president. Of course, this was absurd, and when we visited him and Barbara in their Houston home a few weeks later, we went to Barbara and said we were sorry for all the press reports saying that *we* helped to heal her husband. She replied, "Oh, hogwash, boys—it's true! You *did* help heal George!"

We have always been honored to sing for him. When his son George W. Bush was in office, he invited the Oak Ridge Boys to come and sing for him as well. These have been precious moments in our lives, and I must admit there are really no words to fully express what they mean to us!

Let me tell you about a prayer God answered for me once in the North Atlantic. President Bush 41 had screamed about five miles straight out into the ocean in *Fidelity* before he shut her down to catch some bluefish. We were so far out that all that was visible was rolling blue water, and that, along with the fish smell, was making my stomach turn. I've had plenty of experience deep-sea fishing, and I've also had plenty of experience hurling over the side of a boat at sea—and that was about to happen aboard a presidential vessel.

I was in the seat up front, out of his view, and I began to pray in earnest. "O God, please don't let me be sick out here. I can't blow chunks over the side in front of the president…please, Lord…*please*."

God answered my prayers, and my churning stomach calmed. I am forever grateful. I even caught a few fish before 41 headed back to Walker's Point. The sea breeze felt wonderful on my face on the trip back, and I was feeling pretty good about everything until the president turned to me and said. "You got a little green around the gills out there didn't you, Joe?"

How could I even begin to think I could hide something like that from a former head of the CIA?

★ ★ ★

We sang for President Gerald Ford one time. He was at an event Jim Halsey promoted in Tulsa, and he just loved our show. He came out to the bus afterward and shook our hands and said, "'Man, you boys sure can sing!" It was a great moment, and I believe that was the only time we ever met President Ford.

We first met Bill Clinton when he was governor of Arkansas. He came backstage at the state fair in Little Rock and made us all official Arkansas Travelers. Later, during his presidency, we met him in Philadelphia at the Presidents' Summit for America's Future, an event to promote volunteerism. It was hosted by then General Colin Powell and attended by all the living former presidents—Bush 41, Jimmy Carter, Gerald Ford, and First Lady Nancy Reagan (representing Ronald Reagan). At this amazing event, a ton of volunteers cleaned up a good portion of the city.

The opening ceremonies were held at a football field. We performed a few songs with Boyz II Men, and that was very cool. Kind of an Oak Ridge Boyz II Men sort of moment.

Before we sang, we were standing in the parking lot with George and Barbara Bush as well as Jimmy and Rosalynn Carter. President Clinton arrived with a hundred motorcycles, SUVs, and limos— horns blowing, sirens wailing, and flags waving. Members of the press who were covering the president tumbled out of small busses and ran toward the front of the stage as secret service agents surrounded the presidential limo.

Mrs. Bush turned to her husband and said, "Oh, George, I hope we didn't look that ridiculous!"

Without missing a beat, 41 turned and said, "We did, Barb—we certainly did!"

President Clinton remembered us from Arkansas and was very gracious to us. I will add that neither President Clinton nor President Obama invited us to sing at the White House, but singing for the Clintons that night in Philadelphia was still pretty cool.

We first met George W. Bush on that aforementioned campaign aboard Air Force One with his father. We later performed at his gubernatorial inauguration in Texas. During the eight years of his presidency, we sang at many events at his behest, including yet another congressional barbecue at the White House.

At the White House lawn event when Bush 43 was president, the president's famous dog Barney came running toward us during a sound check. We were all so excited to see the famous little black Scottie that we stopped what we were doing and started to pet and play with the little fellow. Our longtime lighting director, Dave Boots, reached down for Barney just as the president was walking our way, and the dog proceeded to bite the daylights out of Dave.

As he yanked back a semi-bloody hand, all that a smiling Bush 43 could say was, "He must be a Democrat!"

We all laughed so hard because Boots *is* a Democrat!

We made another wonderful memory when President George W. Bush called on us to sing "Amazing Grace" at a huge event in Washington DC. Lady Margaret Thatcher was the speaker that night in what would be her last public appearance, and we were there to be part of it. She was simply amazing, and meeting her was another of the many highlights of our lives.

So there you have it—Ford, Carter, Reagan, Bush 41, Clinton, Bush 43. As for President Obama, we're still waiting for the call.

✳ ✳ ✳

Members of the US House of Representatives and US Senate and state governors and their families—from both sides of the aisle—have been friends and fans of the Oaks. It's always an honor to get to spend some quality time with our leaders and perhaps even get to voice an opinion or two.

We performed at the request of our own Governor Bill Haslam for the 2014 National Governors Association annual meeting held right there in Nashville, Tennessee, and it was really a kick for us to have one governor after another visit our dressing room for a picture.

We have been honored on the floor of the US Senate and on the floor of our own Tennessee State Legislature for our career achievements and our service to America. A very humbling experience for all of us!

A few words here about another great American hero who has become a wonderful friend to the Oak Ridge Boys over the years. He's never been president, but General Chuck Yeager is the greatest aviator in history, and we love him dearly.

Once in Myrtle Beach about 20 years ago, we heard that Chuck was in town having a reunion with his fighter squadron from World War II. We invited them all to the show, and they came.

The general wanted to know what this was going to cost, and we told him it was all on us. As he tells it, "Those Boys welcomed a bunch of old airmen and made us feel appreciated!" Well, yeah—this was Chuck Yeager!

We sang at his eightieth birthday party, and it was a blast. He now celebrates his birthday with the Oaks every year, and we recently celebrated his ninety-first in Nevada. We always have to sing "It Takes a Little Rain" for the general—his favorite song.

Chuck also celebrated his ninety-first birthday by making a trip to South Africa to teach young pilots how to fly F-14s. This is simply astounding.

A few years ago our William Lee Golden flew with Chuck over northern California in a vintage single-engine, open-cockpit airplane. He had a blast! That was a great day for William Lee as they landed at Barron Hilton's Flying-M Ranch, joined up with our tour director, Darrick Kinslow, and had lunch with the *first* and *last* men to walk on the moon—the late Neil Armstrong and Gene Cernan. That kind of right stuff doesn't happen every day.

General Chuck Yeager has introduced us on stages from Alabama to California—about 30 times in all through the years—and it's always fun to watch our audience respond as a real American hero walks out on the stage. He gets the big standing O every single time! We all love and respect the general!

I know this much. If I ever grow up, I want to be like George H.W. Bush or General Chuck Yeager. May God allow them to live and continue to inspire for many years to come. They are some of the best of what is left of our Greatest Generation, and I love them both with all of my being! I am all the better just for knowing them.

16

CRACKER BARREL

"Pass the pancakes"

A book about the Oak Ridge Boys wouldn't be complete without a chapter on our relationship with Cracker Barrel Old Country Stores. There are well over 600 of these family-friendly eateries in 42 states across America. The atmosphere is congenial, and the food and service are down-home and wonderful. But what we Oaks like is that Cracker Barrel has become one of the largest music retailers in America. Many big-box music stores are gone, other large retail outlets are devoting less and less space to CDs, and many music buyers now rely on iTunes to download their favorite songs. In this environment, it's gratifying that Cracker Barrel continues to grow their music space, and the Oaks have been among the beneficiaries.

A few years back, we recorded an album sold exclusively by Cracker Barrel, and it was a huge success. The album was called *It's Only Natural*, and it contained several rerecordings of previous hits as well as five new songs. Duane Allen and Michael Sykes produced most of this project, and a cool thing happened in the process. Julie Craig, who guides Cracker Barrel's marketing, wanted us to record an updated version of "Elvira." We coaxed Ron Chancey out of retirement to get involved. Duane invited Ron to produce two more cuts as well, and things got really nostalgic for us all.

We had a song meeting with Ron, and it was just like the old days again, sitting in a circle with the fifth Oak and laughing and listening to songs. We settled on "Before I Die," "The Shade," and "Elvira" for the Chancey sessions. The swampy-sounding guitars on "Elvira" certainly gave it a facelift, but other than that, it was the Boys singing "Elvira" as usual, and it came out great. (A few years back we recorded a version of "Elvira" with the Dukes of Dixieland. Now *that* was different!)

After recording "Before I Die" and "The Shade" with Ron, I remember thinking that if this had been 1982, we could have celebrated two more number ones before these songs were even released. That's how good they were and are. Both songs became staples of our live show for about two years.

The whole album came out extremely well. Redoing "Gonna Take a Lot of River," "No Matter How High," "True Heart," "Lucky Moon," "Beyond Those Years," and "Louisiana Red Dirt Highway" turned out to be a wonderful idea, and Michael Sykes and the Ace got the sounds and mixes just right. The goal here was to not lose the integrity of the original recordings but to freshen them up and give each song a new glow, and it really worked!

We picked out three more new songs to be produced by Michael and Duane, including the very successful "What'cha Gonna Do," "Wish You Could Have Been There," and my self-penned song "Sacrifice...for Me."

All and all it was a wonderful project, and Cracker Barrel was very pleased when we delivered it. Even the photos on the album jacket came out great. Julie Craig sent a Chicago camera crew to Deadwood, South Dakota, to catch some wonderful scenery and produce some photos of the Oak Ridge Boys like nothing we'd ever seen.

To promote the project, our public relations firm, Webster and Associates, had us running coast to coast doing tons of radio and television and print stuff, and luckily for us the Cracker Barrel jet was available much of the time to help us meet all of the obligations Kirt Webster set up. We also appeared at scores of Cracker Barrel locations. Almost every day, if there was a Cracker Barrel in the city where we were playing, we had lunch there and spent about two hours signing copies of *It's Only Natural.* I ate a *lot* of pancakes during those trips. If you went to eat at a Cracker Barrel during this time, you could *not* get away from us. Our CD was on display as you walked in. An Oak Ridge Boys' display sat on your table as you ate your dumplings. A huge sign and more CDs were waiting for you as you checked out. "Elvira" was even playing in the bathroom—complete with swampy guitars.

Because our album was featured at Cracker Barrel Old Country Stores, our pictures were prominently placed not only throughout the stores but also on billboards all over town. Cracker Barrel is a sponsor of the Grand Ole Opry, so ads for our project ran several times on WSM AM radio during every Opry show. A life-size poster was featured at the Nashville airport. As you descended the escalator to baggage claim, there we were!

When we later released our *Christmas Time's A-Coming* album, Cracker Barrel gave us plenty of shelf space for that as well. For a while Cracker Barrel also sold my book *G.I. Joe & Lillie* as part of their Celebrate America display. During that time I did a bunch of book signings for Cracker Barrel and always managed to have even more pancakes before the crowd lined up. I guess you can tell I *love* Cracker Barrel pancakes.

Cracker Barrel sponsored our Christmas tour for a while as well. Our stage featured a complete Cracker Barrel set too, and it was really fun. We still utilize their rocking chairs on tours today.

17

BRANSON

"Let's go to Branson"

 he Oak Ridge Boys have a long history of doing shows in this all-American, family-oriented town, and we've always done very well there. Branson lies beautifully and strategically in the heart of the Ozark Mountains by Lake Taneycomo, and with its amusement parks, hotels, restaurants, and music theaters, it has become *the* showplace town of the Midwest and a preferred vacation destination for every age group. Mom and Dad and the kids, as well as charter buses full of older folks, descend upon Branson on a regular basis, and music acts of all kinds fill the stages of more than 50 theaters.

Branson first became an attraction in 1912 when people journeyed there to see the Marvel Caves, which lie beneath the Silver Dollar City amusement park—the centerpiece of Branson tourism. (No, we never played the Marvel Caves.)

Nowadays, quite a few entertainment acts live in Branson and play there all the time, including Presleys' Country Jubilee and the Baldknobbers Jamboree Show. These two family acts are pretty much responsible for inventing the Branson variety shows that are emulated by so many others who operate theaters there. These shows feature singing and dancing with lots of country hits, impersonations, comedy, bluegrass, gospel, patriotic songs, costume changes…all stuffed into one fast-paced show.

The Oak Ridge Boys first played Branson in the gospel music days of the late 1960s and early '70s when the Shepherd of the Hills Farm was the centerpiece attraction. With its beauty, history, and gospel music appeal to tourists and music lovers, it was a popular venue for the Oaks of that day. During the heyday of the early '80s, we rocked the Swiss Amphitheater in Branson. Neither of these exist anymore, so add them to the list of venues we have outlived.

But it was the Branson boom in the early '90s, brought on in big part by a popular segment of *60 Minutes*, that brought the Oak Ridge Boys to town on a more regular basis. The Grand Palace was built in 1992 on the famous Route 76 strip. This stunning edifice could seat up to 4000 people, and the stage was enormous. It was built to attract major music acts to Branson, and the very first acts to be booked there were the Oak Ridge Boys and Glen Campbell. Together, we ushered in a new era for Branson. Andy Williams, Bobby Vinton, Ray Stevens, Mel Tillis, Mickey Gilley, Moe Bandy, the Gatlin Brothers, the Osmonds, Jim Stafford, and the Sons of the Pioneers were soon firmly entrenched in Branson, and the town was indeed booming.

The Oaks have been coming to Branson off and on during the year ever since. The Grand Palace started it all. Then we played regularly at the Glen Campbell Theater and the Charlie Pride Theater for several years. We returned to the Grand Palace until it closed in 2007.

The very successful Mansion Theatre group eventually approached us. They had a vision to refurbish the Glen Campbell Theater by adding the most modern sound and lighting and seating available and renaming it the Oak Ridge Boys Theater. We all agreed; the theater reopened as such in 2008, and we've been playing there ever since. We don't actually own the theater, but our name is over the door, and performing there has been a great adventure. Inside the lobby, an Oak Ridge Boys museum of sorts houses all sorts of memorabilia from over the years.

We never moved to Branson, as some performers did. We never even considered it. No one could ever dig us out of the rolling hills of Middle Tennessee, and that's a fact! To us, playing about 27 nights a year in Branson (out of our 150 or so road dates) represents the same management philosophy as when we played Las Vegas for four weeks a year in earlier days. Our manager, Jim Halsey, calls these commitments "anchor dates." We book guaranteed show dates here and there over the course of the year and then work the rest of the tour around them.

We still play Las Vegas on a regular basis in venues like the Golden Nugget, but gone are the days of playing a week or two at a time, as we used to do at Bally's or Caesars Palace or even the Orleans. Branson has pretty much taken the place of Vegas as our anchor dates. (The Golden Nugget also books us in Biloxi, Mississippi, and in Atlantic City, New Jersey.)

As of this writing, our future in Branson is uncertain. A huge hospital and medical center is being built right around the theater site, and there's the possibility it all might be torn down. We will have to see on that, but my guess is that we will still come to Branson on a regular basis because it's a perfect place for us. Maybe the Grand Palace will open up again.

As a Middle America group that appeals to everyone, we present a show that has become a staple of family entertainment. The crowds we see in Branson are pretty much the same crowds we see at the state and county fairs.

We don't change our show in any way when we play in Branson. We play the hits and maybe a new song or two, sing some gospel, and wave the flag a bit. We never have an opening act. We usually play for about an hour or so, take a 20-minute intermission, and complete the two-hour performance. The whole thing usually includes around 25 songs. You'll see the same show in Branson that you'll see at a performing arts center in your town or anywhere else.

Each year we rehearse our Christmas tour in Branson and start adding songs in early November. We usually open our entire full-production Christmas show in mid-November in Branson before we take it out on the road to another 30 to 35 cities.

The fall of the year ushers in the Branson tour-bus crowds, and these bus crowds are usually a bit older. I think it's great that older folks get to go on trips like this, and we always enjoy singing to them. When we were younger, we had a harder time singing to the sometimes older Branson crowd because they often thought we were too loud and not country or gospel enough. Well, that part hasn't changed much, but now we're not much younger than they are...so it's even more fun to rock them a bit! Weren't these folks alive and well through the '70s, '80s, and '90s? I know I was!

Branson is also the destination of many of our military veterans. The town treats vets like royalty (as they should), and it's always an honor to have them at our show. We've had the Military Order of the Purple Heart, the Congressional Medal of Honor Society, American Gold Star Mothers, the Wounded Warrior Project, Soldier's Wish, the American Legion, and various other veterans' organizations make our show a part of their trip. I might add that Branson has a wonderful World War II museum, and it's a must-see place if you're ever passing through.

18

GOING SOCIAL

"What a computer is to me is...it's the most remarkable tool that we've ever come up with. It's the equivalent of a bicycle for our minds."

STEVE JOBS

*T*he Oaks utilize social networking big-time. We have a huge Facebook and Twitter presence, and our online FlipBoard magazine is very popular and well read. We work hard, and we put in a lot of extra personal time keeping our fans and friends updated with news, tour info, public relations, tidbits, logistics, song lyrics, and all kinds of fun stuff they can get only from us. PR firms are great, but it's not like thousands of people are waiting on every word that falls from the mouth of a publicist. No, with the Oaks, it's actually one of the Boys tweeting (or in some cases, *over* tweeting) live and in person right there on your device.

Our very interactive website (oakridgeboys.com) is pretty much the hub of all information relating to the Oaks, and we're thankful to Jon Mir, our webmaster and operations manager, for keeping it up to date and on the cutting edge of today's changing technologies. Jon has been a leader in teaching us all how to use these tools to our advantage—and not just recently. The Oak Ridge Boys have been pioneers in every aspect of technology, and through the years, many other acts have gleaned info by studying how we operate—from our office management to everyday logistics. We owe most of this to Jon.

You can find all four Oaks and many of our team members on

Twitter. Duane and William Lee have a heavy presence on Facebook as well. I'm still debating whether to join Facebook. I am on Linked-In (as is Duane), which is more business and jobs related, so we are always in the loop of vital information with songwriters and music-industry types. One can feel the pulse of Music City by taking a quick trip around LinkedIn.

We're always looking for ways to utilize social networks more efficiently. Don't get me wrong—actually talking to people and writing a personal note of thanks with pen and paper is just as important, and these probably mean more to people now than ever. But in this younger and faster-paced culture, keeping up-to-date online is vital.

Richard is always on the telephone with radio stations and news-papers, doing personal interviews that help promote the Oak Ridge Boys concert that's coming to your town. I handle a ton of online interviews, which I find convenient because I can easily fit them into my personal schedule. But Richard goes that extra mile and takes up a lot of his downtime to provide that personal touch, and reporters and radio station people just love him. Most acts don't do any of this, but they probably should. I believe every little thing you do matters in the big picture of who and what you are and what you're becoming as an entertainment entity. It would be nice if all we had to do was show up and sing, but building a career like ours is like climbing a mountain. A mountain is made up of many little stones, and every stone is important. No stones? No mountain!

Social networking has become an important stone on our mountain. So boot up that laptop or iPad or iPhone or Android or whatever and join us online.

TWITTER
@oakridgeboys @joebonsall @DUANEALLEN @wlgolden
@rasterban

FACEBOOK

facebook.com/oakridgeboys

facebook.com/pages/Duane-Allen-Fan-Page

facebook.com/pages/William-Lee-Golden/

WEBSITE

oakridgeboys.com

We have our own very cool and constantly updated Oak Ridge Boys app for iPhone, iPad, IpodTouch, and Android, and it's free!

Go to FlipBoard, search Oak Ridge Boys, and catch up with our very cool FlipBoard magazine, put together by our own Jon Mir.

A reporter asked me the other day why I was on Twitter at my age. Why? Well…because I like to tweet! I didn't know there was an age limit. I'm also starting to do Google Plus. My friend Jessica Northey, a social-networking guru and the creative force behind the massive online Country Music Chats (#CMChat) and cmchat.com, is trying to teach me how to utilize this Internet tool. Jessica has hosted the Oak Ridge Boys on two different chats on Twitter over the past few years, and between the four of us boys and Jessica, we almost closed down the entire Internet. A tremendous illustration of the power of going social!

One could write an entire chapter on how communications technology has changed the way we do business. It's sure made my home life a lot easier. My home phone used to ring off the hook all day and most of the night, and most calls were relevant and important, but it drove my wife and my cats crazy. Someone always needed me to share an opinion, make a decision, set up an interview, and so on. None of that has changed much, but it's all easier now. A glance at the iPhone reveals, for example, an email from our Jon Mir. "We have an offer to play so and so on such and such for this much…What say ye?"

A quick reply—"Book it!"

Darrick can send a quick group text. "Leaving time has been moved up an hour to 9 p.m."

Answer—"LOL" or "OMG."

He doesn't have to call everyone at home, and my phone doesn't have to ring during dinner. I guess technology today has its downsides, but the only people who ring my home phone now are telemarketers and my mother-in-law. Everyone else knows what to do!

Even our own fans are increasingly discovering our accessibility. In the old days—and I really don't mean all that long ago—people might send a piece of mail to the office to tell us they're coming to a show, and would we either sing a certain song or acknowledge someone in the audience for one reason or another. With greeting cards, fan letters, junk mail, and country artists politicking for our vote for the next awards show, our mailboxes at the office are usually quite full, so many fan letters unfortunately fall through the cracks for one reason or another and are never seen. But with the likes of Twitter, Facebook, website message boards, and even email, these requests are not as apt to get lost. I try to make a note of these requests and do my best to answer them.

"Please sing 'Make My Life with You'—my wife and I are celebrating our fiftieth anniversary."

"Would you wish my dad a happy birthday? He loves you guys."

"Can you sing 'G.I. Joe and Lillie' at the fair? We're bringing a group of veterans to see you."

It happens almost every day. Let me give you an example. I received a tweet from a fan named John. I hear from John every once in a while, so I recognized his name. His request was simple. "I'm bringing my 85-year-old mother to the show at Renfro Valley, Kentucky, and if there is any way you could give her a shout-out, it would mean the world. If you can't, I certainly understand."

I keep a file inside my set-list folder on my laptop called Show Requests, so I open it and enter "Renfro—shout-out to John's mom, Corinne."

Usually on the afternoon of a show, before I make out a set list, I check my Show Requests file to see if I've noted anything for that night. Then I send an email to our crew guys, asking them to please print this note out, and usually Dave Boots, our lighting director, prints the info and places it on my spot onstage so I'll see it every time I take a drink of Fiji Water or Diet Cherry 7 Up during the show. Well, I shouted out that night to John's mom and mentioned that she was 85 and that we were glad she was there (or something to that effect). With John's permission I would like to share part of a note he sent to us the day after the show.

> Joe,
>
> Thank you so much for saying hello to my mom from the stage at Renfro Valley last night. We were totally surprised, but it made my mom's evening. Even though I had said on Twitter that she was ready to sing "Elvira," she sang louder on "The Baptism of Jesse Taylor" and "Where the Soul of Man Never Dies."
>
> I am going to share something you guys did not know. Mom has always been very active and going places. She loves gospel and country music, and when I was growing up, she instilled that same love of music in me. She and her sister took me to many concerts, such as the Oaks, the Stamps, the Blackwoods, and the Prophets. (We even saw Duane Allen sing with the Prophets in 1965!) As late as 2012, she was still driving. Every Sunday she would round up a carload of her friends and take them to Corinth Christian Church, where she played the piano for 57 years…
>
> In April 2012, she suffered a bad stroke at age 83…We already had tickets to see the Oak Ridge Boys at Renfro Valley before she had her stroke, and one day when I was visiting at the rehab facility, she mentioned she was looking forward to the Oak Ridge Boys show. Six weeks after her stroke, on the night before Mother's Day, we took her to Renfro Valley to see the Oak Ridge Boys. It was her first trip out of her house (other than doctor visits) since her stroke. She was singing and clapping so much that my wife and I realized just

how special that concert was to her. We have made sure we got good seats to see the Oaks for both of your Renfro Valley concerts since then.

Several months before the stroke, Mom started talking with me about her funeral arrangements. She told me what songs she wanted sung, one of which the Oak Ridge Boys recorded—"Through It All." That was very sobering…

When you said hello to her from the stage, she didn't know what to say. On our drive home, she asked several times, "How did they know about me?" (She does not understand Twitter at all.) Thank you so much for brightening her day and giving my mom and her family something we will remember the rest of our lives.

So you see, there's just no way to really ascertain just how much a kind word can mean to someone. That's why it's so important to be nice to people every day. I know we miss some things because so much is always going on, but I assure you the Boys try to answer whenever we can. I am so happy I saw John's tweet and so happy I remembered the shout-out to Corrine at the Renfro Valley show. You just never know!

Here's another great story that came through Duane's Facebook page.

In 1976, I was 13 years old. As most 13-year-olds I had difficulty believing everything my dad said. It took many years to realize that my dad is a pretty smart guy. The father–son relationship can be a challenge sometimes (see the movie *Field of Dreams*).

At 13 years old, my eight-track collection included Peter Frampton, ELO, Boston, the Eagles, and REO Speedwagon. My music tastes did not match my father's, to say the least.

As my dad and I were walking out of the grocery store one day, he noticed a poster by the door and exclaimed, "I'm gonna take you to hear some *real* music!" It was a poster from McKendree College. All I knew about McKendree College was that everybody seemed to go there to become a minister.

That's not true of course, but it seemed that way to me. So I went with my dad begrudgingly to hear his favorite group. I thought, *If I go to this, maybe he'll let me go see REO Speedwagon at SuperJam at Busch Stadium.*

So we got to a packed McKendree gym (holds maybe 800 people), and I was going to have to sit through some gospel, Bible-hangin' Oak Ridge Boys concert. I thought, *They're gonna be savin' somebody's soul right here in the aisle! I've seen my dad's albums of these guys wearing identical leisure suits, big turtlenecks, trying to look cool.*

My dad always talked about Willie Wynn and Duane Allen. Best singers ever! When he first listened to the Oak Ridge Boys, there were five of them. William Lee Golden was the only one I barely recognized.

So I had to listen to a concert of gospel music. I wanted no part of it. Little did we know, the week before, the Oak Ridge Boys released their first country album, *Y'all Come Back Saloon.* My Southern Baptist father wasn't too wild about his favorite gospel quartet singin' 'bout no saloon! The first thing I noticed when they came out was...no leisure suits! And hey, some of those guys looked pretty cool! Longer hair, big drums, lots of guitars, a big Afro'd guy at piano, rockin' it out. And man, was it loud (Dad really didn't like that). This cool-looking foursome went into "You're the One," and I was hooked. The gym went crazy, and my dad was ready to leave. He settled down once they did "Just a Little Talk with Jesus" and "The Baptism of Jessie Taylor," which even I enjoyed. They closed the concert with what eventually became their first chart-topping hit, "Y'all Come Back Saloon."

My dad liked Joe Bonsall, but he always followed it up with "He's no Willie Wynn." Bonsall made sure the whole place knew "she played tambourine"—they must have repeated the chorus five times. If that was a gospel concert, I was being saved!

I saw the Oak Ridge Boys at least twice a year through the '80s and '90s. My dad and I always had a funny banter between us—the gospel ORB versus the country ORB. Of course, the number one hits, radio airplay, and appearances on Johnny Carson all supported my stance. But dad never gave in.

About 2008, they released a new gospel CD, recorded at a live studio show with Bill Gaither (another favorite of dad's), and my dad was so happy to say, "See, I told ya—they're gospel."

So here we are, 40 years after that first concert. Dad has moved into a senior living facility with the start of Alzheimer's. He still sings along to any ORB gospel song from 45 years ago. Don't get me wrong, he loves "Leaving Louisiana in the Broad Daylight" and "Bobbie Sue," but not like "Jesus Is Coming Soon."

My kids are required to hear ORB in my car almost all the time. Everybody in my household has seen at least three live shows. This is nowhere close to the 35-plus live concerts I've attended.

I told dad the other day I'm taking him to see the Oak Ridge Boys on October 17. I'll have to remind him several times before then. I haven't told him yet that we're going to a casino to see them! (And you thought the "saloon" was bad!) He asked me if they're going to sing any gospel. Knowing that probably won't happen, I did remind him about "Thank God for Kids."

It's time to pay him back for introducing me to the group that I've enjoyed for more than 40 years.

We love to hear stories like this from our fans. The great thing is that we know this happens a lot to people who never bother to let us know. I'm sure there are lots of stories out there from people whose lives have been impacted by the Oaks. As I've said before, that humbles us greatly. May God bless these dear people!

Now if you'll excuse me, I feel the need to go tweet something.

19

BACKIN' UP

"Slip Slidin' Away"

PAUL SIMON

Over all these years, the Oak Ridge Boys have added our four-part harmony to the recordings of many other artists. Each time we've had the opportunity to do so, we've counted it as an honor. Some of these backup situations have led to long-term friendships and enduring as well as endearing and memorable projects. In chapter 10, I wrote about singing "Same Ole Me" with the legendary George Jones. This performance cemented a friendship that lasted to his passing in the spring of 2013. Anytime we had the opportunity, we would sing it down with the Possum, and it was always memorable.

We sang on Brenda Lee's big hit "Broken Trust" around that same time, so folks heard us on country radio stations several times an hour. "Bobbie Sue" might be followed by George Jones and Brenda Lee, and if a little Johnny Cash or Jimmy Buffet came next...well, there we could be again.

★ ★ ★

We met Paul Simon in 1975 at the Grammy awards. We won a gospel Grammy and even performed a medley of nominated gospel songs on the live CBS show that night. Even though we were struggling on Columbia Records at the time, Paul was a label mate, so we sought him out. He had just had a huge record with "Loves Me Like a Rock," backed by the black gospel group the Dixie Hummingbirds, and we couldn't wait to talk with him. It so happened that he knew our group well, and he was very gracious to us as we surrounded him and begged him to write a song for us. I'll never forget him saying that he was very possessive of his self-written songs and that if he writes a good one, he never gives it away. His legendary success with Art Garfunkel and his own incredible solo career certainly proved that point. We all laughed and became friends right there on the spot. He promised he would call us if he thought of something—and in a few weeks, to our surprise, he did!

He was producing an album for a New York City girls' rock group called the Roches. Paul flew us to New York to record some backup vocals on the Roche project, and we were on cloud nine working with him. Before we left, he told us he might be calling us again soon because he had a great song idea cooking. Sure enough, about a month later, he called. Once again, he flew us first-class to New York and put us up at the Americana Hotel. Remember, this was during our poor days, but here we were, steppin' in all kinds of high cotton. We arrived on a cool September morning at the famous A&R Recording studio, where Paul and legendary producer Phil Ramone were waiting for us.

Paul got out his 12-string guitar and invited us to sit in a circle with him and listen to his new song. We would try to feel out some cool background parts together.

Our jaws dropped as we heard Paul sing "Slip Sliding Away" for the first time. I could go on and on about the process. Taking breaks and pitching baseball cards with a legend. Paul leaving the session early in the evening to go to Yankee Stadium. ("Keep working, Boys. I have to go—the Red Sox are in town!") Learning about the recording process from Paul and Phil Ramone. Feasting on the deli sandwiches and Italian food Paul brought in for us.

I will just say that from late 1976 on into 1977, "Slip Sliding Away" was a worldwide megahit monster, and even though many people had no idea who was singing all the background parts, we knew it was the Oak Ridge Boys, and it became another big stone on our mountain.

We were so encouraged by Paul Simon, just as we were encouraged by Johnny Cash about a year before. "Stick it out, Boys!" Paul said. "You have magic!" To this day, singing on "Slip Sliding Away" with Paul Simon is one of our most cherished memories.

In 1986, the Showtime cable network did a show called "Gospel Jam Session," hosted by Paul Simon and featuring the Oak Ridge Boys. We rocked out "I Would Crawl All the Way to the River" and joined with Paul to sing "Slip Sliding Away." You can find it on YouTube. Just search "Paul Simon & the Oak Ridge Boys—Slip Slidin' Away," and voilà!

Paul Simon always kept a notebook and pencil with him. Anytime a thought entered his head, he immediately wrote it down. He had pages of little sayings and such that could eventually end up as song lyrics.

One such note simply read, "Bat-faced girl." Paul said he saw a girl on the subway who looked like a bat, so he just wrote that down. A few years later on the award-winning *Graceland* album, the hit song "You Can Call Me Al" mentioned "a roly-poly little bat-faced girl"!

We had the honor of working with Ray Charles on his acclaimed *Friendship* album in 1984. We sang with Ray on the song "This Old Heart (Is Gonna Rise Again)," and what an experience that was. Gathered around a piano with the great Ray Charles as he taught us what to sing and exactly how to sing it was another memory for the ages. Ray could hear every part so well, and we were happy and eager to move or change our harmonies to suit him. The *Friendship* album was a huge project, and to be a part of a Ray Charles record was a tremendous honor for the Oak Ridge Boys. Somewhere in the archives sits a CBS-TV special featuring Kenny Rogers, Dottie West, Ray Charles, and the Oaks. It's well worth the watch if you can find it.

We recently added our vocals to former Oaks tenor Willie Wynn's solo project. The song was appropriately called "The Oak Ridge Boys and Me." It was very cool to be singing one down with our brother Willie!

We experienced another great moment when we recorded the great John Lee Hooker's "Boom Boom" on our *The Boys Are Back* project. We've also covered the Kansas hit "Carry On Wayward Son" as well as "Ramblin' Man" (for an Allman Brothers tribute album on Cleopatra Records called *Midnight Rider*).

In the middle '70s, Johnny Cash had a recording studio in our hometown of Hendersonville called House of Cash. It wasn't unusual for us to receive a call from John, asking us to run on over there and sing backup on a song or two, and of course we always dropped everything to work with the Man in Black. Duane once produced an entire gospel album for John with the Oaks singing on every song. I'm not sure what ever happened to it, but perhaps it will see the light of day in the future. In the meantime, you can download songs like "Good Morning, Friend," "Pie in the Sky," and more to hear the Boys sing with Johnny!

We toured quite a bit with Jimmy Dean in the mid-1970s and sang backup onstage with him, but we never recorded with him. However we did record his classic "Big John" with Charlie Daniels. How ironic is that?

Another great honor was recording "Blue Moon of Kentucky" with the father of bluegrass music himself, Mister Bill Monroe. It was late at night, and Bill and his Bluegrass Boys were all dressed alike, complete with cowboy hats—in the studio where no one could even see them. Pretty unforgettable right there now!

Another point of interest was recording with the king of polka, Jimmy Sturr, in 1998. We recorded five songs on his hundredth album, *Dance with Me*, and it won a Grammy award for best polka album.

The early Oaks did a lot of work with Governor Jimmy Davis,

whose song "You Are My Sunshine" was named a song of the century. The cool thing was that Jimmy Davis took the Oak Ridge Boys with him to the *Tonight Show* in the mid-1960s. That was our first *Tonight Show* appearance!

In 1987, we invited Patti Labelle to sing with us on a song called "Rainbow at Midnight" for our *Where the Fast Lane Ends* album. She agreed, and the result was one of the most unique recordings in our history (imagine a duet with Patti Labelle and William Lee Golden). What made the event even more special was that Joe Walsh agreed to play guitar on the song. There is no other recording in our history quite like this one!

Considering the number of people we're recorded with, it's flat-out amazing that we've never recorded with Kenny Rogers. Well, we did, but here's what happened. Kenny and the Oaks were playing a few dates out west together a few years back, and we all got together in a trailer backstage in Pendleton, Oregon, to listen to a new gospel song that Kenny and some of his band guys wrote for an upcoming Cracker Barrel gospel album.

We all loved it, and within the next month we were in the studio putting vocals on a Kenny song at last. But the rest of the album was all hymns, so in the final analysis the song we did with Kenny, which was very contemporary, didn't seem to fit the format, so it was left off. So we *almost* did one with KR!

We've had so many wonderful experiences backing up other performers, and I don't believe we're through. It would be fun to sing one with Garth Brooks or Carrie Underwood one day. Also on our wish list is Little Big Town and Lady Antebellum, and who knows who else might call before the days are done. We are always ready to sing!

Here's a roundup of some of the great folks with whom we've either recorded or performed: Paul Simon, Johnny Cash, the Carter Family, Brenda Lee, Ray Charles, Con Hunley, George Jones, the Blind Boys of Alabama, Billy Ray Cyrus, Jimmy Buffett, Bill Monroe, Little Feat, Joe Walsh, Patti Labelle, Governor Jimmy Davis, Tom T. Hall, Del Reeves, the Grascals, T.G. Shepherd, Shooter Jennings, Barbara Mandrell, Lynn Anderson, Roy Rogers, T. Graham Brown, the

Gatlin Brothers, the Blackwood Brothers, Karen Peck, Bill Anderson, the Chuck Wagon Gang, Jerry Salley, the Dukes of Dixieland, Jimmy Sturr, the McDougal family, Hometown News, Kenny Vaughan, Sawyer Brown (Joe), Peter Cetera (Richard), Alan Jackson (Richard), Trae Edwards (Joe), Charlie Daniels, Lisa Matassa, and Deborah Allen. As of this writing, we're hoping to record a gospel song with Merle Haggard that he wrote just for us. I'm praying that as you read this it will have already happened!

★ ★ ★

We're glad to have had the chance to work with such great performers. In addition, our success has also given us opportunities to appear on television many times. Actually, the Oak Ridge Boys started early on television in the late '60s and early '70s with a very successful weekly syndicated television show out of Shreveport, Louisiana, called *It's Happening with the Oak Ridge Boys*. The show was ahead of its time in sound and production value.

Since then, television has become a huge part of our career, especially in the formative years of the '70s and '80s. Our manager, Jim Halsey, and his crackerjack television team in Los Angeles, headed up by the late and legendary TV agent Dick Howard, were able to get us on every variety show of the day. We also made countless appearances on talk shows, including *The Dinah Shore Chevy Show*, *The Merv Griffin Show*, *The Mike Douglas Show*, *Tomorrow*, and of course, *The Tonight Show*.

We were guests on *The Tonight Show* more than 30 times through the years. Johnny Carson loved the Oaks because we always came in with a great attitude and no demands. We also found out that Carson didn't particularly like talking to several members of a music group all at once, so we always took up what would have been "couch time" with another song.

Jay Leno was also a good friend and was always very good to us as well. As of this writing we are hoping that Jimmy Fallon will invite us to New York to continue our *Tonight Show* legacy.

Once in 1984 at Harrah's Marina in Atlantic City, we taped several songs for the *Jerry Lewis MDA Labor Day Telethon*. Jay Leno was opening for us in those days. The organizers left the cameras all set up and asked the audience to stay over because a major star of the day was coming over to tape a segment as well.

The expected celebrity was running late, so we sang for another hour to keep the people there. After we pretty much exhausted ourselves, the big star still hadn't appeared, but his people assured us he was on his way. Jay volunteered to keep the audience entertained in the meantime. Finally, the star arrived 90 minutes later, and during that 90 minutes Jay Leno did a stand-up routine that was to this day the funniest thing I've ever heard. What a trooper he was. I remember thinking, *This guy is going to be really big one day!*

In the middle to late '70s, we were nicknamed Dinah's Darlings, and Merv Griffin had us on often, but our most meaningful daytime TV appearances may have been on *The Mike Douglas Show* out of Philadelphia. Mike *loved* the Oaks. We would even cohost the show for a week at a time in locations like Miami and London. It's hard to know just how much all these appearances meant to our career, but I know it was huge. Today, it would be like doing *The Ellen DeGeneres Show* a hundred times!

Two of our most popular appearances on television were on *The Dukes of Hazzard* in the late '70s. These shows are repeated to this day, and whenever Boss Hogg makes us sing at the Boar's Nest to get out of a speeding ticket (exactly the same story line on both appearances), the social networks light up!

I love these reruns. A young Joe Bonsall hugging up close with Daisy Duke made me the most admired man in America.

My grandson and his best friend are big fans of *The Dukes of Hazzard*, so my grandson taped the episodes we appeared in and played them for his buddy, bragging all the while that his Pop-Pop was right there with Bo and Luke Duke.

Well, his friend was so impressed he wanted to meet me. My grandson (also named Luke) brought him over and introduced us.

The little boy looked so disappointed and proclaimed, "That's not him! That *can't* be him!" He almost started crying. That's what adding 30 years does to a man.

Last year an episode of the popular *Mike and Molly* show was based entirely on the Oak Ridge Boys and "Elvira." It was a real hoot! Talk about Twitter lighting up!

Somewhat related to TV, the Oak Ridge Boys have been a regular piece of the *TV Guide* crossword puzzle since around 1980. The ___ Ridge Boys, or the Oak _____ Boys, or quite often it's the Oak Ridge ____ . Yet another sign of lasting success!

Over the past three years, we've dipped into reality television as guests on *Diners, Drive-Ins and Dives* (with Chef Guy Fieri) and *Pawn Stars*. These shows are hugely popular. For "Triple D," we took the famous chef to one of our favorite eating places in our hometown of Hendersonville—Café Rakka—and the show came out great.

As for *Pawn Stars*, we have made friends with the Harrisons because the Old Man, Navy veteran Richard Harrison, and his wife are huge Oaks fans. In fact, the day we stopped by the shop, we weren't planning on being on the show. We didn't even know they were taping that day. We were there to pay a surprise visit to Mr. Harrison, and they ended up taping us.

Another side note regarding *Pawn Stars*—the car expert, a big, good-looking kid with a do-rag on his head and lots of tattoos, is Danny Koker. His father, also named Danny Koker, was a member of the original Cathedral Quartet. Young Danny now has his own spin-off show called *Counting Cars* on the History Channel, and over the past several years we've become great friends. He comes out to see us often, and we always talk about his dad. Tears are usually shed. Danny is very successful, and his dad would be so proud of him.

Both *Diners, Drive-Ins and Dives* and *Pawn Stars* have huge ratings, and they have both replayed about a hundred times. We seem to always be on one or the other, and it's really been fun. Maybe next we can tape an episode of *Ice Road Truckers* or *Hillbilly Handfishin'*. To be honest, *Duck Dynasty* is a real possibility.

There has actually been talk of a possible Oak Ridge Boys reality show. I'm not certain this will ever happen. We'll just have to wait and see.

Two of America's favorite TV programs are *Wheel of Fortune* and *Jeopardy*, and we have a history with both. We've been an answer on *Jeopardy* and a puzzle on *Wheel of Fortune* several times. Here was one of the *Jeopardy* answers:

"In 1981, this group burned up the country and pop music charts with a song about a girl named 'Elvira.'"

Do do do do do do do dooo…They didn't get it! Three guys who could probably recite the table of elements or guess the volume of water contained in the Bay of Fundy did *not* know the answer!

Which brings us to Pat Sajak and Vanna White.

We once made a live appearance on the set of *Wheel of Fortune* while playing in Las Vegas. Our name was blanked out in the famous word puzzle in four words under the category Music. Our job was to wait in the wings, and when someone guessed the puzzle, we were to run out onto the set and congratulate the winner.

We waited as one letter after another was turned. Nobody was even close. We were really sweating it. I almost bailed and headed for the exit. They were finally down to THE _AK R_DGE B_YS when a girl buys a vowel.

"I would like to buy an 'O'!" She bought an O! "I would like to solve the puzzle."

Well, duh! "THE OAK RIDGE BOYS!"

With confetti falling and "Elvira" playing loudly, we all ran onstage. Thankfully, the audience stood and cheered. A real piece of show biz, right? And I got to hug Vanna White!

20

PRICES PAID

"Sacrifice for Me."

JOE BONSALL

*I*n our 2003 patriotic-flavored album, *Colors*, we pay tribute to our military, our veterans, our flag, and America, which we love dearly. We're so thankful for the freedoms of this great land, and we never take them for granted. With songs like "Colors," "An American Family," "This Is America," "American Beauty," "G.I. Joe and Lillie," and more recently, "Sacrifice…for Me," we love to take our audience on a musical side trip and pay tribute to the prices paid and the sacrifices made so that we may live in the land of the free.

The very meaningful and poignant song "This Is America" was written by Duane's wife, Norah Lee. Norah Lee is not only a great singer who has performed on the stage of the Grand Ole Opry for decades but also a songwriter who has captured the feeling of the entire country after 9/11 in this one song. It doesn't matter what the enemies of freedom throw our way, we cry out, "This is our homeland, this is America, we won't give up, we won't give in"—*ever*!

Yes, we love our America. It's as plain as that. It has to do with the way we were raised. My mom always said I could be anything I wanted to be in this great country if I worked hard, told the truth, and honored God in my life. Then she would point to my daddy in his wheelchair and remind me that it was because of guys like him that we have this freedom to begin with. Prices paid!

We never take politics to our stage, and we rarely express our heart-felt opinions to the press. We believe people pay to see a musical performance, not to hear an artist ramble on as to why he or she leans left or right on the issues. But on these pages, I can tell you that all four Oak Ridge Boys lean to the conservative side. We believe in lower taxes and less regulation to spur the economy. We believe in legal immigration, the key word being "legal." We believe strongly in family values. We believe in second-amendment rights to responsibly own guns, and the key word here is "responsibly." And we believe in a strong military.

And you already know the Oaks are men of faith. We believe it's imperative that prayer and Jesus Christ be at the forefront of our thinking and in the way we live our lives. There is a loud element today whose desire is to move America further away from God and the Bible at a time when we should be moving *closer* to God and His holy Word!

Even with the problems facing America today, the Oaks are very optimistic. Unlike many folks, we have the opportunity to look Middle America right in the eye on a daily basis, and overall we love what we see. Sometimes watching a 24/7 news channel can lead you to believe this country is sliding downhill, and yes, our leaders need very badly to address some serious issues. But I must tell you that from the stage of a state fair or a performing arts center, watching an audience stand and cheer after we've just performed a song about the flag or our military or our veterans is very encouraging and makes our hearts swell with joy. From the big city to the farmlands, the hardworking American family is still the backbone of all that's right with America, and when our music touches that vein and people respond as they do, it's quite rewarding and, as I said, encouraging.

Most people realize that freedom is not free and never has been. Someone has always paid a price, and that price is often paid in personal sacrifice and bloodshed. As Jesus Christ shed His blood for our sins on Calvary's cross, so many brave souls have shed their blood for the cause of our American way of life, and it has been this way throughout history. Prices paid!

This is why we so love our veterans and our brave young men and women serving around the world, putting their lives on the line every day while we're eating our pancakes and watching baseball. No matter how you see things politically, you must love these kids and pray for them and their families on a daily basis.

I wear a black memory bracelet on my right wrist in honor of Corporal Jonathan W. Bowling, USMC, from Stuart, Virginia, killed in action in Iraq on January 26, 2005. His father, Darrell Bowling, has become a friend and a brother, and even though I know him so well, I can't possibly imagine the dark part of his heart that cries every single day for a lost son. Jesus called it "no greater love," and He would know, for He Himself laid down His life for His friends. For *us*.

It's hard to believe I've worn this bracelet for nine years now. And I will continue to wear it, for when I see it, I not only think about Darrell and his son Jon but I also remember that many families have suffered this same loss, and it moves my heart in ways I cannot explain. When Gold Star moms and dads or Wounded Warriors come out to our show, we do our best to honor them. Prices paid!

My mother loved veterans and taught me to love and appreciate them too. My daddy wasn't killed after taking Utah Beach on D-day more than 70 years ago, but after that day of days, he fought the hedgerows of France and got hit hard in Saint-Lô. He was never the same after that. My mom was the WAC who married him and looked after him until the day he died. Their bodies both rest in Arlington now. They gave so much of themselves, as have so many of the Greatest Generation and the many who have since taken up the clarion call to accomplish something way beyond themselves for the cause of the red, white, and blue. Prices paid!

So that gives you a small insight into why the Oak Ridge Boys care so much about our country and for those who serve and have served. Rest assured that when you see us onstage, we're thankful deep in our souls for the opportunity this great nation has given us to pursue our dreams, sing our songs, live our lives without fear, and raise our children beneath the rockets' red glare of freedom. Sorry to say, we have never traveled overseas to sing for our troops because every time the opportunity presented itself the logistics were prohibitive. However, we did sign on with a wonderful organization called Spirit of America that afforded us the opportunity to put on shows at military bases right here in America. This organization is no longer in operation, but for several years it allowed us the honor to place dates right in the middle of our touring schedules in places like Fort Knox, Whiteman Air Force Base, Fort Leonard Wood, and Marine Corps Base Camp LeJeune.

Whitman Air Force Base is the home of the B-1 stealth bombers, and we not only made friends with all the pilots there but also were given a tour of the cockpit of the B-1. *Nobody* ever gets to do that.

A few years later they were out on maneuvers while we were onstage at the Missouri State Fair in Sedalia. The B-1s did a low fly-by while we were singing. It gave all of us as well as the grandstand crowd a big thrill, and yes, we found out later that buzzing our show was all part of the plan. You have to love these men. They are the best!

Veterans are always welcome at an Oaks show. Sharing time with these incredible men and women over the years has provided some of the most precious moments imaginable. There is no greater honor than to share time with these vets and have them open up to us a bit about their experiences. These old warriors seem to realize that we appreciate their service to America, and I must tell you some vets have shared stories with us that their own families have never heard. What could possibly be a greater honor than this? God bless our veterans!

Prices paid!

21

ANTHEM SINGERS

"Oh say, can you see..."

FRANCIS SCOTT KEY, "THE STAR-SPANGLED BANNER"

There's nothing we enjoy more than standing upright with our hands over our hearts while facing Old Glory and singing our national anthem. The Oak Ridge Boys have performed our simple version of unison and harmony at hundreds of events over the years, and each time, our hearts swell with pride, honor, and that special emotion that comes from a true love of country and tradition. Singing "The Star Spangled Banner" never gets old to us, and we always say yes to an invitation to do so if it's at all logistically possible.

I joke that we get some great seats to sporting events in the deal, and that's the truth. We've never been paid to sing our anthem, nor would we request to. This is a perk that comes with being the Oak Ridge Boys. We've sung our anthem at huge festivals, on political campaigns, at major-league and minor-league ballparks, and National Football League games. We've performed the song for the National Hockey League and for the National Basketball Association as well as many National Collegiate Athletic Association events—football, hockey, baseball, and basketball. And when we're not there, many ball clubs consistently play our recorded version to open a game.

We have some great stories and memories associated with singing the national anthem. One story involves a recording of the anthem. It was in our early days of singing the anthem, when we would sometimes lip-sync over a recorded version. The idea behind this was that we just didn't want to mess it up, so we played it safe—we thought. Well, one night at a major-league baseball game the tape went crazy in the middle of the song. It made a whirring sound and skipped to the end.

Lesson learned. We dumped that idea while wiping the egg off our faces and decided we would sing it live forever after—and we have! Our motto is now, "If you can't sing it live, don't sing it at all!" However, if you can't hear us sing it live, our version is heard on countless radio and television stations, and it's also recorded on our *Colors* album. It can even be downloaded on iTunes.

This chapter is titled "Anthem Singers" because of something that happened one Sunday afternoon at a Kansas City Chiefs game at Arrowhead Stadium. We were almost late, but the local police came to the rescue and guided us into the stadium and down to the field while yelling, "Get out of the way—the anthem singers are coming through." To this day we refer to ourselves as the Anthem Singers.

We also had an escort in New York. We were playing a show there, and the Mets invited us over to Shea Stadium to sing the anthem for a Yankees–Mets game. The only way we could do it was to have a police escort guide us to the game and back to the gig. Well, we missed watching the game that night of course, but we did sing our anthem before 40,000 crazed New York baseball fans, and the police escorts through New York City were pretty exhilarating. It felt like an episode of *Law & Order: Special Victims Unit*.

In 1983, we performed the anthem at the All-Star Game in old Comiskey Park in Chicago, and for a bunch of baseball addicts, sitting in the dugout with the best players in the game was almost an overload. The only thing more amazing than that was a dinner the night before for all of the Hall of Famers in attendance. We were invited as well, and that was an overload for certain. I remember getting on an elevator with Brooks Robinson, Mike Schmidt, and Ernie Banks and actually fighting back tears! By the way, the Oak Ridge Boys sang the anthem at the last game of old Comiskey Park and the first game played at the new Comiskey Park, now known as US Cellular Field.

More trivia—since Harry Caray passed away, a different artist sings "Take Me Out to the Ball Game" at every Cubs game during the seventh-inning stretch. One day we were at a Cubs game at the famed Wrigley Field to sing the anthem, and we were also invited to lead the crowd in the middle of the seventh-inning stretch. It so happened that right before that, the young man who was supposed to sing "God Bless America" came down with a stomach problem, so they asked us to sing that patriotic tune as well. It was the only time that the same act pulled off the Wrigley Field trifecta! A one...a two...a three...

For many years we performed the anthem all around the Twin Cities of Minnesota, and every time we did, the home team lost. This includes the Vikings, the old NHL North Stars, and even the Minnesota Gophers college hockey team. Back when we played the Carlton Theater, we went over to the old Twins ballpark and sang the anthem for the Twins on several occasions. They always lost. So it came to pass in 1991, when the Twins hosted the Atlanta Braves in the World Series, they asked us *not* to come and sing the anthem. They won that World Series!

The great thing about being a group is that no matter how much echo and slap-back there might be in a huge arena or stadium, if we just look at each other and concentrate on what we are doing, we can get through it just fine. The worst slap-back ever was at the Triple-A All Star game in Las Vegas at Cashman Field. A local beauty queen had been asked to sing the Canadian national anthem before we sang. She started singing but got so lost in the echo that she broke down crying and ran out of the ballpark halfway through "O Canada." Her little crown was still on the field. We were not very optimistic as we walked out toward home plate, but before I blew an A-flat on the pitch pipe, Duane implored us to look at him. We did just that and got through it just fine. I was looking pretty funny wearing the crown though. (Yes, we sing "The Star Spangled Banner" in the key of A-flat. God help us if I ever blow a B-flat!)

We have performed the anthem for our hometown NFL team, the Tennessee Titans, many times here in Nashville at LP Field over the years, and they of course always make us feel at home. We are all huge Titans fans, and we often appear on the huge TitanTron screen during a game yelling, "Go, Titans, go!"

Then there was the time the Pittsburgh Steelers invited us to Heinz

Field and provided us with bags of Steelers swag. As fate would have it, our Titans were the visiting team, and as we were waiting to go out and sing our anthem, the Titans came running by us. We were all properly adorned in Steelers yellow-and-black jerseys. "When in Rome" and so forth. It was a long time before the Titans let us live that one down.

Another anthem story was at my expense. In January 2012, the Ringling Brothers and Barnum and Bailey circus would make their annual appearance in Nashville, and our manager, Jim Halsey, wanted the Oak Ridge Boys to take part in the opening night's ceremonies. In an email blast, Jim described how we would first sing the national anthem, and then each boy except for Richard, who had a torn Achilles tendon, would take part in the circus. He went on and on about how this would kick off our year in style.

Jim was a lot more stoked about it than I was because he had me going up with the high-wire act and riding on top of a guy's shoulders from one side of the roof to the other. I was aghast and rebelled against this big-time. The other guys had small things to do—but I was to be part of a high-wire act? My emails of rebellious refusal were not answered except for one small blurb from our Nashville publicist, Kirt Webster, that *Country Weekly* magazine would be covering the event. It was all confirmed and okayed by everyone, and I would just have to go along. My Mary thought I was crazy, and I thought Jim was crazier…but we are a group and a democracy, and I was out-voted, so I began to prepare myself mentally for the high wire.

It wasn't until the afternoon of the opening day that I realized everyone had snookered me! The real plan was that we would just hang out with the circus folks and animals, take pictures, and sing the anthem. That had been the plan from the very beginning. So we did sing the anthem, and we did get a nice four-page spread in *Country Weekly*, and thankfully I did not have to fall off of a high wire and crack my head open on the Bridgestone Arena floor as I had imagined might happen!

There are so many Anthem Singers stories, but I will tell just one more. It's actually my favorite, so I saved it for last. The year was 1985, and the World Series between the Saint Louis Cardinals and the Kansas

City Royals was known as the Interstate 70 Show Me Series. We were invited to perform the National Anthem for game seven—if it went seven. Well, the Cards held a 3–2 game lead in game six, and all of us were at home watching on TV. It would take a Royals win to send it to KC for game seven.

Then a miracle happened. The Cards were winning when an umpire made a bad call, sending the game the Royals' way and sending the Oak Ridge Boys to Kansas City the following night to sing the anthem. The Royals went on to win that historic game seven—the most exciting game we have ever been a part of—and as a result the Royals have invited us back many times over the years to sing the anthem.

They had not been back to the World Series until 2014. They would play seven games against the National League champions, the San Francisco Giants, and don't you know we figured they would call us to sing the national anthem for that deciding game seven!

What a story line, right? The Royals have not even made it to a playoff game since 1985, and as superstitious as baseball fans are, it would have been a natural for the Oaks to return to what is now Kauffman Stadium. The whole theme in KC was "Party like It's 1985," so it was a natural to invite us back, right?

Wrong! Some opera singer girl sang the anthem, and alas, mostly because of an outer-space pitcher named Madison Bumgarner, the Alcatraz Giants prevailed, winning their third World Series in five years (which is downright amazing).

Bottom line here is, the Oak Ridge Boys should have performed the national anthem on that cool October 29 evening in the City of Fountains. But to be honest, I sincerely doubt we could have gotten past Bumgarner either.

The truth is, we've sung the anthem so many times, we've become associated with "The Star Spangled Banner," and it's an association we're proud of. In fact, because of our efforts to sing it well and to sing it right, the National Music Council (NMC) has named us the official singers of "The Star Spangled Banner." NMC Director David Sanders made this special proclamation:

The Oak Ridge Boys have been global ambassadors of American music and culture for decades. Cultural diplomacy is more important now than ever before, and this designation is a way for us to highlight the role that musicians, creators, and artists play in bettering our nation's relationship with the world. The singing of "The Star Spangled Banner" is emblematic not only of the pride we all take in our own country, but also of the appreciation and respect we have for other cultures and musical genres that have played such an important role in shaping America's own distinctive musical voice. This proclamation recognizes the Oak Ridge Boys' contribution to the preservation of patriotic American music, as well as their longstanding advancement of musical culture and their commitment to celebrating the global diversity of music traditions. It also celebrates the group's continued service as ambassadors of American culture.

Now…how big of a WOW is *that*?

Many years before this proclamation, the National Association for Music Education (NAfME) named the Oaks the official spokesmen for "The Star Spangled Banner." Over the course of many years, we were directly involved in educating students about the history and tradition behind our anthem. Our image appeared in special printed materials, and we even shot classroom videos, teaching kids how to sing the song with gusto and respect.

So there is more than just a ticket to the big game involved here, although again, the big game *is* a special bonus. But keep in mind the importance of the song to our national heritage. Remove your cap, place your hand over your heart, stand at attention, face the flag, and sing Francis Scott Key's lyrics with gusto and pride.

I heartily recommend a book called *America's Star Spangled Story* by Jane Hampton Cook, celebrating 200 years of the national anthem, for everyone in your family, especially the children. We must help our young people grasp the importance of our great flag and how this song of tribute celebrates the freedom for which it stands!

22

SHERMAN

"Goodbye, Brother"

Sometimes it seems unfair that performers like the Oak Ridge Boys get so much acclaim while many of the behind-the-scenes people who make it all happen are rarely known. One of those important people in our history was Sherman Halsey. He was the son of our manager and godfather, Jim Halsey, so he grew up right before our eyes, and his untimely death a few years ago at the age of 56 stunned us beyond words. We all miss Sherman. He was like a son to all of us. And he was a great son to Jim. They were as close as a father and son could possibly be. We rarely saw Jim without Sherman.

Sherman would grow up to become important to many in our business. In fact, his creative contributions are legendary in Nashville and Los Angeles music circles. Sherman came up with the original concept of the music video long before there were such outlets as Great American Country, County Music Television, or for that matter, MTV or VH1. In fact, Sherman's first video came out way before cable television ever took over our living rooms, and here is how it happened.

In 1977, the *Y'all Come Back Saloon* album was smoking hot. There's a song on the album called "Easy" that started hitting big in Australia. Jim thought we needed to do something for Australia, and Sherman came up with an idea. He said, "Let's shoot a video of the song and send it over. MCA Records can get it shown on popular TV shows there!"

So under Sherman's direction, we proceeded to shoot the first-ever concept video. First, we set up a stage in a Tulsa hotel, and while we lip-synced the song, Sherman recorded the performance on film from about ten different angles, utilizing close-ups as well as long shots.

Then, Sherman hired an actress, and we shot little vignettes all over Tulsa with the story line portraying a budding romance between Duane Allen, who sang the lead on the song, and the girl, while his three friends walked along the street with him, singing "Easy." Sherman then interspersed the vignette scenes with the stage performances. Sound familiar? You bet! You can still see this first-ever concept video on YouTube.

As time went by, Sherman became one of the most sought-after directors in the business. He was the force behind the early success of Dwight Yoakam, and he directed almost every Tim McGraw video and network TV special that Tim has ever done. Sherman once shoehorned us into one of Tim's videos called "The Cowboy in Me." We had no business being in that video, but hey, Sherman was a brother and an Oak Ridge Boy in his heart, so there we were waving and frolicking while Tim sang.

Sherman also became a successful manager, like his dad, but it was his creative, directorial genius that elevated him to the success and respect everyone strives for. Hundreds of music videos have his hand on them, and most of the directors today continue to use his style and pacing techniques. Sherman was a master of lighting effect. He would wait for just the right sunlight at just the right time or catch a sunset at just the right moment.

Yes, he could see things that most others couldn't see. In fact, a story from his childhood backs that up. Sherman's sister, Gina, said that since he was a little boy, Sherman's vision was very keen. He could see four-leaf clovers within a second of looking down after others had been searching for hours.

One of the first Oak Ridge Boys videos to gain a lot of traction was our remake of the Fiestas' hit "So Fine" in 1982. Sherman directed this very funny video, and though the song didn't do as well on radio as we might have liked, the video became somewhat of a cult classic in the early days of TNN and CMT.

During the Rodney King riots in Los Angeles in 1992, only one white-skinned boy was carrying a ton of video gear and getting documentary footage throughout those dangerous neighborhoods. When asked about the danger, Sherman always said, "They didn't pay me any mind. I think they thought I was insane!"

Sherman went on to direct all the *Feed the Children* television specials we did over many years, including the patriotic and Christmas shows shown over and over all around the world. We received a ton of great exposure while feeding hungry children everywhere.

Sherman also directed every episode of our very successful weekly TV show that premiered in January 1998, called *The Oak Ridge Boys Live from Las Vegas* for TNN. We taped almost 20 episodes with more than a hundred guests in less than two weeks at the Las Vegas Hilton. The logistics alone were staggering, and so was the $3 million budget. But we pulled it all off without a hitch thanks to the leadership of Jim Halsey and the sheer energy and talent of the director, Sherman Halsey.

Sherman's passing stunned the entire music industry. The Oak Ridge Boys sang "Farther Along" at Sherman's funeral in Independence, Kansas. We also sang "Have a Little Talk with Jesus" with Roy Clark. Tim McGraw was there as well.

So many times I run into young, aspiring artists who ask for advice in making it in the music business. I always take the time to share my thoughts, but it's a younger business now, and so often I think to myself that I need to call Sherman and glean some knowledge and direction from him. Well, Sherman isn't around to call anymore, so I say to you, my friends, celebrate life and celebrate it every day. It's God's greatest gift to us this side of salvation.

Never take anyone for granted. If you love them, tell them you love them. Just realize that in a heartbeat…in an instant…in an eye blink, they could be gone. No man or woman is guaranteed the next second, so make every second count while you and your loved ones and friends are still here.

Rest easy, Sherm. Thank you for all you have done for us. But most of all, thanks for the love and friendship and fun. We will see you again, as is His promise!

23

THE BIG QUESTION

"If I can still play, then why not play?"

W e've been asked so many questions over the years by friends, fans, and of course, the men and women of the entertainment press. I want to answer a few of those here. First the simple ones and then what I consider the *big* question we're often asked.

"So, where did you come in from?" This is usually coupled with "So, where are you boys going from here?" Easy answers that obviously change on a daily basis.

Q: "Do y'all sleep on that bus?"
A: Yes!

Q: "Does your family ever travel with you?"
A: Yes, on rare occasions.

Q: "How long has William Lee been growing that beard?"
A: Since around 1980.

Q: "How does he keep it looking so nice?"
A: He brushes it and sleeps with it outside the covers so it can breathe.

Q: "Can I touch it?"
A: Sure.

Q: "Can I pull it?"
A: You can—at your own risk.

It's amazing how many people compare William's beard to either ZZ Top or the *Duck Dynasty* guys, when in fact he has the nicest beard of any of them. By the way, the *Duck Dynasty* family has made William Lee an honorary Robertson. Maybe we can start calling him Bayou Bill...or not!

Q: "What do think of country music today?"
A: See chapter 12.

Q: "How long have you guys been together?"
A: More than 40 years. It won't be long until I can say, "Half a century!"

Q: "How'd y'all meet?"
A: Long story—it's in the book.

Q: "Didn't you guys used to be all gospel?"
A: Yes. That's in the book too.

Q: "Are y'all from Oak Ridge?"
A: No, but the original guys...well, read the book.

Okay, by now you can see the big one coming. Here it is:

Q: "When are y'all going to retire?"

Several years ago, when our peers the Statler Brothers retired and our friends Alabama announced a farewell tour, we made big news by stating that we had leased brand-new buses. But all these years later, as the Statlers are still at home and our brothers in the Alabama band have started to tour again, the big question persists.

A few years ago, Brooks and Dunn went their separate ways, and more recently King George Strait rode off into the sunset. The press still wants to know why we keep on singing.

Kenny Rogers and Merle Haggard and Willie Nelson are still singing as well, and don't you know they keep getting asked the same question? What about Tony Bennett? Ray Price just passed recently, and he was singing well into his nineties. He still sounded great too. George Jones announced a farewell tour, but the Possum passed on with a lot of unplayed concerts still in his datebook.

I'm so happy that my dreams of playing second base for the Philadelphia Phillies never panned out, or I would have been washed up in my thirties. God sure knew what He was doing. As Garth Brooks might say, "Unanswered Prayers."

The retired athlete metaphor is a good one though. A 40-year-old major leaguer recently proclaimed that he could still play the game and added, "If I can still play, then why not play?"

This particular player really *can* still play, but I guess it's the word "if" that's in question. Age and gravity take their toll on even the stoutest heart, especially in professional sports. Some old quarterbacks *think* they still have the big arm, but on the field they may come up short. However, the Oak

"Whether it is on the Grand Ole Opry stage or in a performing arts center or at a big festival or a stadium…Wherever it's at…it's a thing! When we hit the stage at night, we're all serious about it, because it's like we try to outdo ourselves from what we did the day before, wherever *that* may have been, because we feel like we're constantly growing as the Oak Ridge Boys, and we never tire of the growth in what we are doing every single day, and it's important to feel that way. It's energizing!"

WILLIAM LEE GOLDEN

Ridge Boys can still sing, and we're not delusional about it. So if we *can* still sing, then why not keep singing?

That's one of the simple answers to the big question. Here are some others.

A: We love what we do! We four are still living our dream.

A: We've never really been able to plan how to stop doing this. We don't even know how to slow down.

A: We're singing our songs—doing what we love—to earn a living. Why should we stop?

These simple answers are all true, and I've heard these very words spill out of our mouths on many occasions. But I want to explore a deeper reason why the Oak Ridge Boys still tour and sing today even though we are older men. The Old Kids on the Block, so to speak.

"We are traveling down roads we've never traveled before. New music puts life and new energy into us. In the process of reinventing ourselves, we do not change. We stay true to who we are and to ourselves,"

RICHARD STERBAN

To begin with, our hearts are young. We're still excited about we do, and we are to a man somehow driven to keep this legacy alive.

Duane Allen, William Lee Golden, Richard Sterban, and I feel as if we were destined by God to meet and to excel as one entity, and this frame of mind daily pushes us on to be the best we can be. Our love and respect for each other and for what each man brings to the table every single day is now engrained in our very DNA, and I seriously don't believe we will ever be able to stop being the Oak Ridge Boys unless God says it's time by taking one of us home to heaven.

Even then, the remaining three would probably consider going on with a new member in place. However, thank God, we haven't had to travel down that road, so there's really no way to know if that would happen or not.

I must admit, if something happened to one of my three partners, I may find it very hard to move on without them. However, if I were to go first, I hope they would find another guy and keep on singing for as long as they continue to enjoy it.

Just like everyone else, we've all had to deal with the deaths of friends, loved ones, and colleagues from the music world through the years, and it's never easy. A death of one of the four Oaks would be devastating and life changing. I'm thankful to our Lord and Savior Jesus Christ for the good health He's given us thus far and for our ability to continue touring and performing at a level worthy of being out here. Singing is an incredible blessing from on high, and we never take for granted one day, one show, one song, or one breath.

So the answer to the big question isn't easy. When people wonder why at our age we aren't fishing or playing golf instead of riding on a tour bus and singing songs, the answer isn't all that simple. The big question is very shallow in comparison to how deep this river runs. (Besides, we still fish whenever we feel like fishing—but we do *not* golf!)

My friend Jeff Myers has an interesting take on the matter.

> Any day that the Oak Ridge Boys spend actually being the Oak Ridge Boys—doing press, a photo shoot, a recording session, or singing in front of an audience—is a day spent doing what they did at 25, at 35, at 45, and even 55 and 65. Most jobs, however satisfying or well paid, at some point become work. But in this job, they pay you every single day to be 35 again. Why would you stop doing that? After all, when you retire, it's a long time between shows. On this never-ending tour, the compass doesn't point north or south. It doesn't point east or west. The compass, as ever, points forward.

Perspective is important when considering the big question. I'm not an Oak Ridge Boy every minute of every day. I'm just Joe Bonsall most of the time, taking out the trash, cutting grass, weed eating, writing, picking my banjo, and expediting honey-do lists. I try not to take things too seriously, though I will continue to do all I can to keep the Oaks alive and do my job well.

I've always wanted to be worthy of the blessings God has provided this Philadelphia street kid who has been blessed to live in the rolling hills of the great state of Tennessee for more than 40 years now. We have all been so very blessed to experience big-time success this long, and the perks have been appreciated. I'm not just talking about limos, tour buses, nice hotels, health insurance, and great food. I'm also talking about being able to pay all my bills, live comfortably, and put my children and even my grandchildren through college.

"We've been able to plan almost every step of our career for decades, and the only thing we haven't been able to plan for is how to stop."

DUANE ALLEN

I believe our work ethic, faith, and talent have earned us our success, but I still thank my Lord for every show and every song and every dollar ever earned from living a life of music. So if it all ended today and we considered retiring, I think I'd be okay with that. I would continue to write and continue to be a father, "pop-pop," and husband. I would keep picking my banjo no matter what my cats might think about it, and I would still enjoy working on my farm. Would I miss being an Oak Ridge Boy? Yes. Probably every single day until God calls me to glory!

So I guess the bottom line is that God will tell us when it's time to stop. He is the one who holds the compass, and He's the one who directs our future and yours with His strong hand. So the answer to the big question all begins and ends with God. And that is a fact.

I know this much. I can assure you that as long as God gives us strong voices and the good health we need to keep on grinding and plowing forward, the Oak Ridge Boys will be out there somewhere singing our songs.

24

RONNIE AND THE MOB

The Force Behind the Music

*T*he Oaks have always had the greatest instrumentalists playing on our stage. In fact, back in 1986, the Oaks Band won the Country Music Association Instrumental Group of the Year Award. That was the last year that award was given.

Band members have changed over the years, but every player has always been among the finest you will hear on any stage anywhere. Actually, the Oaks Band was the first-ever band in southern gospel music. Comprised of John Rich, Don Breland, Mark Ellerbee, and Tony Brown, they blazed a solid pathway for all that was to come. Tony went on to be a major record-company executive and top-tier producer, creating astounding hit-record success for the likes of Reba McEntire and George Strait. He also discovered Nanci Griffith and Lyle Lovett, just to name a few.

THE OAKS BAND TODAY

Rex Wiseman
guitar, pedal steel, and fiddle

Roger Eaton
lead guitar

Jeff Douglas
stage manager, production manager,
rhythm guitar, and dobro

David Northrup
the ultimate drummer

Scotty Simpson
bass guitar

Ronnie Fairchild
keyboards

Ronnie is *always* on keyboards! From our heyday to the present, he's always been there for us—almost 35 years. He took a few short breaks along the way, but he always came back. We love Ronnie. He's a musical genius and a master in the recording studio. We've done a lot of work at his Ron Fairchild Music studio in Hendersonville, and the results have always been great.

Ron's father, Tommy Fairchild, played piano for the Oak Ridge Boys in the late 1950s and early '60s!

I know this much—we could take Ronnie just about anywhere in the world and probably perform our entire catalogue. *The man remembers everything.*

Because Ronnie is so important to the success of the Oak Ridge Boys, I asked him to write something for this book, and he took me up on it. I knew he would have a unique perspective on the Oaks as a 35-year member and leader of the Mighty Oaks Band—also known as The Mob—and he didn't let me down.

In the summer of 1979, I was playing with the late Dottie West, and we were working a lot with Kenny Rogers. It was certainly a wonderful time with good players, huge crowds, and Dottie singing her heart out every night. The word came down that we were to pick up the Oaks in Shreveport, Lousiana. This was great for me because of the long history I already had with the Oak Ridge Boys.

When the date came, we went on first. The building was terrible acoustically. Built for sports and not for music—like many others we've played.

After our set, I stayed around to watch the Oaks. They came on like a freight train. It was bold and in your face! We had done a great job as the first act, but when they came on, it was a different ball game. I felt something that night that was undeniable.

Not long after that we played the Omni in Atlanta, and all three acts put on our best show for about 15,000 people.

Somewhere around November of that year I played with Dottie West and Mel Tillis at the old Frontier Hotel in Las Vegas. We played two shows a day for 28 days in a row. One night at the lounge after the second show, I was told that the Oaks were in town to do a TV show and were staying at the Desert Inn. I got bold and called across the street and asked for Duane Allen's room. He answered rather groggy and tired. Naturally I felt bad, but he was very nice, and we had a short chat. I remember him telling me, "I know why you're calling." Frankly, I didn't have any agenda for the call, but he told me to call Mickey Baker (their road manager at the time) when I got back to Hendersonville.

I didn't think much more about it, but two weeks later I did call Mickey, and he said, "Ronnie, you're coming with us."

I replied, "But I kind of have a job already!"

Mickey said, "It's a done deal!"

And it was. I gave notice to Dottie and spent the next week in Hawaii at the Royal Hawaiian Hotel. When I returned home, I was whisked straight into rehearsals with the Oak Ridge Boys. The parameters of my world had just changed in a big way. Things would never be the same again for me.

We went back out on the Full House tour with Kenny and Dottie, but this time the Oaks had a new, beefed-up band, and we absolutely killed it. I am serious. Kenny is one of the classiest and greatest artists ever, but the Oak Ridge Boys were a hard act to follow. Only an artist of Kenny's stature could have felt comfortable following us, and certainly he did. I'm fond of saying that the Oaks "took" the stage and didn't give you a chance to breathe or pontificate. In those days there was simply nothing like the power that the group gave off. Imagine a huge freight train coming at you with four blinding spotlights and a steam engine of a band behind them. The listener didn't have a chance. Game, set, and match!

Now, 35 years later, the group still continues to amaze audiences. Certainly we're all a little older, but the Oaks still work more than any group out there. If there's a law of physics in the music business, the Oak Ridge Boys make a mockery of that law. Many people shake their heads and wonder, "How do they do it?"

I've now been a part of this group for 35 years. That seems amazing to me. One by one the guys I started playing with in the band have gone their own way. I still love every one of the people I have worked with in this group—in different ways perhaps, but I still love them all.

Somehow I still remain after all of this time. If I were to write my own script, it might read, "It was simply meant to be!"

I owe much to the Oak Ridge Boys. They have taken me to places that most people can only dream of reaching. Few people would ever be able to understand what we have been through together. I'd like to think that I have made my own way with them. Truthfully, I've always felt that it was pretty cool that people spent time trying to figure out how we did it! As William Lee Golden has so famously said, "Anyhow, as long as they spell my name right!"

When the world does come to an end, I feel certain that only a few things will remain. There will still be four singers up front with a single piano player behind them, and there will be dates to play and people to sing to. And that piano player will be me!

25

WHAT IS HARD AND WHAT IS NOT

"Home is where the heart is"

I was sitting on my couch watching baseball, sipping a nice cabernet with a cat on my lap, and my wife, Mary, was preparing ice cream and berries in the kitchen. I had been away a lot of late, and I was content and happy. I didn't feel like leaving for good ol' Somewhere, USA, even though my bags were packed and already in the truck for another eight-day run. So I threw a tweet out there that said something like, "Most of what I do is easy, but leaving home is always hard."

The responses to my tweet were mixed, as is usual in the social-network universe. Most tweets were supportive. But several people laid into me.

"Don't you know how blessed you are?"

Um, yes—that's my point!

Most people, especially those who know me, got it. I love my home life, and it's always tough to leave. So yes, leaving home *is* hard. It always has been and always will be. But it's the only thing that's hard about being an Oak Ridge Boy.

Most people look at our busy schedule and assume that everything we do borders on the abnormal. I would tend to agree. But what is really hard about being a 40-plus-year member of the Oak Ridge Boys and what is not?

When I joined the Oaks in October 1973, I was 25 years old. Now I'm in my late sixties. Richard Sterban and Duane Allen are now both in their early seventies. William Lee Golden is in his late seventies. This is amazing to me, and I hope it is to you too. Even if we were to decide to end it all right now, music history buffs would have to shake their heads at what we've accomplished over the past four decades—and are *still* accomplishing as we continue to put new stones on the mountain every single day.

Our date book remains full. People still want to hear us sing our songs and tell our stories. We have a schedule that many acts would give anything for. We have a history that will be hard for upcoming acts to duplicate. We thank God for our success, but we've worked hard to be where we are today.

What's hard about singing songs for a living? There's nothing hard about that part. My daddy worked in a factory, so by comparison, singing songs is easy as long as my health is holding up and my voice is strong. It can get a bit difficult if I catch a cold or something else hits hard and I have to force my singing instead of just letting it flow. But isn't good health the key with everyone? To perform at a high level, I *must* be feeling good, and that is a fact. Age has nothing to do with it either. Bad health is not a respecter of age. Just visit any children's hospital for proof of that.

But overall, walking onstage and singing songs is not really hard for me. It's what I do. It's what I've wanted to do since childhood, and that I can still do it is a blessing beyond words. I cannot describe the warmth of a standing ovation from an audience when we simply walk onstage.

I can't speak for my singing partners, but I always thought I was in my absolute prime between the ages of 36 and 42. Now, don't get me wrong—I can still bring it pretty good in my late sixties, but in those days I swear I could run three miles in the morning, play several sets of tennis in the afternoon, and still be able to jump through the roof while singing "Dancing the Night Away" that night. Believe me, I don't want to go back there again, but the memories are all good ones.

However, I must follow some rules. The human voice is *not*

electronic! Vocal chords can wear a bit, so I need to get some quality sleep after a big show. I also find that a bit of quiet time every afternoon is helpful, and for me that's often difficult.

Getting enough sleep isn't hard though. For me and my singing partners, riding (and sleeping) in a big, custom tour bus is not hard, no matter how far we roll on any given trip. Our clothes hang in closets. We have WiFi and plenty of satellite TV, along with laptops, iPhones, iPads, iPods…iEverything. Our bunks are comfy, and we truly have a home away from home.

Flying is another story. Early morning flights mean not enough sleep, and the hassles of flying with all kinds of show gear, security checks, and soaring costs are monumental. However, it's necessary on certain occasions, so we just suck it up and go. If we never had to board another commercial flight again, I would be good with that. Give me my bunk on the bus any day—even for a road trip of several hundred miles.

I don't mind spending my days in a hotel room or eating out. I don't mind rehearsing music or taping television shows. I don't mind meeting with the press or other folks. That's all part of the job description and part of living my dream.

I don't much care for photo shoots, but again, they come with the job. When we do a photo shoot, we try to take a ton of different shots that can be utilized for a long time to come. It's not really very hard, though. We just plan it out and do it. I'm not much of a male model though, as pictures throughout the years will illustrate.

Spending each day around a bunch of guys who are brothers and friends is also definitely not hard. Each guy supports the other in every way possible, and quite frankly, this is a phenomenon on every level. We are closer than brothers, and that is a fact.

Brothers tend to fight, but I can tell you that there are no bad words said or felt among any of us. Not that we don't have a disagreement here and there, but honestly, right now I can't even remember one of those. These guys are all honest and true and totally dedicated to doing things right. Pretty decent work environment, huh?

From the time I was a little boy, I dreamed about traveling around with a group of men whom I could trust with my life. Men who were true friends and who had my back at all times. True friends whom I would die for if it ever came to that. So that part of being an Oak is not hard. Not hard at all.

I can honestly say without hesitation that being away from my home and my family is the only thing that's hard. There is a price to pay for continued success in any field of endeavor, and my sacrifice is missing a lot of precious family moments.

Graduations, anniversaries, birthdays...these are treasured events that never return once they have passed. My wife sleeps alone most nights, and so do I. My Mary is prone to nightmares, which probably stems from her childhood, and when I'm there I always gently wake her and tell her it's all right. Many nights, as I roll down the highway, safe and secure in my bunk, thoughts of her without me beside her during a nightmare keep me awake. This is something I've never admitted. Nothing in the world is sweeter than hearing your loved one say, "I'm so happy you are home, honey!" That's worth every mile away.

So being an Oak Ridge Boy isn't hard at all. Being away from Mary, our daughters, our grandkids, our cats, and our farm—that's the only hard part.

I've come to think about it like this. In a way, I live three separate and distinct lives.

There's my life at home with Mary and our kitties. That's the Joe Bonsall who eats gourmet home-cooked meals, expedites honey-do lists, pays bills, watches TV, and plays with the cats.

Then there's my life working my behind off on the farm. I love caring for the land and communing with God and nature.

Then there's the third life, the one you see. It's my life as one of the Oak Ridge Boys—riding in a bus, writing words, singing songs, and playing banjo.

Yes, there are three of me, but praise God, all three are very happy!

Success in any endeavor requires hard work and sacrifice. There's always a price to pay for anything worthwhile in life. Nothing just happens. It takes a team, it takes a supportive and loving family…but most of all it requires being *willing*. Willing to step out there when the odds seem against you. Willing to pay your dues and build your career, whatever it is, one step at a time.

Most of all, you must be willing to put Jesus Christ first in *all* things. Lean on Him and allow Him to lead you into His will for your life. Let Him be the light for your path, and good things *can* and *will* happen!

I'm glad my folks taught me a good work ethic. They taught me that you have to work hard for what you get. There's no way of getting around that. Hard work is what makes it all happen, and the more successful you are, the harder you've worked to get there. That's why I don't ever begrudge anybody their successes—I know success doesn't just happen on its own. Maybe it does for a chosen few who seem to come out of nowhere, and all of a sudden, bingo, they hit the big time. But most of the time, they pay their dues and put on the miles. Miles in an old Buick pulling a U-Haul trailer full of gear. Miles crammed into a van with a bunch of other dudes and playing some of the seedier places just to feed yourselves and get enough gas money to make it to the next gig.

And then suddenly you're riding around in a big, private, beautiful bus, and the world's your oyster. But boy, I tell ya—that doesn't happen overnight. And when it finally does happen, you appreciate it. You don't take stuff for granted anymore. Every day, you know what it took to get here, and you know that it takes even more to stay here. So it instills a work ethic that builds on itself.

I think that's the basic story of the Oak Ridge Boys. Each of us brings something different to the table—a different talent, a different background, a different attitude…each guy is as different as night from day, but everybody melds together as one. We're like spokes in a big wheel, and that big wheel is the Oak Ridge Boys, and we all know it. We all know that what we do individually is important, but we also realize that what we do together is even more important. We are a good team.

FROM MY HEART

I write not with the prose of the more learned
For I am but a simple man
To utilize words wherein the meaning is unknown
Would be sheer folly to me
So I write simply...from my heart

I grew up roughly but not wounded
Grief has come to me, yet laughter has ruled
I have seen much of the world
But certainly not all
So I write simply...from my heart

I am an expert of not one single thing
Yet I certainly know my way
I don't always understand God
Yet He dwells within me despite my shortcoming
So I write simply...from my heart

I am a man of the streets who dwells in the hills
I am a child of labor yet my toils do not scar
My energy is unabated and I own a star
My weakness is kept in shadow
So I write simply...from my heart

I have placed stones on the mountain
I have supped with my friends
I am loved and I have loved
Therefore my heart keeps singing
So I write simply...from my heart

My loved one is my garden
And my children are the flowers
Keep in mind my yarns and ramblings
Lest the light be dimmed
I will always write simply...from my heart

JOSEPH S. BONSALL

A FINAL, PERSONAL NOTE FROM JOE

"Born to Climb"

I love to write. However, I've never been taught or never even thought very much about the finer points of putting ink to scroll, and yet the blank page constantly calls out to me as a mother might call for her lost child.

The words come in a vortex of constant movement, and it's only the openness of my own heart and mind that keeps the door ajar. I pray that it never closes on me. One doesn't usually write as a reward to one's ego, although I imagine some do. One doesn't write just to pontificate or to make unnecessary noise. One doesn't write just to hear one's own voice speaking, although again many do indeed love the sound of their own voice droning on and on into the abyss.

The true creative process in the writing, as far as I am concerned, is to fill a blank page with words that are meaningful to the reader, or at the very least, words that tell a good story. I seriously work toward a good mix of the two. I want to entertain the reader with a well-woven yarn or, at best, provide a laugh or two. But if somewhere in that blend of words I haven't moved or inspired the reader in some way, then the writing is just an empty voice that becomes forgettable and meaningless very quickly.

I sense the same philosophy behind an Oaks show. We want to take

231

you on a fun and exciting journey with the music and such, but somewhere along the way we want the Oak Ridge Boys to touch your heart. We hope you leave a show—and I want you to leave these pages—with something meaningful you can apply to your life. I would hope that along with the storytelling and the singing, you would see a glimpse of the love of Jesus in all things, and that perhaps that light shines through and touches your heart.

I pray every day for the light of His leadership in all I do, and most times I sincerely do believe that these prayers are answered as I keep on writing words and singing songs and breathing air.

I count on the presence of the Holy Spirit and perhaps a few angels to help me translate my sometimes jumbled thoughts into readable prose, and I'm so thankful for constant inspirations that guide me down these sometimes shadowy pathways.

Life itself is often shrouded in darkness and uncertainty, and I believe that's God's master plan. Or why else would we have reason to seek His Light? We bob and weave through the high weeds, praying constantly for a clearing. We seek a parting of the clouds and a ray of sunlight to shine down on us, and we long for a comforting voice to whisper to us that everything will turn out okay.

There are those, however, who choose to languish in the dark, and for them I feel pain and remorse. But blessed is the man or woman who strives to be better even when the pathway is long and tedious and full of sorrow.

The decent soul strives to be better. Yearns for more. The hungry heart is never satisfied until certain goals are reached. The stouthearted strives for that light, and the darkness is only a metaphor. This person is constantly looking upward and sees above the darkness even when the brambles are tugging at the ankles and the thorns are tearing at the cloak. Still, this brave-hearted person is not deterred or discouraged. His or her vision isn't dimmed in the pursuit of purpose, nor is mediocrity accepted as an option.

Many people just die little by little with each passing day and don't even consider their legacy of failure, even as they constantly fail themselves and those around them. They accept shortcomings as if that were the natural order, and they plod along without meaning or purpose. Sadly, love eludes them, and their pathway shortens and becomes meaningless. They lose all sight of hope, and I would say that faith and even love are downright impossible without hope.

A friend once called me a climber, so yes, I am a climber. By choice I am a climber. Yet I know that no matter how positive I strive to be, the journey is not easy and never has been. If I hadn't loved what I do, I would have stopped climbing long ago.

Since childhood I have always believed in myself, yet because my heart has always been wide open, the help I have needed has always been there for me. I have never been alone in my quests and visions—no, not once. I'm so very thankful for the many who have been there for me to guide and lead and share and love and constantly point me in the right direction. I've written about some of these folks in the preceding pages. But I reiterate that one must be cognizant and willing, and above all, one must believe and have faith, or many opportunities and relationships are never experienced. And when they are missed, more times than not, they are never realized again.

Did I mention *love*?

Perhaps love is the most important element of all, as our small vapor passes through this dimension of flesh and blood and bone on to eternity. Faith, hope, and love—and as the Bible says, it is love that matters the most, and there has never been a greater love than that of our Shepherd and Master.

Many times Jesus spoke in a simple fashion for those around Him, for human beings are relatively simple folk in comparison to God's all-seeing plans and visions. Such a unique way to express to His followers that one day He would take the sins of the world upon Himself while He hung in pain, suspended between two worlds, on a crude Roman cross fashioned out of a dogwood tree. He was nailed to the tree while wearing a crown of thorns that had been tightly pressed into His very skull. Even as a spear pierced His side, He spoke of forgiveness while all the time He was bearing my sins and yours. What kind of unreal *love* is that?

I do wonder though what pained Him the most. Was it the physical pain He endured? Or was it the incredible weight of our sin that He bore deep?

He who was perfect and unblemished in every way had now become the worst of sinners as He hung there. When He said, "It is finished," I believe He meant this part of the process had ended at last. And I believe that when His spirit left the human body and He once again regained the power of heaven, He must have been oh so ready for the battle ahead.

The pain part was over. The prophecies had been fulfilled. It was now time to reign as King! He had paid the price asked of Him. He obeyed the Father and completed His mission. I can't even fathom what it must have been like for Jesus during all of this.

Then, while the angels and the entire spiritual world looked on in awe, He paid a visit to hell itself, confronted Satan, and let it be known then and there that He, Jesus Christ, God's only begotten Son, now held the keys of life and death and that He was the beginning and the end of everything.

I'll bet the devil was quaking in fear in that moment. The fallen angel would recover and continue his demonic course of battling the light. But in that moment? It's all just too impossible to fathom. This was no ending, but a beginning for Jesus. Then He proceeded to do that which we might have thought was impossible. He rose in victory from the tomb on that third day after the cross!

Yes, I am a climber. I choose a more positive frame of mind. Even when things around me collapse and disappoint, I climb onward, and I give my Lord all the credit for anything I have been or am or might become, because in Christ there is perfect light. My Bible says there is no darkness at all in His realm—only light! I choose the light.

Oh, to live in the light of His glory. Because of what He did on that cross and on that day we call Easter, a new road was paved for each one of us.

Fear is perhaps our biggest stumbling block as we run our earthly marathon. Jesus has told us so many times that we needn't be overcome with fear. But alas, we're human, and a certain amount of fear seems natural. To be victorious over fear we must constantly seek Jesus

Christ and His will in our lives. We must commit ourselves to Him in all things, and fear and sorrow and sin and chaos will dim in His light.

So as I continue to climb and to write and to sing, I strive to seek more of God in my life. I actually think it's easier to believe in the final place He has prepared for me than *not* to. The world will tell you that death is the end, but to me, that is the tougher pill to swallow.

Someday I will see my mother and father and celebrate with long-lost friends and loved ones forever in a new time zone of eternal life that has been promised to me by the cross and the empty tomb of my Lord Jesus. As Jim Hill once wrote, "What a day that will be!"

So even though most of my earthly journey is behind me now, I continue to peer forward. My earthly sight has been dimmed, yet the pathway ahead seems always clear and bright, and for this I'm thankful.

So how about you, my friends? I invite you to climb with me. Accept Jesus Christ into your life and begin to shine as the stars with a new purpose and a new goal.

Onward and upward! May God bless you, and I sincerely thank you for reading about the Boys!

Acknowledgments

Thank you to Bob Hawkins and everyone at Harvest House for giving me the honor of writing this book and the platform to do it. A very special thank you to Nick Harrison for being with me at the very beginning of this project and for expertly guiding me through the process with kind words and a great edit! Thanks, too, to Joan Yoder, Nick's mother-in-law and Oak Ridge Boys fan.

To Kathy Harris, my book agent, associate, and friend, as well as an Oak Ridge Boys marketing guru, thank you for putting me together with Harvest House. To be published by this historic and blessed company is an honor beyond words, and it would not have happened without you.

Thanks to my counselor and longtime friend, S. Gary Spicer, for always looking after Joseph and Mary.

To Duane Allen, William Lee Golden, and Richard Sterban—my singing partners, brothers, and friends—thank you for the years and the music and the love and support you have always provided. Thank you for the positive input on this book, which is, after all, about all of us. May our light continue to glow long after we are gone. I love you guys with all of my heart.

Thank you to Darrick Kinslow, friend and brother and scholar of all things related to The Oak Ridge Boys, southern gospel music, and tour buses. Your help with some of these pages has been most appreciated.

To my Mary Ann, I thank you for loving me all of these years and for giving me the freedom to live my life of songs and words while sacrificing so much in the process. I love you and will love you throughout eternity. I could not live without your companionship and counsel and humor.

To my daughters, Sabrina and Jennifer, and my grandchildren, Breanne and Luke, thank you for the constant love. I'm very blessed to have you all in my life. I love you more than one can ever imagine.

Most of all I want to thank my Lord and Savior, Jesus Christ. I'm so undeserving of all He has done for me. I praise Him and thank Him for my family, my friends, and this amazing life I have lived thus far. But mostly I thank Him for the cross and for making my many sins vanish into the light of His forgiveness and amazing grace. I'm standing on the promises of Christ my King! I love You, Lord!

IN MEMORY

Larry Anderson, Annette Rich Arboe, Ron Baird, Trevor Boulanger, Todd Brewer, Richard Brown, Darla Burris, Bobby Clark, Charlie Daunis, Mark Ellerbee, Jim Fogelsong, Noel Fox, Sally Fox, Lon "Deacon" Freeman, Smitty Gatlin, Curtis Green, Robert Green, Sherman Halsey, Jim Hamill, Dewayne Hamilton, Herman Harper, Larry Harris, John Hitt, Dick Howard, Howard Hughes, Betty Kaye, Don Light, George Mallard, Jolene Mercer, Bob Montgomery, Harry "Hap" Peebles, Harley Pinkerman, Frances Preston, Don Romeo, Sol Saffian, Steve Sanders, Ray Sanderson, Nelson Sears, Sonny Simmons, Billy R. Smith Jr., E. O. Stacey, Kyle Tullis, Jerry Webb, and Leo Zabelin

✳ ✳ ✳

A very special thank-you to the following for sharing our lives over all of these years and for your love, friendship, and miles. Nothing just happens. It takes a lot of sacrifice and hard work from a huge team of folks to keep these wheels greased and turning for more than 40 incredible years. Everyone on this list has played some part in the career of the Oak Ridge Boys. If I have forgotten someone, I sincerely apologize.

Aaron Brown, Aaron McCune, Abby Wells-Baas, Akiko Rodgers, Al Zar, Alan Branton, Allan Sine, Alex Luebbert, Allan Bregman, Amy Willis, Andy McMahan, AnnJanette Toth, Anne-Marie Gebel, Annette Rich Arboe, Ari Emanuel, Armando Moreno, Art Gower, Ashley Shealy, B. James Lowry, Barrett Sellers, Barry Jeffrey, Barry Jennings, Barry McCord, Beckie Collins, Becky Gardenhire, Ben Isaacs, Bernie Rothkof, Beth Blinn, Betty Kaye, Bill Carter, Bill Coben, Bill Covault, Bill Fitch, Bill Gaither, Bill Harrah, Bill Magann, Billy Blackwood, Billy Helbig, Billy James, Billy

Sherrill, Billy Smith Jr., Billy Smith Sr., Billy Sudekum, Bob Bell, Bob Burwell, Bob Gottschalk, Bob Kaltenbach, Bob Kaminsky, Bob Kinkead, Bob Montgomery, Bob Siner, Bob Towery, Bobby Brantley, Bobby Hynds, Bonnie Sugarman, Brad Bissell, Brad Coombs, Brad Harrison, Brad Siemens, Braeden Rountree, Brenda Hall, Brenda Woods, Brett McMahan, Brian Jones, Britt Kisshauer, Brooks Thomas, Bruce Hinton, Bruce Phillips, Bruce White, Bruno Burnett, Bud Billings, Buddy Hardison, Butch Spyridon, C. K. Spurlock, Calvin Newton, Cam Shillington, Carl Stothart, Carrie Hickman, Carrie Ann Porter, Cathy Gurley, Cathy Highfill, Celeste Winstead, Chad Smith, Charlie Bryan, Charles Blum, Charles Hailey, Charley Jacobson, Charlie Daunis, Charlie Green, Cheryl Ground, Chester Reiten, Chip Brown, Chris Demonbreun, Chris Golden, Chris Hamrin, Chris Nole, Chris Zar, Christina Lam, Cindy Buck, Clark Gallagher, Claudia Hilton, Clay Campbell, Clay Harper, Cliff Hall, Colin Reed, Connie Ray, Curly Jones, Curtis Green, Dan Foster, Dan Gattis, Dan Liebhauser, Dan Taylor, Dana Burwell, Danny Finnerty, Danny Watkins, Darla Burris, Darlene Fort, Darrell Bowling, Darrick Kinslow, Dave Boots, Dave Douds, Dave Emerson, Dave Gibson, Dave McAllister, Dave Newman, Dave Snowden, Dave Steuer, Dave Watson, David Alley, David Cobb, David Deforest, David Ecrement, David Evitts, David Green, David Itkin, David Keller, David Musselman, David Northrup, David Payne, David Ponder, David Robinson, Dean Hartley, Debbye Scroggins, Dee Allen, Del Bryant, Del Delamont, Dennis Grubb, Dennis Winters, Derek Bruner, Dewayne Hamilton, Dewey Dorough, Diana Pugh, Diane Hadley, Dick Howard, Don Breland, Don Hart, Don Kronberg, Don Light, Don Romeo, Donna Jean Kisshauer, Donna Sterban, Donnie Carr, Doug Brown, Doug Bushhousen, Doug Garard, Doug King, Doug Neff, Doug Pierce, E. O. Stacey, Earl Jones, Ed Benson, Ed Dougherty, Ed Finney, Eddie Haddad, Edgar Struble, Ellen Hairr, Erma Smith, Ernie Smith, Erv Woolsey, Fran Romeo, Frances Preston, Frank Breeden, Fred Cameron, Fred Satterfield, Fred Woods, Garland Craft, Garry Jones, Gary Carnes, Gary McSpadden, Gary Musick, Gary Osier, Gary Sisco, Gary Trusler, Gayle Holcomb, Gene Bicknell, Gene Clair, Gene McDonald, Gene Roy, Geoff Bridge, George Hampton, George Mallard, George Moffatt, Gerald Roy, Gil Cunningham, Gina Keltner, Ginger

Anderson, Ginger Key, Glen Tadlock, Glenn Meadows, Gordon Mote, Grant Hinch, Greg Cothran, Greg Gordon, Greg McGill, Greg Oswald, Harley Pinkerman, Harold Pickens, Harold Workman, Harry McClure, Harry "Hap" Peebles, Harvey Krantz, Harvey Martin, Helen Farmer, Herb Frank, Herb Gronauer, Herman Harper, Holly Hamilton, Holmes Hendrickson, Howard Hughes, Irving Azoff, J. Edgar, Jack Faust, Jade Nielsen, James Taylor (JT), James Yelich, Janet Kinslow, Janet Lamar, Janice Gray, Janet Williams, Jay Jackson, Jeff Douglas, Jeff Olsen, Jeff Panzer, Jeff Walker, Jeffrey Kruger, Jeremy DeLoach, Jeremy Westby, Jerry Bailey, Jerry Bentley, Jerry Davis, Jerry Flowers, Jerry Pope, Jerry Webb, Jill Curtis, Jim Black, Jim Cotton, Jim Fitzgerald, Jim Foglesong, Jim "Pappy" Glass, Jim Halsey, Jim Hamill, Jim Krueger, Jim Leamy, Jim Martin, Jim Moore, Jim Thompson, Jim Waits, Jimbeau Hinson, Jimmy Bowen, Jimmy Fulbright, Jimmy Jay, Jimmy Tarbutton, Jo Walker-Meador, JoAnn Berry, Jody Williams, Joe Dieters, Joe Galante, Joe Higgins, Joe Hupp, Joe Jestus, Joe Lake, Joe Madden, Joe Scaife, Joel Fischman, Joey Hemphill, John Ascuaga, John Daines, John Ferriter, John Gimenez, John Hitt, John Logan, John McCain, John Rich, John Ristoff, John Tevis, John Webb, Jolene Mercer, Jon Mir, Josh Whitmore, Joyce Martin, Joyce Morgan, Judi Pofsky, Judy Seale, Julie Craig, Karen Hicks, Karin Warf, Karrie Waszkowski, Kathy Gangwisch, Kathy Harris, Katie Gillon, Kay Waggoner, Kay West, Keith Miller, Ken Harding, Kent Breeding, Kent Wells, Kevin Arrowsmith, Kevin Meads, Kirt Webster, Kjell Samuelson, Kristin Semako, Kristy Merritt, Kyle Tullis, Lance Alleman, Lane Wilson, Larry Anderson, Larry Barr, Larry Chandler, Larry Crocker, Larry Frank, Larry Harris, Larry Hughes, Larry Jones, Larry Patton, Larry Wilhite, Lauren Hamilton, Lee Brantley, Lee Ragonese, Lem Kinslow, Len Owsley, Leo Zabelin, Leon Jones, Les Wethington, Linda Covault, Linda Elliff, Linda Kirkpatrick, Lisa Boult, Lisa Campbell Creasy, Lon "Deacon" Freeman, Manuel, Marc Dennis, Marc Speer, Marc Whitmore, Marcia Olienberger, Mark Bass, Mark Bishop, Mark Brown, Mark Dice, Mark Ellerbee, Mark Fetto, Mark Furnas, Mark Gray, Mark Roeder, Marko Hunt, Marshall Dutton, Martha Moore, Mary Ann Bonsall, MaryAnn McCready, Mary Lou Woodard, Melissa Chambers, Melissa Mattrazzo, Mervyn Conn, Michael Brame, Michael "Sweet Mikey" Campbell, Michael Foster, Michael Jasper,

Michael Saleem, Michael Strickland, Michael Sykes, Mickey Baker, Mike Benedict, Mike Flood, Mike Stahl, Mindy Benson, Myles Harmon, Nate Towne, Neil Vance, Nelson Sears, Nick Dorr, Nina Ground, Noel Fox, Norah Lee Allen, Norman Brokaw, Norman Weiser, Pat Bruner, Pat Halper, Pat Melfi, Pat Roberts, Paul Bryski, Paul Cowen, Paul Jackson, Paul Martin, Paul Moore, Paul Pavis, Paul Sizelove, Paul Uhrig, Paulette Carlson, Peggy Kaltenbach, Pete Burgen, Pete Cummings, Pete Fisher, Pete Green, Phil Citron, Phil Johnson, Philip Lyon, Ramona Simmons, Randy Wright, Ray Clevenger, Ray Sanderson, Ray Schelide, Raymond Hicks, Reggie Churchwell, Rex Wiseman, Rhonda Benson Carroll, Rich Bay, Rich Carpenter, Rich Hervieux, Rich Mischell, Richard Anthony, Richard Brown, Richard Haire, Richard Landis, Richard Sturm, Richard Wooten, Rick Bain, Rick Bundy, Rick Modesitt, Rick Shipp, Risha Rodgers, R. J. Kaltenbach, Rob Battle, Rob Beckham, Rob Hall, Robert Frost, Robert "Sodbuster" Conroy, Robert Green, Robert Romeo, Robert Rosenthal, Robin Wolkey, Roger Eaton, Rolf Samuelson, Ron Baird, Ron Bledsoe, Ron Chancey, Ron Page, Ronnie Fairchild, Roy Clair, Roy Jernigan, Roy Wunsch, Rusty Golden, Ryan Gardenhire, Ryan Pierce, Ryan Schatz, S. Gary Spicer, Sabrina Carver, Sally Fox, Sandi McDerman, Sanford Brokaw, Sarah Brosmer, Scott Borchetta, Scott Chancey, Scott Munz, Scotty Simpson, Sharon Allen, Sheldon Davis, Shelia Shipley, Sheri Calogne, Sherman Halsey, Simone De Staley, Skip Mitchell, Smitty Gatlin, Sol Saffian, Sonny Anderson, Sonny Simmons, Starr Griffy, Stennis Little, Stephanie Lauffer, Steve Buchanan, Steve Earle, Steve Englert, Steve Garard, Steve Gudis, Steve Highfill, Steve Hauser, Steve Kelley, Steve "Rabbit" Easter, Steve Lassiter, Steve Pritchard, Steve Robinson, Steve Sanders, Steve Tolman, Steve Zweifel, Steven Haddad, Stuart Eckard, T. Rat, Taylor Seale, Ted Hacker, Terry Calonge, Terry Cline, Terry Jenkins, Terrye Seigel, Thad Edwards, Therese Maller, Tilman Fertitta, Tim Cotton, Tim Thomas, Tim Wendt, Tim Yasui, Timmer Ground, Tinti Moffat, Todd Boltin, Todd Brewer, Tom Fowler, Tom Peley, Tommy Fairchild, Tony Brown, Tony Byworth, Tracey Denton, Tracy Gideon, Tracy Johnson, Tracy Trost, Travis Medlin, Trent Hemphill, Trevor Boulanger, Tricia Walker, Troy Bailey, Walter Kane, Warren Stitt, Wayne Creasy, Wayne

Halper, Wayne Hilton, Wesley Osler, Willie Wynn, Windy Johnson, and Zeke Hamilton

A very special thank you to these folks for extra book input as well as valuable help, insight, and personal contributions: Duane Allen, William Lee Golden, Richard Sterban, Ron Fairchild, Brian McKinney, Cameron Dole, Jeff Myers, John Herndon, Ronnie Nutt, Gerald Wolf, Michael Booth, Emily Sutherland, Jessica Northey, Celeste Winstead, Phil Elmore, Kathy Harris, Jon Mir, Darrick Kinslow, and Carl Cartee.

I refer to a group of people in our nation as Oak Ridge Boys scholars. A few of them are related, and most have loved this group since their early childhood. I swear they know more about the Oaks and our history and our music then any of us. So thank you, scholars: Kyle Boreing, Reggie Brann, Bruce Burner, Ed Funderburk, Eric Hall, Martin Ratcliff, Jennifer Stevens, Ronnie Booth, Darrick Kinslow, Michael Booth, Les Butler, Richard Haire, Rick Dominic, Dee Allen, Rex Kamstra, Lauren Sterban, John Vairin, Edward Wille, Matthew Gillian, Chris Logli, Russell Reed, Irl Grundy, Kris Rutherford, Michael O'Neal, and the late Chip Gardner.

A special thank you to my cats…Blackie, Crockett, Baybe, Mitty, Ted, Sunny, and Sally Ann for being good kitties.

This book was written from April to August of 2014. Much of it was written on the road, but I wrote quite a bit more at home than I usually would do on such a project, so more thanks go to my wife, Mary Ann, for putting up with a more absentminded husband than usual during the creative process. There is nothing much worse for a man than to hear the words, "What did I just say?" and not have the answer.

About the Author

Joseph S. Bonsall, a.k.a. Joe, Joey, Daddy, Honey, Pop-Pop, and Ban-Joey, lives in Hendersonville, Tennessee, on Old Hickory Lake with his wife, Mary Ann, and their seven cats. He has two grown daughters, Jennifer and Sabrina, and two grandchildren, Breanne and Luke. He has been an Oak Ridge Boy for more than forty years and also plays banjo and does public speaking engagements when time and schedule allow. Joe and Mary Ann also spend quality time on their 350-acre farm on the Tennessee–Kentucky line.

Joseph is the author of nine other books, including the Molly the Cat series, *An Inconvenient Christmas*, *An American Journey*, *Christmas Miracles*, *G.I. Joe and Lillie*, and *From My Perspective*.

Email the author at **josephsbonsall@aol.com**

Visit him online at **oakridgeboys.com** and **josephsbonsall.com**

Follow him on Twitter **@joebonsall** and **@oakridgeboys**

★ DISCOGRAPHY ★

Y'all Come Back Saloon * +	September 1977
Room Service * +	May 1978
Oak Ridge Boys Have Arrived * +	March 1979
Together *	March 1980
Greatest Hits ** +	October 1980
Fancy Free *** +	May 1981
Bobbie Sue * +	February 1982
Oak Ridge Boys Christmas * +	September 1982
American Made * +	January 1983
Greatest Hits Two ** +	July 1984
Deliver * +	October 1984
Step On Out	March 1985
Seasons	March 1986
Christmas Again	September 1986
Where the Fast Lane Ends	February 1987
Heartbeat	September 1987
Monongahela	August 1988
Greatest Hits Volume Three	May 1989
American Dreams	September 1989
Unstoppable	April 1991
Collection * +	April 1992
The Long Haul	June 1992
Country Christmas Eve	November 1995
Revival	March 1997
Voices	July 1999
Millennium	August 2000
From the Heart	May 2001
An Inconvenient Christmas	September 2002
Colors	May 2003
The Journey	July 2004
Common Thread	May 2005

Christmas Cookies	October 2005
Definitive Collection	August 2006
Front Row Seats	September 2006
Gold	January 2007
The Gospel Collection	April 2008
A Gospel Journey	April 2009
The Boys Are Back	May 2009
It's Only Natural	September 2011
Back Home Again	May 2012
Christmas Time's A-Coming	September 2012
Celebrating Faith, Family & Freedom	July 2013
Boys Night Out	April 2014
Rock of Ages	March 2015

*Indicates Gold **Indicates Platinum ***Indicates Double Platinum
+ Sales certified by the Recording Industry Association of America

✦ AWARDS ✦

ENTERTAINMENT AWARDS

Academy of Country Music Awards
Top Vocal Group, 1978
Album of the Year (*Y'all Come Back Saloon*), 1978
Single of the Year ("*Elvira*"), 1981
Cliffie Stone Pioneer Award (for lifetime achievement), 2007

American Music Awards
Country Group of the Year, 1982
Best Country Music Video Artist, 1985

American Entertainment Magazine
Best Music Act, 2007

Boy Scouts of America
Silver Buffalo Award, 2001

Country Music Association Awards
Vocal Group of the Year, 1978
Instrumental Group of the Year (Oaks Band), 1978
Single of the Year ("*Elvira*"), 1981
Instrumental Group of the Year (Oaks Band), 1986

Grammy Awards
Best Vocal Performance by a Country Group or Duo ("*Elvira*"), 1982

Grand Old Opry
Induction into the Grand Old Opry, 2011

Music City News Fan Awards
Band of the Year (Oaks Band), 1978
Best Single of the Year ("*Elvira*"), 1982

TNN Viewers' Choice Awards
Favorite Group, 1988
Favorite Group, 1989

American Guild of Variety Artists
Best Country Vocal Group of the Year, 1981

Billboard
Breakthrough Award, 1977
Number One Country Group, 1980
Number One Country Group/Singles, 1980
Number One Country Group/Albums, 1980
Bill Williams Memorial Award, 1981

Broadcast Music Incorporated (BMI)
Most Performed Song of the Year ("*Elvira*"), 1981

Cashbox
Country Vocal Group/Singles, 1978
Country Vocal Group/Singles, 1979
Country Vocal Group/Albums, 1979
Country Vocal Group/Singles, 1980
Country Vocal Group/Albums, 1981
Country Crossover Group Pop/Singles, 1981
Country Crossover Group Pop/Albums, 1981
Country Crossover Group Pop/Singles, 1983

Disc Jockey Awards
Group of the Year/Country, 1980

International Entertainment Buyers Association
Living Legend Award, 2005

International Fan Club Organization
Tex Ritter Award, 1993

National Association for Music Education
Fame Award, 2006

Juke Box Operators of America
Country Group of the Year, 1980
Song of the Year ("Elvira"), 1981

National Association for Campus Activities
Best Major Country Performance, 1983
Best Major Country Performance, 1985
Best Major Country Performance, 1986

National Music Council
American Eagle Award, 1997 ·

National Committee to Prevent Child Abuse
National Voice Award, 1997

Performance Magazine Readers Poll
Country Act of the Year, 1981

Radio & Records Country Music Poll
Country Group of the Year, 1978–1980
Single of the Year ("Elvira"), 1981

Radio Programmers' Choice Awards
Vocal Group of the Year, 1981

Record World
Country Singles Award, 1977
Country Vocal Group/Singles 1978
Country Vocal Group/Albums 1978
Country Vocal Group/Singles 1980
Country Vocal Group/Albums 1980
Country Vocal Group/Albums 1981
Most Promising Male Group/Albums, 1981
Top Country Crossover Group, 1981

Vocal Group Hall of Fame
Inducted, September 2001

GOSPEL AWARDS

Christian Country Music Awards
Mainstream Artist of the Year, 2004

Dove Awards
Album of the Year, 1969
Album Jacket Design, 1969
Male Group of the Year, 1970
Album of the Year, 1972
Male Group of the Year, 1972
Album of the Year, 1973
Country Album of the Year, 2002
Country Recorded Song of the Year, 2007
Long Form Music Video of the Year, 2010

Gospel Music Hall of Fame
Inducted, 2000

Grammy Awards
Best Vocal Performance by a Group or Duo/Gospel, 1971–1979 (four awards)

Southern Gospel Music Association
James D. Vaughan Impact Award, 2012

Southern Gospel Music Guild
President's Award, 2010

INTERNATIONAL AWARDS

Billboard/Wembley Festival of Country Music
Best Country Group, 1975

Country Rhythms International Fan Awards
Best Country Group, 1982

Kountry Korral Magazine, *Sweden*
Number One Country Group, 1975
Number One Gospel Group, 1975

International Federation of Festival Organizations
Award of Excellence, 1986

★ OAK RIDGE BOYS TRIVIA ★

1. **The Oak Ridge Boys have recorded with:**
   a. Country legend Johnny Cash
   b. Pop icon Paul Simon
   c. Polka entertainer Jimmy Sturr
   d. All of the above

2. **In the 1940s, the group that evolved into The Oak Ridge Boys was called:**
   a. Sharon, Lois, and Bram
   b. The Four Tops
   c. The Georgia Clodhoppers
   d. The Ridge Riders

3. **The Oak Ridge Boys were once known as a:**
   a. Bluegrass band
   b. Gospel quartet
   c. Celtic group
   d. Hip-hop act

4. **In his spare time, William Lee Golden likes:**
   a. Playing banjo
   b. Collecting old cars
   c. Painting & photography
   d. Long distance bike riding

5. **The Oak Ridge Boys' first big Country hit was:**
   a. You're the One
   b. Cryin' Again
   c. Bobbie Sue
   d. Y'all Come Back Saloon

6. **Lead singer Duane Allen studied opera in college.**
   a. True
   b. False

7. **Which Oak once worked in an upscale men's store and still has an interest in fashion?**
   a. Joe Bonsall
   b. Richard Sterban
   c. William Lee Golden
   d. Duane Allen

8. **As a young man, tenor Joe Bonsall wanted to be a veterinarian.**
   a. True
   b. False

9. **Bass singer Richard Sterban sang soprano as a young boy in church choir.**
   a. True
   b. False

10. **The Oaks' official autobiography, written by Joe Bonsall and published in 2004, was called:**
    a. *An American Journey*
    b. *Harmony and Hits*
    c. *Days of Our Lives*
    d. *Acorns to Oaks*

11. **The Oaks have performed in which foreign country?**
    a. Russia
    b. Sweden
    c. England
    d. All of the above

12. The Oaks' backup band is known as:

    a. Solid Oak

    b. Rockland Road

    c. The Mighty Oaks Band

    d. The Acorns

13. The Oak Ridge Boys tour how many days a year?

    a. 150 or more

    b. 365

    c. Less than 50

    d. 10

14. According to *Billboard* Magazine, how many number one hits have The Oak Ridge Boys had?

    a. 6

    b. 13

    c. 18

    d. 25

15. Match the Oak with their birthplace:

    Duane Allen

    William Lee Golden

    Joe Bonsall

    Richard Sterban

    Philadelphia, PA

    Camden, NJ

    Taylortown, TX

    Brewton, AL

16. Which Oak Ridge Boy has the nickname "Mountain Man"?

    a. William Lee Golden

    b. Joe Bonsall

    c. Richard Sterban

    d. Duane Allen

17. Which Oak Ridge Boy performed with the Stamps Quartet backing Elvis Presley?

    a. Joe Bonsall

    b. William Lee Golden

    c. Duane Allen

    d. Richard Sterban

18. Which Oak Ridge Boy is an antique car buff with more than two dozen classics?

    a. Duane Allen

    b. Richard Sterban

    c. Joe Bonsall

    d. Richard Sterban

19. Which Oak Ridge Boy wrote a series of children's books about the adventures of Molly the Cat?

    a. William Lee Golden

    b. Richard Sterban

    c. Joe Bonsall

    d. Duane Allen

20. What organization awarded the Oak Ridge Boys the Silver Buffalo Award, its highest honor, for outstanding service to youth?

    a. VISTA

    b. Boy Scouts of America

    c. Campfire

    d. Royal Rangers

21. Which Oak Ridge Boy has the nickname "Ace"?

    a. Richard Sterban

    b. Duane Allen

    c. Joe Bonsall

    d. William Lee Golden

22. "Elvira" was written by Dallas Frazier. He wrote the song about what?

a. His daughter
b. His wife
c. A street in Nashville
d. His grandmother

23. Match the Oak with the year he joined the group.

a. Joe Bonsall   1972
b. Richard Sterban   1965
c. William Lee Golden   1966
d. Duane Allen   1973

24. The Oak Ridge Boys toured throughout 1979 on the Full House Tour with whom?

a. Garth Brooks and Wanda Jackson
b. Kenny Rogers and Dottie West
c. The Rolling Stones
d. Oingo Boingo

25. In the 1980s, the Oaks, band, and crew formed a softball team to play charity events, both at home and on tour. What was the name of the team?

a. Oak Ridge Team Spirit
b. Boys Will Be Boys
c. ORBITS (Oak Ridge Boys Is Tough Stuff)
d. Mighty Oaks at Bat

26. Which is the only Oak to have a bobblehead doll named after him?

a. Joe Bonsall
b. Richard Sterban
c. Duane Allen
d. William Lee Golden

27. The Oaks have performed for 40 straight years at what event:

a. The season opener for the Tennessee Titans
b. The Oscar ceremonies
c. The Kentucky State Fair
d. Groundhog Day in Punxsutawney, Pennsylvania

28. The legendary Oak Ridge Boys logo was designed by Gary Huerta, who also designed the logo for what other famous band?

a. The Kingston Trio
b. The Beatles
c. Chicago
d. Alabama

Answers

1. d.
2. c.
3. b.
4. c.
5. d.
6. a.
7. b.
8. a.
9. a.
10. a.
11. d.
12. c.
13. a.
14. d.

15. **Duane Allen—**
Taylortown, TX
William Lee Golden—
Brewton, AL
Joe Bonsall—
Philadelphia, PA
Richard Sterban—
Camden, NJ

16. a.
17. d.
18. a.
19. c.
20. b.
21. b.
22. c.
23. Joe Bonsall—1973
Richard Sterban—1972
William Lee Golden—1965
Duane Allen—1966
24. b.
25. c.

26. b. Richard was once a part-owner of our Triple-A ball club, the Nashville Sounds. He is now more of a goodwill ambassador for the team, and one night they had a special game honoring Richard with his own bobblehead doll. To this day he is the only Oak with a bobblehead likeness.

27. c.

28. c. Columbia Records commissioned these two logos at the time, and both are used extensively to this day.

To learn more about Harvest House books and
to read sample chapters, visit our website:

www.harvesthousepublishers.com

HARVEST HOUSE PUBLISHERS
EUGENE, OREGON